As Bob Parr, Mr. Incredible misses being a real hero.

Bob remembers the good old days.

Raising two Supers isn't easy.

At least Jack-Jack is normal.

Mirage recruits Mr. Incredible for a top-secret assignment.

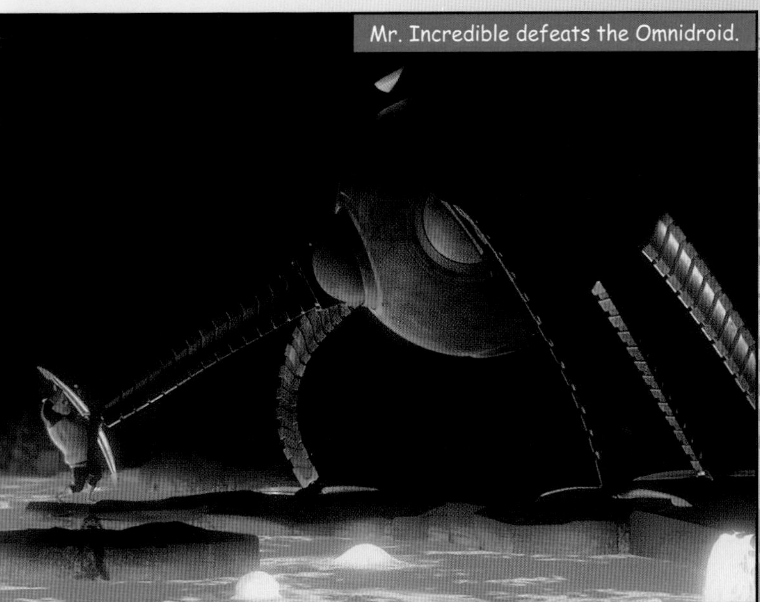

Mr. Incredible defeats the Omnidroid.

Bob starts getting into shape.

Edna decides to make a new suit for Mr. Incredible.

Mr. Incredible is back for his next Super assignment.

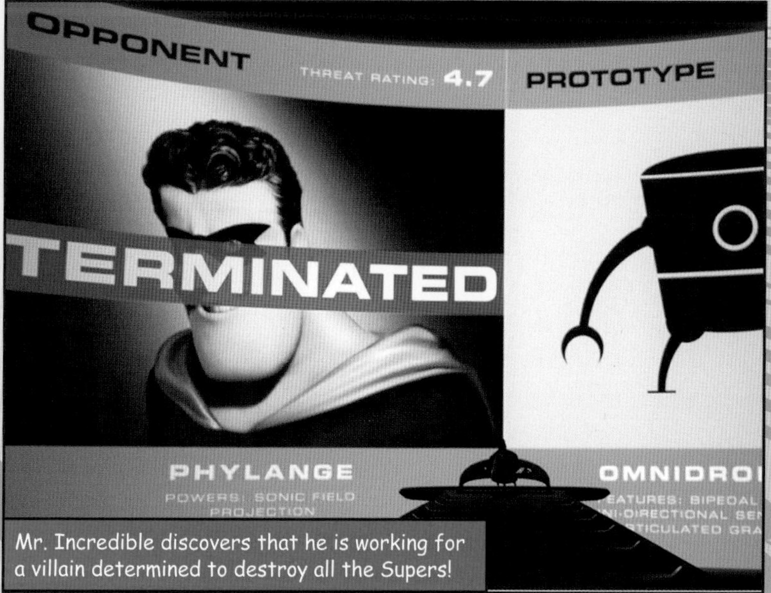
OPPONENT
THREAT RATING: 4.7
PROTOTYPE
TERMINATED
PHYLANGE
POWERS: SONIC FIELD PROJECTION
Mr. Incredible discovers that he is working for a villain determined to destroy all the Supers!

Syndrome taunts Mr. Incredible with his evil plan.

Elastigirl stretches to the rescue!

Dash and Vi use their powers to escape Syndrome's guards.

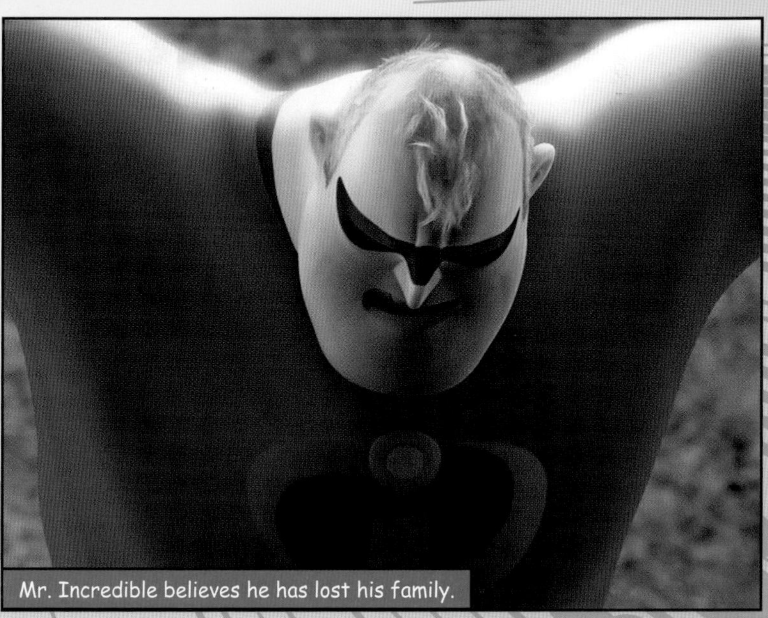

Mr. Incredible believes he has lost his family.

Together, the family battles Syndrome's guards.

Mr. Incredible and Frozone face the deadly Omnidroid.

DISNEY PRESENTS A PIXAR FILM

THE INCREDIBLES

Adapted by Irene Trimble

ISBN 979-11-86701-83-6 14740

Longtail Books

The sun was just beginning to set over the city of Municiburg. A **powerful**ly built, **handsome blond bachelor** wearing a tuxedo★ **maneuver**ed his **sporty** little car through the streets of the city, listening to the radio. He was on his way to a very important **appointment**, when suddenly—

"We **interrupt** for an important **bulletin**!" The man listened for details. A high-speed car **chase** between police and **gunmen** was in **progress** on San Pablo **Boulevard**.

★tuxedo 턱시도. 남자가 입는 야간용 약식 예복. 모양은 양복과 비슷하며 연미복의 대용으로 입는다.

Without **hesitation**, the man **punch**ed a button on the **dash**. The radio **immediate**ly **convert**ed into an **electronic aerial** map. The map's **sophisticate**d radar★ system **lock**ed **on** two red **dot**s **speed**ing through the city. "Yeah, I've got time," the man decided, giving his watch a **glance**. He could still make his appointment.

He hit another button, marked AUTODRIVE, and the car began to drive itself. Then he typed **MERGE PURSUIT** into the **control**s. The autodrive immediately began to **plot** a course to **intercept** the trouble.

Next, the seat backs of the car **snap**ped down **flat**. Two steel bands suddenly **wrap**ped around the man's **waist** and **slid** over his body in **opposing** directions, removing his clothes to **reveal** a **slick** Super **suit** underneath. He wore a dark **mask** over his eyes.

The seat backs returned to an **upright** position. The man in the driver's seat was **none other than** Mr. Incredible. And he was ready for action!

Mr. Incredible smiled as his **vehicle** converted into

★radar 레이더. 전자기파를 물체에 발사해 그 물체에서 반사되는 전자기파를 수신하여 물체와의 거리, 방향 등을 알아내는 무선감시장치.

the **sleek futuristic** Incredibile. As he hit the turbo★ button, afterburners✻ **flame**d and the car **rocket**ed down the street.

Then something **caught his eye**.

A sweet gray-haired woman was **frantic**ally **waving** at him and pointing at a tree. Mr. Incredible hit the **brake**s, **reverse retro**-thrusters❋ **fire**d, and the Incredibile **stop**ped **on a dime**. A darkly **tint**ed window slid down. "What is it, ma'am?"

"My cat, Squeaker, won't come down," she cried.

Mr. Incredible glanced up at the **wild-eyed** Squeaker, who was **stubborn**ly **grip**ping the tree, then at the screen on the dash of the Incredibile. Red dots from the car chase were now headed their way. A **blazing** car-to-car gun **battle** would **rip** down this street within moments.

"I suggest you **stand clear**," he said to the cat's owner. "There could be trouble."

Suddenly, the **squeal** of **screech**ing tires could be

★turbo 터보차저. 배기가스를 이용하여 터빈을 돌리고 혼합 기체를 실린더 안으로 보내어 압력을 높이는 엔진의 보조 장치. 출력을 높이고 연비 향상에 도움을 준다.

✻afterburner 애프터버너. 자동차의 배기가스를 재연소하는 장치.

❋thruster 반동 추진 엔진.

heard. The **headlight**s of the cars were moving toward them fast. In one **sweep**ing **motion**, Mr. Incredible **tore** the **enormous** tree out of the ground and gently shook Squeaker into his owner's **outstretched** arms. Then he **slam**med the tree onto the **hood** of the **oncoming** car, **stop**ping the **criminal**s **in their tracks**.

As he carefully **replant**ed the tree, Mr. Incredible accepted the usual thanks from the police. "Just here to help," he said, giving each of them a **nod**. "**Officer**s, ma'am . . . Squeaker." He **was about to** leave the **scene** when the radio began to **blare**, "Tour bus **rob**bery in the **vicinity** of Howard and Chase streets."

Mr. Incredible looked at his watch again. *I've still got time*, he thought, deciding to take the call. He jumped into the Incredibile, but just before he **pull**ed **out**, someone *in* the car said, "Cool! Ready for **takeoff**!"

Mr. Incredible turned to find a **pudgy** kid sitting in the **passenger** seat of the Incredibile.

"Who are you?" Mr. Incredible asked.

"I'm Incrediboy!" the kid answered **enthusiastic**ally.

"What? No . . . ," Mr. Incredible said as he looked

him over. The redheaded kid was wearing a mask and a **homemade** Super suit. Then Mr. Incredible **recognize**d him.

"Buddy?" he asked.

Buddy, the **president** of the Mr. Incredible Fan Club, answered with a **frown**. "My name is INCREDIBOY!"

"Look," Mr. Incredible said, trying to be **patient**, "I've stood for every photo, **sign**ed every **scrap** of paper, but this is a bit much."

But Buddy wasn't listening. "You don't have to worry about training me," he answered quickly. "I know all your moves—your **crime**-fighting style, everything!" The volume of Buddy's voice suddenly **crank**ed **up** to ten. "I'm your number-one fan!" he **yell**ed.

Suddenly, the door of the Incredibile **whoosh**ed open, **eject**ing an angry Incrediboy onto the side of the road.

Mr. Incredible hit the afterburners and **peel**ed **out**.

Chapter 2

The bus **rob**ber was hiding on a **rooftop**, **root**ing through a stolen purse. The **crook** never saw Mr. Incredible's shadow **loom**ing over him.

"You can tell a lot about a woman by the **content**s of her purse. But maybe that's not what you had in mind," Mr. Incredible said. The crook pulled a gun and backed away from the **formidable** hero. ***Whack!*** A **punch** seemed to come from nowhere, dropping the **thief**.

But the punch hadn't come from Mr. Incredible.

Mr. Incredible looked over his shoulder. Then he smiled. A **dazzling mask**ed woman smiled back.

"Elastigirl," he said **knowingly**.

"Mr. Incredible," she replied as she **stretch**ed out an arm to lift the **thug** to his feet.

"It's all right," he told her. "I've got him."

"Sure you've got him," she said, **snap**ping her arm back. "I just **took** him **out** for you."

The two heroes stepped back and **playful**ly argued about who would **take** the bus robber **in**.

"We could share, you know," she said, stretching toward him with **graceful ease**.

"I work alone," Mr. Incredible said coolly.

"Well," Elastigirl said, **loop**ing herself around him in one **fluid motion**, "I think you need to be more . . . **flexible**."

"You doing anything later?" Mr. Incredible asked, raising an **eyebrow**.

"I have a **previous engage**ment," she **whisper**ed **pointed**ly as she stretched across the rooftops and disappeared.

Mr. Incredible watched in **admiration** as the beautiful Super woman left. Then he turned his attention back to the bus robber and **handcuff**ed him.

The **crack** of **gunfire** filled the air as a black helicopter **armed to the teeth buzz**ed the rooftops, **zoom**ing away from something—or someone.

Mr. Incredible looked up. "Frozone," he said with a smile.

Frozone **swoop**ed down, traveling on **sheet**s of ice he threw from rooftop to rooftop. A **fellow** Super, Frozone could create ice from the **moisture** in the air. Ice **bolt**s shot from his **palm** as he **chase**d the **flee**ing helicopter.

Frozone **notice**d Mr. Incredible as he passed. "Shouldn't you be getting ready?" he shouted.

Mr. Incredible **yell**ed back. "Hey . . . I've still got time!"

The sound of a woman's scream caught Mr. Incredible's attention. He turned to see someone pointing to the top of a giant **skyscraper**. A man on a **ledge was about to** jump. A **crowd** was quickly forming in the street.

The crowd **gasp**ed as the man stepped off the ledge and **tumble**d toward the **pavement**.

Mr. Incredible **burst** into action with a **calculate**d

jump from the **roof** of a lower building. He **tackle**d the jumper in **midair** and **sail**ed across the street, **crash**ing through a window. In a **shower** of glass, they **land**ed in the empty lobby of a bank.

"I think you broke something," the jumper **moan**ed.

"With **counsel**ing, I think you'll come to forgive me," Mr. Incredible told him. Then his **crime** sense **kick**ed **in**. Something was wrong.

He was taking a look around the bank when suddenly there was a **boom**ing **explosion**. A huge safe door flew through the air and landed on Mr. Incredible, **pin**ning him to the ground. Out of the **smoke** and **rubble** stepped **Bomb** Voyage, a super **villain** from France. It seemed Mr. Incredible had **stumble**d **into** a bank robbery in **progress**.

Mr. Incredible rolled the safe door aside. "Bomb Voyage!" He stepped forward to stop the villain.

"Monsieur★ Incroyable," replied the **notorious** thief.

"And Incrediboy!" said a voice from behind Mr. Incredible.

★ monsieur 프랑스어로 남자를 부르는 표현으로 '~씨' 또는 '~님'이라는 뜻. 영어의 'Mr.' 또는 'Sir'와 비슷한 말.

"Incrediboy?" Bomb Voyage **mock**ed.

Buddy was back. **Flash**ing his **homemade rocket boot**s, he asked Mr. Incredible, "Aren't you **curious** how I get around so fast?"

"Go home, Buddy," Mr. Incredible told him.

"This is because I don't have powers, isn't it?" Buddy said angrily. "You can be Super without them. I **invent**ed these." Buddy lifted one of his rocket boots so Mr. Incredible could get a better look. "I can fly! Can *you* fly?"

"Fly home, Buddy," Mr. Incredible told him. "I work alone."

"I'll show you," Buddy **insist**ed. "I'll go get the police!"

But Bomb Voyage wasn't about to let either of them **ruin** his day. As Buddy **dash**ed for the **shatter**ed window, Bomb Voyage secretly **clip**ped a small bomb to Buddy's **cape**.

Mr. Incredible **spot**ted the bomb. He **race**d after Buddy and **grab**bed the cape, yelling, "Buddy, don't!" But it was too late. Buddy jumped, **activating** his rocket boots in a shower of **spark**s and lifting Mr. Incredible into the air with him.

Mr. Incredible fought to **get hold of** the bomb as he and Buddy **streak**ed across the sky.

"Let go!" Buddy shouted. "You're **wreck**ing my **flight** pattern!"

Mr. Incredible reached the bomb and **tore** it from Buddy's cape. The bomb fell, as did Mr. Incredible. Both landed on the **track**s of an **elevate**d train. The bomb exploded. The **blast rip**ped through a huge **section** of track just as a train was approaching. Mr. Incredible had to stop the train before it came to the missing tracks!

Using his Super strength, Mr. Incredible held his body up against the **oncoming** train. *Screeeeeeeee!* The sound of **screech**ing metal filled the air as Mr. Incredible used every **ounce** of his Super strength to **halt** the train.

Thanks to Mr. Incredible, the train was stopped and no one was seriously hurt. Mr. Incredible had Buddy by the back of the neck. "Take this one home," he said to a police **officer**, "and make sure his mom knows what he's been doing."

"You're making a mistake," Buddy **protest**ed. "I could help you!"

Mr. Incredible told the police about the **injure**d jumper and the bank robbery. "The **blast** in that building was caused by **Bomb** Voyage. We might be able to **nab** him if we **set up** a **perimeter**."

"You mean he **got away**?" an officer asked.

"Well, yeah," Mr. Incredible answered, **nod**ding at Buddy. "Skippy here made sure of that."

"Incrediboy!" Buddy said again.

Mr. Incredible turned to Buddy. "You're not **affiliate**d with me!"

A **tiny alarm** sounded. Mr. Incredible checked his watch. "Holy smokes!★ I'm late!" he said. "Listen, I have to be somewhere." He **signal**ed the Incredibile, and the **futuristic vehicle** came **roar**ing around the corner and up to its owner.

"But what about Bomb Voyage?" asked one of the officers.

"Any other night I'd go after him myself," Mr. Incredible answered as he climbed into the car. "But I've really gotta go. Don't worry, we'll get him **eventually**!"

Mr. Incredible **fire**d the afterburners and **sped** off.

"You're very late," Frozone said **flat**ly. Mr. Incredible

★holy smokes '이런!', '세상에!'라는 뜻으로 놀라움을 나타내는 표현.

fumbled with his **bow** tie.★ "How do I look?" he asked.

"The mask!" Frozone said, stopping him. "You've still got the mask on!"

Frozone pulled the mask off Mr. Incredible. Mr. Incredible took a deep breath and pushed open the **chapel** doors. **Smart**ly dressed in a black tuxedo again, he took a step down the **aisle** of the large **cathedral**.

Frozone, his **best man**, followed him.

They walked to the **altar**, where Mr. Incredible's beautiful **bride** was waiting. The **ceremony** began. "Robert Parr, will you have this woman to be your **lawful**ly **wed**ded wife?"

His wife-to-be, Elastigirl, also known as Helen, **whisper**ed, "**Cut**ting **it** kind of **close**, don't you think?"

Mr. Incredible smiled. "You need to be more . . . **flexible**," he replied with a **wink**.

The ceremony **conclude**d: "As long as you both shall live?"

"I do," answered Mr. Incredible, taking Elastigirl in

★bow tie 나비넥타이. 날개를 편 나비 모양으로 가로로 짧게 매는 넥타이.

his arms. The **crowd** of Supers in the cathedral stood up and **cheer**ed.

"As long as we both shall live," Elastigirl promised. "No matter what happens."

"We're Supers," Mr. Incredible said **confident**ly. "What could happen?"

"This **flash** from the news desk: In a **stun**ning **turn** of events, a Super is being **sue**d for saving someone who, **apparent**ly, did not want to be saved. The **plaintiff**, who was **foil**ed in his attempted **suicide** by Mr. Incredible, has **file**d a **suit** against the **fame**d hero in **Superior Court**."

On the crowded steps of the **courthouse**, a **lawyer** spoke to the **media**. "My **client** didn't ask to be saved. He didn't want to be saved," he said dryly.

A masked Mr. Incredible appeared on the courthouse steps in a blue business suit and tie. "I saved your life!" he said, pointing at his **accuse**r.

"You **ruin**ed my death!" the man shouted back.

Five days later, the injured **victim**s of the train accident also filed a suit. Mr. Incredible's court losses cost the

government millions.

Suddenly, it seemed to be **open season** on Supers everywhere. The newspapers were filled with **headline**s accusing the Supers of harming, not helping, people. The lawsuits began to **pile** up.

Even the government **turn**ed **against** them. "It is time for their secret **identities** to become their *only* identities," one **congresswoman** demanded. "Time for them to join us, or go away."

There was some protest in **favor** of the Supers, but finally, under **tremendous pressure** and a mountain of lawsuits, the government quietly **initiate**d the Super **Relocation** Program (otherwise known as the SRP). Supers promised never to use their Super powers again, in exchange for **anonymity**.

The Supers found themselves with new names and identities. From now on, they would live **average** lives, quietly **blend**ing **in** with the rest of society.

And just like that, the **golden age** of Supers was over.

Fifteen years later, Mr. Incredible, now known as Bob Parr, sat in his small **cubicle** at the Insuricare **insurance** company, **stamp**ing the word DENIED in red ink on everything that passed his desk. His white **collar** was a bit too tight, his uncomfortable chair a bit too small. Bob Parr, an insurance **adjuster**, was sixty-four pounds★ **overweight** and losing his hair. It was hard to believe he was the man the world had once known as Mr. Incredible.

A **frail elderly** woman sat in Bob's cubicle. She held

★pound 무게의 단위 파운드. 1파운드는 약 0.45킬로그램으로, 64파운드는 약 29킬로그램이다.

in her hand a piece of paper stamped with red ink.

"Denied?" asked old Mrs. Hogenson, **confuse**d and **upset**. "You're denying my **claim**?"

"I'm sorry, Mrs. Hogenson," Bob told her, "but our **liability** is **spell**ed **out** in **paragraph** seventeen." He was about to explain when the phone **interrupt**ed him. It was Helen.

She held the phone in the **crook** of her neck as she tried to get baby Jack-Jack out of the bath. The mask she had once worn as Elastigirl was gone; her shiny red **thigh**-high **boot**s had been **replace**d by a pair of **sensible** shoes.

"I'm calling to **celebrate** a **momentous occasion**!" she said as Jack-Jack **squirm**ed. "We are now **official**ly **move**d **in**. I finally un**pack**ed the last box!" The Parrs had moved a number of times since they'd entered the SRP. Helen **had high hopes** that this move would **stick**.

"That's great, honey," Bob answered, "but I have a **client** here. . . ."

"Say no more," Helen said brightly. "Go save the world one **policy** at a time. I've gotta go **pick up** the kids from school. See you tonight."

"Bye, honey," Bob said into the phone, and then looked at the sad face of Mrs. Hogenson. "Excuse me, where were we?"

Mrs. Hogenson explained that she **desperate**ly needed the money from her insurance policy. "If you can't help me, I don't know what I'll do," she said quietly.

Bob thought for a minute, checked to make sure that **the coast was clear** outside his cubicle, and then quickly whispered to Mrs. Hogenson every possible **loophole** she could use to get Insuricare to pay her claim.

"Oh, thank you," Mrs. Hogenson said **graceful**ly.

Bob gave her a little smile and then told her to pretend to be upset just **in case** anyone was **eavesdrop**ping.

"I'm sorry, ma'am, but there's nothing I can do," Bob said, loudly enough for people to hear him. Mrs. Hogenson **pat**ted Bob's hand and left the office.

Bob's boss, Gilbert Huph, a small and **mean-spirited** man, suddenly **barge**d into Bob's cubicle.

"Parr!" he yelled. "You **authorize**d **payment** on the Walker policy?"

"Their policy clearly **cover**s them against—" Bob

began.

"I don't want to know about their coverage! Tell me how you're keeping Insuricare **in the black**." Huph continued angrily. "Tell me how that is possible with you writing **check**s to every Harry Hardluck and Sally Sobstory★ that gives you a call."

Huph **storm**ed off, leaving Bob **mute**—a **typical** day at the office.

★Harry Hardluck and Sally Sobstroy 여기에서는 평범한 이름과 함께 'hard luck(불행)'과 'sob story(눈물 나는 이야기)'라는 표현을 성으로 사용하여 '운이 없는 사람들'이라고 비꼬아서 말했다.

Chapter 5

Helen Parr had been hoping to **pile** the kids into her station wagon★ and get home **in time** to make dinner. Instead, she was heading to the **principal**'s office. Dash, the Parrs' older son, was in trouble again.

Dash had been born with the Super power of **lightning**-fast speed. But of course, since Supers weren't supposed to be Super, he was never allowed to use it, and the Parr family *had* to keep it a secret.

"What's this about? Has Dash done something

★station wagon 스테이션왜건. 뒷좌석 뒤에 화물칸을 만들어 사람과 화물을 동시에 운반할 수 있게 제작된 자동차.

wrong?" Helen asked the school principal when she got to the office, where Dash was waiting.

"He put **thumbtack**s on my **stool**!" Dash's fourth-**grade** teacher, Bernie Kropp, told Helen. "And this time I've got him!" Mr. Kropp continued **triumphant**ly. "I hid a camera!"

He dropped a disc into a player. Helen and Dash **held their breath** and **stare**d at the TV screen. There was Mr. Kropp, about to sit in his chair. He sat . . . and screamed. No **sign** of Dash at all. *"See?"* Mr. Kropp shouted, replaying it.

The school principal looked at Mr. Kropp. The teacher sounded completely **nuts**. Helen breathed a **sigh** of **relief**.

"Bernie . . . ," the principal said.

"Don't 'Bernie' me!" Mr. Kropp **protest**ed. "This little rat★ is **guilty**!"

The principal turned to Helen. "You and your son can go now, Mrs. Parr. I'm sorry for the trouble."

As Helen hurried Dash out the door, she could hear

★ rat '배신자' 또는 '비열한 인간'이라는 뜻의 속어.

Bernie Kropp yelling, "You're letting him go *again?* He's guilty! You can see it on his **smug** little face! Guilty! Guilty! Guilty!"

"Dash!" Helen **exclaim**ed when she got him into the car. "This is the third time this year you've been sent to the office! We need to find a better **outlet**."

Dash **slump**ed in his seat. "Maybe I could, if you'd let me go out for sports," he **mutter**ed **glum**ly.

"Honey," Helen answered. "You know why we can't do that."

"But I promise I'll slow up!" Dash offered. "I'll only be the best by a **tiny** bit."

But Helen knew the world didn't want them to be their best, not even by a little bit.

She shook her head. "Right now, honey, the world just wants us to **fit** in."

"But Dad always says our powers are nothing to be **ashamed** of. Our powers made us special."

"Everyone's special," Helen sighed **wearily**.

"Which is another way of saying no one is," Dash

said, **sulk**ing.

Helen drove the station wagon to the junior high★ to **pick up** Dash's older sister, Violet. Helen looked around. Violet was nowhere to be seen—but then, that was one of her **talent**s. Violet had the power to turn in**visible**. This came in **handy** when she felt **shy** around boys, especially Tony Rydinger.

Violet also had the power of **generating force field**s, but that was only good for fights with Dash. He hated it when she used her force fields.

Violet was invisible now, as she **peek**ed over the top of a **bush** and watched Tony Rydinger come down the school steps. He stopped for a second and then looked over his shoulder. Seeing nothing, he walked away. Violet shyly re**materialize**d and **blush**ed. Then she **scamper**ed into her mother's car.

★junior high 미국에서 12~14세의 학생들이 다니는 학교. 한국의 중학교에 해당한다.

It was dinnertime at the Parr home.

"Do you have to read at the table?" Helen asked Bob as she quickly used a spoon to **scoop** up **dribbling** baby food from Jack-Jack's face.

Bob, who was reading his newspaper, didn't hear the question. He **was lost in** the news.

"Uh-huh, yeah," he said **distract**edly.

Helen **sigh**ed and turned to Dash. "Smaller **bite**s, Dash," she suggested. But Dash didn't seem to hear her either. "Bob, could you help the **carnivore** cut his **meat**?"

Bob sighed, put down his paper, and reached over to

Dash's **plate** with a fork and knife.

"You have something you want to tell your father about school?" Helen asked Dash.

"Uh . . . we **dissect**ed a frog . . . ?" Dash asked, hoping to **divert** his mother's line of questioning.

Helen raised her **eyebrow**s. "Dash got sent to the office again," she said **matter-of-fact**ly.

"Good . . . good," Bob answered, still reading the paper **out of the corner of his eye** as he cut the meat on Dash's plate.

"No, Bob. That's bad."

"What?" Bob said, finally looking up.

"Dash got sent to the office again," Helen repeated.

"What for?" asked Bob.

"Nothing," Dash said quickly.

"He put **thumbtack**s on his teacher's chair *during class,*" Helen said.

"Nobody saw me," Dash argued as Bob continued cutting. "You could **barely** see it on the tape!"

"They caught you on tape and you still **got away with** it?" Bob said with some **pride**. "Whoa! You must have been **book**ing!"

"Bob!" Helen said. "We're not **encouraging** this."

"I'm not encouraging," Bob said, trying to hide his excitement. "I'm just asking how fast—" A sudden ***crack*** interrupted the conversation. Bob stopped cutting Dash's meat and looked down. **Inadvertent**ly using his Super strength, he had cut through the plate, and the dining room table, too.

"I'm getting a new plate," Bob said, and headed for the kitchen.

Helen turned to Violet, who was **poking** at her dinner, her long hair **cover**ing most of her face. "How about you, Vi? How was school?"

Violet **shrug**ged. "Nothing to report."

"You've **hardly** touched your food," Helen said.

"I'm not hungry for meat loaf,★" Violet answered.

Helen offered to get Vi something else. "What are you hungry for?"

"Tony Rydinger!" Dash **tease**d.

★meat loaf 미트로프. 곱게 다진 고기에 우유에 적셔서 꼭 짠 식빵과 달걀, 양파 등을 넣고 잘 반죽하여, 식빵 모양의 덩어리를 만들어 오븐에서 구운 요리.

"Shut up!" Vi said to him.

"Well, you are!" Dash laughed.

"I said shut up, you little **insect**!"

"Do *not* shout at the table!" Helen said **firm**ly, and called Bob, who was still in the kitchen. "Honey!"

"She'd eat if we were having Tony loaf!" Dash **giggle**d.

"That's it!" Vi shouted in **frustration**, **lunging** at Dash and then **vanish**ing. Dash **wrestle**d free and ran around the table in a **blur**. Jack-Jack giggled happily. Violet stopped Dash with her **force field** as Helen **stretch**ed her arms in all directions, trying to catch them. They **dove** under the table, continuing to wrestle.

In the kitchen, Bob was **fixated** on the newspaper. Under the **headline** PALADINO MISSING, Bob read, "Simon J. Paladino, long an **outspoken advocate** of Supers' rights, is missing." Bob couldn't help wondering what had happened. Simon Paladino was the secret **identity** of Gazerbeam, a **former** Super and one of Bob's friends.

Then he heard Helen. "Bob?" she was calling **desperate**ly. "It's time to **engage**! Do something!"

Bob **snap**ped out of it and entered the dining room.

He **hoist**ed the dinner table and his family over his head. Helen hung over the table as Dash and Vi **dangle**d from her stretched arms. They were still fighting, **twist**ing Helen's arms into a **hopeless**ly **tangle**d **knot**. Jack-Jack, loving the excitement, **shriek**ed with joy.

Then the doorbell rang.

Everyone **froze**. Bob lowered the table, and the family **resume**d a "normal" dining position. Dash calmly stood up and answered the door.

"Hey, Speedo! Hey, Helen!" said a voice in the **doorway**. Everyone in the Parr house relaxed. It was Lucius Best, formerly known as Frozone!

"Hey!" shouted Bob warmly. "*Ice*★ of you to **drop by**!"

"Ha!" answered Lucius. "I never heard that one before."

Lucius Best, the guy who **wrote the book** on "cool," hadn't changed much since the old days. Sure, he had to hide the **chill**ing Super powers he had used when he was known to the world as Frozone, but as with everything else, he was cool with that.

★ice 'nice'를 'ice'로 바꾼 농담.

Bob ran to the hall **closet** and quickly **grab**bed his coat and **bowling** bag. "I'll be back later," he said to Helen.

Helen seemed **confuse**d.

"It's Wednesday," Bob **remind**ed her.

Helen shook her head, remembering. "Oh . . . !" she said. "Bowling night."

She looked back at Dash and Vi, who were still ready to **go at** it, and then sighed.

"Say hello to Honey for me," Helen said to Lucius as he and Bob headed out the door.

"Will do," Lucius answered. "Good night, Helen. G'night, kids!"

Helen turned back to Dash. He wasn't going to get out of discussing his trip to the **principal**'s office.

"I'm not the only kid who's been sent to the office, ya know," Dash said.

"Other kids don't have Super powers," Helen said, trying to be **patient**. "You were almost caught. Now, it's perfectly normal for you to feel—"

"What does anyone in our family know about being

normal?" Vi interrupted. "The only normal one is Jack-Jack."

Jack-Jack, the only member of the Parr family who didn't seem to have any Super powers, **gleeful**ly **spit** a **mouthful** of baby food onto his **chin** and giggled.

Lucius drove to a **run-down** part of the city and parked in an **alleyway**. He and Bob weren't really going **bowling**. Instead, they sat in the car and **reminisce**d about the old days while a **portable** police **scan**ner **hiss**ed **dispatch** calls.

"So now I'm in deep trouble." Lucius laughed, telling Bob a story from his past. "I mean, one more **jolt** of this death **ray** and I'm an **epitaph**. So what does Baron Von Worthless do?"

"He starts **monologuing**!" Bob **crack**ed **up**.

"He starts monologuing! He starts this, like, prepared

speech about how **feeble** I am compared to him, how **inevitable** my **defeat** is, how the world will soon be his, yadda yadda yadda.★"

"**Yammer**in'!" Bob said, loving the story.

"Yammerin'," Lucius said even more loudly. "I mean, the guy has me on a **platter** and he won't shut up!"

A call suddenly **crackle**d over the scanner: "Twenty-three fifty-six in **progress**."

"Twenty-three fifty-six," Bob repeated. "What is that . . . **rob**bery? Wanna catch a robber?"

"Tell you the truth," Lucius answered, "I'd rather go bowling. What if we actually did what our wives think we're doing for a change?"

As the **former** Supers continued to talk, they didn't even **realize** they were being watched. A beautiful **blonde** in a black sports car spoke into a **headset**.

"He's not alone," she said. "The fat guy's still with him."

The words "Fire at Fourth and Elias" came across

★yadda yadda yadda '어쩌고저쩌고'라는 뜻으로 별로 중요하지 않거나 뻔하다고 여겨지는 세부 사항들을 이를 때 쓰는 표현.

Lucius's scanner. Bob lit up like a **bulb**.

"A fire! Yeah, baby!" Bob said, pulling on a ski **mask**. Lucius did the same, turned on the car, and headed in the direction of Fourth and Elias.

"We're gonna get caught," Lucius said.

As they **tore** down the street, the black sports car followed them.

Bob and Lucius could see the orange **glow** of the **burn**ing apartment building from a **block** away. They were the first to arrive at the **scene**. Together, they ran into the burning building, found the un**conscious** apartment **dwell**ers, and **stack**ed them on their shoulders.

"Is that everybody?" Lucius shouted to Bob.

"It should be," Bob answered through the thick **smoke**, trying to **make his way** back into the street. "Can't you **put** this **out**?"

Lucius tried to ice the **flame**s. "I can't lay down a **layer** thick enough!" he said. "It's **evaporating** too fast!"

"What does that mean?" shouted Bob.

"It means it's hot and I'm **dehydrate**d, Bob!"

"What?" **yell**ed Bob. "You'**re out of** ice? I thought you could use the water in the air!"

"There is no water in this air! What's your **excuse**? **Run out of muscle**s?"

Then the two heard an **incredible roar**. They looked up. The flaming **roof was about to collapse** and **trap** them inside. Lucius shook his head and looked at Bob. "I wanted to go bowling!" he said, **scowl**ing.

A large **chunk** of the **ceiling** suddenly **smash**ed to the floor in a burning **heap**. Bob looked around and **spot**ted a way out. He **shift**ed his stack of unconscious **victim**s to one shoulder and looked at Lucius.

"All right," Bob shouted, taking **charge**. "Stay right on my **tail**, this is going to get hot!"

Bob suddenly ran full speed down the flaming **hallway**. Lucius was right behind him. As they ran through the flames, Bob focused on the **brick** wall ahead. He **pick**ed **up** speed, gave a huge yell, and lowered his free shoulder into it. The heroes and their **rescue**d fire victims smashed through the brick wall just as the burning building collapsed behind them.

Saved! Bob thought for an **instant**. Then an **alarm went off**. Bob and Lucius looked around. They had smashed through the wall of a **jewelry** store.

A **rookie** police **officer** who had responded to the fire alarm suddenly **spied** the two ski-masked men and **drew** his **pistol**. "**Freeze**!" he shouted.

Lucius **notice**d a **watercooler** and managed to **convince** the rookie officer that he needed a cup of water. Lucius slowly brought the cup of water to his mouth and smiled.

"Okay, you had your drink now," said the rookie officer.

"I know," replied Lucius. "Freeze."

A **frigid blast split** the air.

On the street, **firefighter**s **tend**ed to the fire. Several more police officers had arrived. They heard a **gunshot**. Drawing their guns, the officers entered the jewelry store. But once inside, they stopped and looked at each other, **bewilder**ed. In front of them was a heap of rescued fire victims at the base of an **enormous** hole in the wall. Standing **nearby** was the rookie, **stun**ned and **blink**ing under a layer of ice. The **bullet** and its **vapor trail** were frozen in **midair** in front of them.

Bob and Lucius jumped back into their car and pulled off their ski masks.

"That was way too close," Lucius said, **hit**ting **the gas**. "We're not doing that again."

As the **taillight**s of Lucius's car **sped** away, the cool blonde in the black sports car **radio**ed in to her **headquarter**s. "**Verify** you want to **switch target**s? Over," the voice on the radio said.

"Trust me," she answered. "This is the one he's been waiting for."

Bob **tiptoe**d through the kitchen. He had grabbed the last **chunk** of chocolate cake from a **plate** on the **counter** and was quietly **making his way** into the living room when the lights suddenly snapped on. It was Helen. She was sitting in a living room chair in her **bathrobe**.

"You said you'd be back by eleven," she said.

"I said I'd be back later," Bob answered.

"I **assume**d you'd be back later," Helen said, **peeved**. "If you came back at all you'd be back later."

Helen's arm stretched to Bob's shoulder and pulled a piece of concrete* off his coat. "Is this . . . **rubble**?" she asked him **accusingly**.

"It was just a little **workout**," Bob replied. "Just to **stay loose**."

Helen closed her eyes. "You know how I feel about that, Bob! We can't **blow** our cover again!"

Bob looked down at his **singe**d coat. "The building was **coming down** anyway," he said, trying to explain.

"You **knock**ed down a building?"

"It was on fire!" Bob argued. "**Structural**ly **unsound**! I performed a public service. You act like that's a bad thing."

"It is a bad thing, Bob. **Uproot**ing our family again so you can **relive** the **glory** days is a very bad thing!"

Some **loose** papers on the coffee table suddenly **rustle**d as a **breeze** came through the room.

Bob sighed. "All right, Dash. I know you're listening. Come on out."

"Vi, you too, young lady," Helen added.

Dash moved out from behind a door as Violet

★concrete 콘크리트. 시멘트에 모래와 자갈, 골재 등을 적당히 섞고 물에 반죽한 혼합물.

re**materialize**d from behind the **couch**.

"It's okay, kids," Bob said gently. "We're just having a discussion."

"Pretty loud discussion," Violet said.

"But that's okay," Bob told them, trying to sound **upbeat**. "What's important is that Mommy and I are always a team, always **unite**d . . . against . . . uh . . ." Bob wasn't sure where he was going with this. "The forces of . . ."

"**Pigheaded**ness?" Helen suggested.

Bob **hesitate**d. "I was going to say '**evil**' or something."

Helen stood up and stretched her arms around the kids' shoulders. "We're sorry we woke you," she told them. "Everything's okay. We should all be in bed."

Chapter 9

The next day, Bob was back at his **tiny** desk in his tiny **cubicle** at Insuricare. His **intercom** suddenly **beep**ed. Bob hit the answer button.

"Mr. Huph would like to talk to you in his office," a voice said **flat**ly.

"Now?" Bob asked.

"Now," the voice replied.

Bob **roll**ed **his eyes**, got up, and walked from his windowless cubicle to Huph's office. He didn't notice the **mysterious attractive** blonde who **slip**ped into his cubicle as he left.

Huph's office was larger than Bob's cubicle, but **painful**ly **tidy** and completely **joyless**—a lot like Huph himself.

"Sit down," Huph told Bob.

Bob took a seat as Huph stood up at his desk. This put Bob at about eye level with the little man.

"I am not happy, Bob," Huph **announce**d. "Not happy. Ask me why, Bob."

Bob **blink**ed slowly. "Okay . . . why?"

"Why what? Be **specific**, Bob," Huph said, **cross**ing his arms and **glaring** at Bob.

Bob knew a visit to Huph's office always required **patience**. Suddenly, he noticed something going on outside Huph's window. A **stocky** man was **suspicious**ly **hang**ing **around** the back **alley**.

Keeping **an eye on** the guy in the alley, Bob answered, "Why are you unhappy?"

"Your **customer**s make me unhappy, Bob."

"You've had **complaint**s?" Bob asked.

"Complaints I can **handle**," Huph answered. "What I can't handle is your customers' in**explicable** knowledge of Insuricare's inner **workings**. They're **experts**. Experts, Bob! **Exploit**ing every **loophole**, **dodging** every **obstacle**! They're **penetrating** the **bureaucracy**!"

"Did I do something **illegal**?" Bob asked him calmly.

"No," said Huph, **irritate**d.

"Are you saying we shouldn't help our customers?"

Huph **grit**ted his teeth. "The law requires that I answer no."

"We're supposed to help people," Bob said.

"We're supposed to help *our* people!" Huph **explode**d. "Starting with our **stockholder**s.

"You know, Bob," Huph **went on**, taking a breath and **composing** himself, "a company is like—"

"An enormous clock," Bob said **dull**y, finishing the sentence for him. Bob had heard Huph's "enormous clock" **lecture** before.

Huph **drone**d on about **cog**s and **wheel**s: ". . . cogs that **fit**, Bob. **Cooperative** cogs." But Bob's attention was on the **thug** outside the window, who was now **mug**ging a **citizen**. Every **muscle** in Bob's body **tense**d for action.

"You know what I mean by cooperative cogs?" Huph

asked, **mesh**ing his fingers together. "Bob? Bob! Look at me when I'm talking to you, Parr!"

"That man out there!" Bob said, his eyes on the **victim**. "He needs help. He's getting mugged."

"Well, let's hope we don't cover him!" Huph said coldly as Bob suddenly stood and **bolt**ed for the door.

"I'll be right back," Bob said.

"Stop right now or you're **fire**d!" Huph **threaten**ed.

Bob hesitated. He thought about Helen and the kids. Huph **narrow**ed his eyes, sensing he had the **advantage**. **Confident**ly, Huph said, "Close the door."

Bob slowly let go of the door**knob** that he had **crush**ed in his **powerful** hand.

"Get over here, Bob," Huph told him.

Bob turned to face Huph. Through Huph's window, he could see the **helpless crime** victim lying on the street. The mugger had **gotten away**. Bob could feel his **blood pressure** rise. Suddenly, his enormous right hand **flash**ed out and **clamp**ed around Huph's **scrawny** neck. Huph let out a tiny **squeak**.

The office **staff** watched as Huph **crash**ed through

four office walls before he **slam**med into a **file cabinet**, sending **document**s everywhere.

"Uh-oh," Bob **mumble**d.

"How is he?" Bob asked.

"He'll live," replied Rick Dicker.

"I'm fired, aren't I?" asked Bob.

Rick Dicker, a **government agent** of the SRP, was a "tell it like it is" kind of guy, and he told Bob he was, indeed, fired. "We **appreciate** all you did in the old days," he said, "but from now on, Bob, you're on your own."

Bob **nod**ded. He knew how **complicated** and expensive it was to **relocate** a Super once the Super's **cover** had been **blown**. Rick had done it for Bob more than a few times.

Dicker was in the hospital elevator when he said,

“Listen. Maybe I could relocate you, for old times’ **sake**.”

Bob smiled and shook his head. “I can’t do that to my family again. We just got **settle**d. I’ll make it work. Thanks,” he said, and headed home.

Bob **pull**ed **into** his **driveway**. A **neighborhood** kid on a **trike** was **staring** at him. “What are you waiting for?” Bob asked, getting out of his car.

“I dunno,” the kid answered, looking around. He had once **spied** Bob lifting his car with one hand. “Something **amazing**, I guess.”

A smile flashed over Bob’s face and then **fade**d. “Me too, kid. Me too.”

Bob walked into the house. Helen was in the kitchen **fix**ing dinner. He headed down to his **den**. It was the one place where he could proudly **display** his **memento**s of the old days.

They were all there: the amazing photos, the **front-page headline**s, the **countless** magazines, thank-you letters, and all his other **triumph**s. But the **centerpiece** hung on the wall, **mount**ed behind a **sheet** of glass. It was his old blue and black Mr. Incredible **suit**. Seeing it today was almost more than Bob could take.

Bob set his **briefcase** on his desk, opened it, took out his Insuricare **employ**ee **manual**, and **toss**ed it and everything else in his briefcase into the **trash**. But something hit the bottom of the trashcan with a **clunk**. Bob looked. It was a large manila★ **envelope**.

Bob picked it up and tore it open. Inside was a **flat** metal **panel** with a small circle in its center. Bob tried to read the tiny words inside the circle. He **squint**ed and read, "'Hold still,'" out loud.

Suddenly, the panel **project**ed a blue laser✳ **grid** over Bob's face. A **robotic** voice began to speak. "**Match**. Mr. Incredible."

Bob jumped and dropped the panel onto his desk. A small **rod** rose from the panel and **scan**ned the den. "Room is **secure**," the voice said. "**Commence** message."

The panel **turn**ed **into** a video screen. On it was the beautiful blonde from the black sports car. Bob

---

★ manila 마닐라지. 목재 펄프에 파초과의 여러해살이풀인 마닐라삼 줄기에서 뽑은 섬유를 섞어서 만든 질긴 종이.

✳ laser 레이저. 증폭기 안에서 유도 방출을 반복하여 증폭된 빛 또는 그러한 빛을 내는 장치.

was stunned. "Hello, Mr. Incredible," she said warmly. "Yes, we know who you are. **Rest assured**, your secret is safe with us. My name is Mirage. We have something in common. **According to** the government, neither of us exist. . . ."

Bob moved closer to the screen, **mesmerize**d. "I **represent** a top-secret **division** of the government **design**ing and testing **experimental technology**, and"—she **pause**d—"we have need of your **unique** abilities."

"Honey?"

Bob jumped. It was Helen calling from the kitchen. "Dinner's ready!"

Bob turned back to the screen as Mirage continued. "Something has happened at our **remote** testing **facility**. A highly experimental **prototype** robot has escaped our **control**—"

"Honey!"

"Okay! Okay!" Bob shouted to Helen.

"It **threaten**s to cause **incalculable damage** to itself and our testing facilities," Mirage said.

"Is someone in there?" Helen shouted.

"It's the TV! I'm trying to watch!" Bob yelled back. He put his face closer to the screen. He **grab**bed a pencil. He didn't want to miss any of this message.

"Because of its highly **sensitive nature**, this **mission** does not, nor will it ever, exist."

"Well, stop trying!" Helen said. "It's time for dinner!"

"One minute!" Bob yelled.

"If you accept, your **payment** will be **triple** your **current annual salary**." Bob's **jaw** dropped, and he **blank**ly **scribble**d "BIG $$$$" on a **pad**.

"Call the number on the card," Mirage **instruct**ed as a **business card spit** out of the bottom of the video screen. "Voice matching will be used to **ensure security**. The Supers aren't gone, Mr. Incredible. You can still do great things. You have twenty-four hours to respond," she said **smooth**ly. "Think about it."

Bob finished scribbling. His mind was **reel**ing. Then the robotic voice came on again. "This message will **self-destruct**," it said.

From outside Bob's den, the family could hear a **muffle**d **boom**!

From inside his den, Bob could hear the family suddenly scream as the sprinklers★ over the dining room table **went off**.

Bob and Helen finished drying out the inside of the house. "You're one **distract**ed guy," Helen said as she used a hair dryer on the kids' books.

"Hmm? Am I?" Bob said. "Don't mean to be."

Helen put her arm around him. "I know you miss being a hero and your job is **frustrating**. I just want you to know how much it means to me that you **stay at it** anyway."

"Honey," Bob said, looking away, "about the job . . ."

Helen was suddenly alarmed. "What?"

"Uh, I . . . uh," Bob **stammer**ed. "Something's happened."

"What?" Helen asked.

Bob **gulp**ed hard. "Uh, the company's sending me to a **conference** out of town," he said finally. "I'm just gonna be gone for a few days."

★sprinkler 스프링클러. 화재가 발생했을 때 이상고온을 감지하여 자동으로 물을 뿜는 자동 소화 장치.

"A conference? This is good, isn't it?" she said **hopeful**ly. "You see? They're finally **recognizing** your **talent**s!" She gave him a **hug**.

"Yes," Bob said, hugging her back.

Bob went down to his den. He picked up the phone and **dial**ed the number on the card. A female voice answered.

"This is Mr. Incredible," Bob said. "I'm in." He **hung up** the phone and **glance**d at his Mr. Incredible suit on the wall.

Chapter 11

Bob sat back in a **sleek luxurious jet** as it **slice**d through the sky. He was on his way to a **remote** secret **location**. **Clad** in his old Super suit, now a little tight around the middle, Bob faced the beautiful Mirage. She began **brief**ing him on his **upcoming mission**.

"The Omnidroid★ 9000 is a top-secret **prototype battle** robot," she told Bob. "Its **artificial intelligence enable**s it to solve any problem. And **unfortunately**—"

"Let me guess," Bob said. "It got smart enough to

★ droid 드로이드. 공상 과학 영화 등에 등장하는 인공 지능을 갖춘 로봇들을 가리키는 말.

wonder why it had to take orders."

Mirage nodded. "We lost control and now it's **loose** in the **jungle**."

"How am I going in?" Bob asked in a cool **tone**.

"An **airdrop** from five thousand feet,★" Mirage said. It had been a long time since Bob had been air-dropped into anything. He played it cool, but secretly he couldn't wait.

"We're pretty sure it's on the southern half of the island," Mirage told Bob. "One more thing," she said. "**Obvious**ly it **represent**s a **significant invest**ment."

Bob understood. "You want me to **shut** it **down** without completely destroying it."

Mirage smiled. "You *are* Mr. Incredible."

Bob confidently entered the drop-**pod bay**. Getting into the pod **prove**d a Super **feat** in itself. After a few un**successful** attempts at **squeezing** himself in, he was finally **cram**med inside the pod. **Admittedly**, he wasn't in top Super form. Mirage entered the drop-pod bay and

---

★feet 길이의 단위 피트. 1피트는 약 30.48센티미터이다. 5,000피트는 1,524미터를 말한다.

pressed the speaker **switch**.

"Remember," she said, "it's a learning robot. Every moment you spend fighting it only increases its knowledge of how to **beat** you."

Bob nodded and repeated his **instruct**ions. "Shut it down. Do it quickly. Don't destroy it," he said.

"And don't die," Mirage added. Bob flashed her a smile, and the pod **blast**ed from the jet into the clouds above the island of Nomanisan.

The pod dropped and disappeared into the thick jungle. Bob had to **tear** the pod apart to get out. **Free**d, he quickly began to **track** the robot. Mr. Incredible was ready for action.

Unfortunately, he was also **out of shape**. By the time Mr. Incredible found the first **sign** of the Omnidroid, he was breathing heavily. Then, crashing out of the jungle, the robot attacked him. Mr. Incredible, **overweight** and a little **rusty**, **struggle**d with the large spiderlike robot. He hadn't fought like this in a long time. He managed to throw the robot into a **nearby lava pool**, but hurt his back in the **process**.

"Ow! My back!" he cried.

The robot **emerge**d, red-hot from the lava, and grabbed him with two **claw**s, trying to break him in half! Mr. Incredible's back **crack**ed. He smiled. The Omnidroid was better than a chiropractor!★ With newfound strength he **slip**ped under the robot and tore his way inside the machine. The Omnidroid began attacking itself to get at Mr. Incredible, **eventually** pulling itself apart in the process.

In a secret room in the island's **headquarter**s, Mirage and her **mysterious employ**er watched a video **display** of the battle.

"Surprising," the **mystery** man **comment**ed to Mirage as they watched Mr. Incredible. "We must bring him back." He smiled. "Invite him to dinner."

Later that evening, Bob, **handsome**ly dressed in a tuxedo, opened the door to an **enormous** dining room. No one was there. He glanced at his watch. He was early. The

★ chiropractor 척추 지압사. 척추 신경 압박으로 인한 신체의 이상을 치료하고 장애를 예방하기 위해 해당 부위를 전문적으로 지압하는 사람.

dining room had a **terrace** that **overlook**ed a **lush tropical** jungle. The **lavish**ly set table was placed in front of an **impressive waterfall** of **molten** lava.

Suddenly, there was a **rumble**. The hot lava **part**ed like a curtain, **reveal**ing a **passageway**. Bob slipped out of the room and **peek**ed through a crack in the door. He could see two **figure**s behind the falls. He recognized one of them as Mirage. The other was **obscure**d by the lava's **glow**. Bob closed the door. Mirage opened the door moments later to see Bob—**seeming**ly just arriving at the room.

"Am I **overdressed**?" he asked as he stepped into the dining room.

Mirage smiled **approving**ly. "Actually, you look rather **dashing**."

They sat at the dining room table, the red lava falling behind them. "I take it our **host** is—" Bob began.

"I'm sorry. He's not able to dine with us tonight," Mirage said with a **wave** of her hand. "He hopes you'll understand."

"Of course," Bob said **casual**ly. "I do usually **make it**

a point to know who I'm working for."

Mirage explained that their host preferred **anonymity**. "Surely you of all people understand that," she said, smiling.

Bob looked at the **surroundings**. "I was just wondering . . . of all places to **settle** down," he said, "why live—"

"With a **volcano**?" Mirage laughed. "He's attracted to power. So am I." She **lean**ed toward Bob. "It's a weakness we share."

"Seems a bit un**stable**," Bob said.

"I prefer to think of it as **misunderstood**," Mirage said, looking at Bob over her raised glass.

Bob returned home and felt like a new man. Over the next few weeks, he began **work**ing **out**, **get**ting **in shape** again. He bought the **brand-new** sports car he'd always dreamed about for himself and a new car for Helen. For the first time in years, he felt ***incredible***.

As he dressed the next morning in a **tailor**ed business suit, Bob **notice**d a tear in his Mr. Incredible suit.

"Hurry, honey, or you'll be late for work!" Helen called. Bob quickly **stuff**ed his old Super suit into his **briefcase** and **snap**ped it shut. He still hadn't told Helen he'd been fired from Insuricare. He'd been pretending to go to work every morning.

Helen **hug**ged him at the **doorstep**. "Have a great day, honey! Help **customer**s! Climb **ladder**s!" she said, **brighten**ed by Bob's new **attitude**.

Bob waved from his new sports car, **rev**ved the engine a bit, and backed down the **driveway**.

An hour later, he **pull**ed **up** to an enormous gate of **web**bed laser **beam**s and **lean**ed out his window toward the video **security** monitor.

The screen flashed on. "Do you have an **appointment**?" a **guard** asked **stiff**ly.

"I'm an old friend," Bob answered. "I just wanted—"

"Get back, Rolf!" a **husky** voice suddenly **bark**ed over the speaker. "Go check the **electric fence** or something."

Bob couldn't see anyone on the screen but the guard. But a familiar face wearing huge dark-**rim**med glasses rose into the bottom half of the screen. It was his old friend, **international**ly famous fashion **design**er Edna Mode.

"What is it?" she asked in her **brusque** but **fabulous accent**. "What do you want?"

Bob took off his sunglasses and **grin**ned at the security

camera.

Edna, known to her good friends simply as E, was **stun**ned. “My God, you have gotten fat!” she said. “Come in! Come!”

The laser beams **shut down**. Bob drove through the gate and up the long driveway. E, now in her sixties, **greet**ed Bob warmly as he entered her modern, gallery-like home. She reached up and took Bob’s arm. She led him into her **gigantic** living room.

“Yes, things are going quite well, but”—she **sigh**ed—“you know, it is not the same. Not the same at all.”

Bob nodded. “Weren’t you just in the news?” he asked. “Some show in Prague?★”

“Milan,✻ **darling**, Milan. Supermodels—*Hah!* Nothing *Super* about them. *Feh!* I used to design for gods!” Then E looked at Bob **hopeful**ly. “But perhaps you come with a **challenge**, eh?”

Bob held up his suit. “E, I just need a **patch** job.”

★Prague 프라하. 체코의 수도. 국제 교통의 요충지로, 자동차 · 기계 · 맥주 등의 공업이 발달하였다.

✻Milan 밀라노. 이탈리아 롬바르디아주에 있는 도시. 예로부터 교통의 요지이며 이탈리아 제1의 상업 · 금융 · 공업 도시로 발전해 왔다.

E grabbed the torn suit. "This is **megamesh**," she told him **impatient**ly, "**outmode**d but very **sturdy**, and you have torn right through it."

She looked up. "What have you been doing, Robert? **Moonlight**ing hero work?"

Bob tried to sound **casual**. "Must've happened a long time ago."

"Ah," E said **knowingly**. "I see."

E stood up. "This is a **hobo** suit," she **announce**d **firm**ly. "You cannot be seen in this. I won't allow it. Fifteen years ago, maybe. But now!" She shook her head and dropped the suit into the **trash**.

"What do you mean?" Bob asked, **rush**ing to **retrieve** it. "You designed it."

"I never **look back**, darling," she said with a wave of her hand. "It **distract**s me from the *now*. You need a new suit. That much is certain."

"A new suit?" Bob was shocked. "Where would I get—"

"Ask me now before I again become **sane**," E said. It was a **hint**.

"Wait," Bob said, **confuse**d. "You want to make me a suit?"

E suddenly began **gesturing** with her tiny arms. "It will be **bold**. **Dramatic**! **Heroic**!"

"Yeah!" Bob agreed **enthusiastic**ally. "Something **classic**, like Dynaguy. He had a great look. The **cape** and the **boot**s—"

"No capes," said E, **cut**ting him **off**.

"Isn't that my decision?" Bob asked.

E **stiffen**ed and **remind**ed Bob of all the past caped Supers. "Do you remember Thunderhead?" she asked.

Bob **cringe**d.

"Tall? **Storm** powers? Nice man," E said. "Good with kids. His cape **snag**ged on a **missile fin**."

"Thunderhead was not the brightest **bulb** in the—!" Bob said, hoping to change her mind.

E raised an **eyebrow** and ran down the list of **doom**ed Supers.

"Stratogale," she said. "Cape caught in a **jet** turbine.★"

★turbine 터빈. 물 · 가스 · 증기 등의 유체가 가지는 에너지를 유용한 기계적 일로 변환시키는 기계.

Bob sighed.

"Metaman," E continued. "Express elevator. Dynaguy—snag on **takeoff**."

E **glare**d at Bob. *"No capes!"* she said with a **finality** Bob **wasn't** **about to** argue with. Then she smiled. "Well, **go on**," she told him. "Your new suit will be finished before your next **assign**ment."

"I only need a patch job, E," Bob said, looking at his old suit. "For **sentimental** reasons."

"Fine," E sighed, taking the suit from Bob. "I will also **fix** the hobo suit."

Bob smiled at his old friend. "E, you're the best of the best!"

E closed her eyes and smiled. "Yes, I know, darling. I know."

Chapter 13

Helen was home doing laundry. She was about to hang Bob's sports coat when she saw it: the **glint** of something shiny on his jacket—a long **blond** hair. The phone rang. Bob **yell**ed that he'd get it and picked it up in the **den**. Helen **sly**ly picked up the bedroom phone anyway.

She heard a woman's voice say, "How soon can you get here?"

"I'll leave tomorrow morning," Bob answered quickly, and then **hung up** the phone.

"Who was that, honey?" Helen asked as Bob came out of his den. "The office?"

Bob **shrug**ged. "Another **conference**," he said. "Short notice, but **duty** calls." Bob smiled, but Helen was growing **suspicious**.

The next morning, Mr. Incredible found himself once again in the **luxurious surrounding**s of the **sleek** jet. But this time, he was wearing his newly made and completely redesigned Super suit—**dramatic**, **heroic**, red—no cape. Mr. Incredible **sip**ped his drink as the jet cut through the sky.

A voice came over the **autopilot**. "This is your **automate**d **captain** speaking. **Curren**tly seventy-eight degrees★ in Nomanisan. Please **fasten** your seat belt. We're beginning our **descent**."

Mr. Incredible glanced out the jet's window as it began to drop. He could see the **lush volcanic terrain** of Nomanisan coming up fast.

Suddenly, Mr. Incredible heard the autopilot cut the engines. The jet **plunge**d, **nose** down, into the sea. As

---

★ seventy-eight degrees 화씨 78도(℉). 섭씨온도로는 약 25도(℃)이다.

it hit the **surface**, the jet **convert**ed into a high-speed **submersible**.

The jet-sub **maneuver**ed through rock **formation**s as it headed toward the island of Nomanisan. Mr. Incredible watched the **spectacular underwater scenery** as it passed his window.

Ahead, an underwater **dock**ing **bay** opened. The submersible passed through a blue curtain of **bubble**s created by the cooling **lava**, and settled to a **land**ing. The water **drain**ed from around the ship. Mr. Incredible heard the **clunk** of a docking **tube** as it **attach**ed to a door.

"Hello, Mr. Incredible," Mirage said as the door opened. "Welcome back."

They stepped into a waiting mono**pod** that **zoom**ed from the **lagoon**, through the **jungle**, and into the island **headquarter**s.

Mirage **escort**ed Mr. Incredible to his **quarter**s and told him he'd be **brief**ed in the conference room at two o'clock.

Helen's day wasn't quite as exciting. She was **tidy**ing up Bob's **den**, **dust**ing the glass case, when she noticed the case was open. She took a closer look and saw a long, nearly **microscopic stitch** in his old Super **suit**. Helen was shocked. It had been newly **repair**ed.

"Edna," she said to herself. Helen knew that type of **craftsmanship** couldn't have been done by anyone else.

Helen decided that if Bob was doing Super work **on the side**, she wanted to know. There was only one thing to do. She picked up the phone and **dial**ed a number she had never thought she would dial again.

"Hello," Helen said. "I'd like to speak to Edna, please."

"This is Edna," E replied.

"E, this is Helen."

"Helen who?" E asked in her usual **husky** voice.

"Uh, Helen Parr, er, uh . . . you know . . . Elastigirl."

E was **thrill**ed. "**Darling**!" she said. "It's been such a long time. So long!"

"Yes, it has been a while," Helen said, **hesitating**. "Listen, there's only one person Bob would trust to **patch** his Super suit, and that's you, E."

"Yes, yes, yes. **Marvelous**, isn't it? Much better than those horrible **pajamas** he used to wear. They are all finished; when are you coming to see me? Do not make me **beg**, darling, I will not do it, you know!"

"Beg? Uh, no, I'm calling to beg about—I'm calling about Bob's suit!" Helen said finally.

"You come in one hour, darling," E said. "I **insist**. Okay? Okay. Bye."

Back in an **enormous** Nomanisan **conference** room, Mr. Incredible was waiting to be **brief**ed on his next dangerous **mission**. He checked his watch. It was exactly two o'clock.

Two huge doors at the end of the conference room suddenly **slam**med open. But it wasn't Mirage. Another Omnidroid stood in the **hangar**like **doorway** that opened to the jungle, but this one was not like the other Omnidroid.

"It's bigger!" a voice **echo**ed over a **loudspeaker** as Mr. Incredible tried to **maneuver** around the robot. "It's badder!*" the voice continued as the Omnidroid seemed to **anticipate** the Super's every move.

"It's too much for Mr. Incredible!" the voice **boom**ed as the Omnidroid **grab**bed Mr. Incredible with a huge **claw** and **flung** him into a jungle **clearing**. It **seize**d the Super in one of its giant claws as two **spin**ning claws **close**d **in** on his neck. A **chunk**y, wild-haired **figure** in a bright suit suddenly appeared.

"It's finally ready!" The caped stranger laughed. "After you **trash**ed the last one, I had to make some major **modification**s. Sure, it was difficult, but you're worth it. **After all**—I am your biggest fan."

A dark look of **realization** fell over Mr. Incredible's face. "Buddy?"

"My name is not Buddy!" he said, and **press**ed a button on his thick platinum✻ **wrist**band. The Omnidroid flung Mr. Incredible again. "And it's not Incrediboy either," Buddy went on. "That ship has **sail**ed. All I wanted was to help you. I only wanted to help! And what did you say to me?"

★badder 'bad'의 비교급은 'worse'이지만 여기에서는 'bigger'와 운율을 맞추기 위해서 이렇게 쓰였다.

✻platinum 백금. 은백색의 금속으로 은보다 단단하며 녹슬지 않는다.

Mr. Incredible remembered his words: *"Fly home, Buddy. I work alone."*

"I was wrong to **treat** you that way. I'm sorry," the Super said.

"See? Now you **respect** me. I'm a **threat**. That's the way it works. **Turns out** there are a lot of people, whole countries, who want respect. And they will **pay through the nose** to get it. How do you think I got rich? I **invent**ed **weapon**s. Now I have a weapon that only I can **defeat**, and when I un**leash** it, I'll get everyone's respect. I am Syndrome!"

Mr. Incredible suddenly reached for a fallen **log** and **hurl**ed it at Syndrome with all his Super strength. Syndrome **duck**ed and shot a **beam** from his **index finger**, hitting the hero in the chest. Mr. Incredible **froze** in **midair**.

"You **sly** dog! You got me **monologuing**!" Syndrome **chuckle**d with **admiration**. Then, **jerk**ing his index finger, he **effortless**ly **toss**ed Mr. Incredible into a tree with **tremendous force**.

"Cool, huh? Zero-point energy.★ I save the best

inventions for myself!"

With a **slight** move of his finger, Syndrome caught Mr. Incredible in his immobi-**ray**✻ again, freezing him in midair. "Am I good enough now? Who's Super now?" Syndrome **taunt**ed as he slammed Mr. Incredible into the ground over and over.

"I'm Syndrome! Your **nemesis**! And . . ."

Syndrome suddenly **caught himself** monologuing again and realized he hadn't heard Mr. Incredible's body land. He flew over the jungle **canopy** to watch Mr. Incredible **dive** off a **massive waterfall**. Syndrome looked over a **ledge** as the Super **crash**ed into the water below the falls. **Furious**, Syndrome **engage**d a small **lollipop**-shaped **device** from his wristband and dropped it into the water. It was a very **powerful explosive**.

The shock **wave** from the explosion **blew** Mr. Incredible through a **cave** into a **grotto** above the water. **Exhaust**ed, he was looking for a possible way out when he saw the

---

★zero-point energy 영점에너지. 양자역학에서 입자가 바닥상태에서 지니는 에너지이다. 불확정성원리에 의해 바닥상태라도 입자는 최소한의 에너지를 갖게 되는데, 이로 인해 절대영도에서도 초전도 현상이나 초유동 현상이 일어난다.

✻immobi- 여기에서는 'immobile(움직이지 못하는)'이라는 단어를 줄여 쓴 말이다.

skeleton of Gazerbeam. He **recognize**d the glasses that hung on the old Super's **skull**. He remembered reading that Gazerbeam was missing, and shook his head sadly. But Mr. Incredible **had to hand it to** his old hero friend—in Gazerbeam's dying moments, he had used his laser eyes to **burn** the word *KRONOS* into the cave wall. Mr. Incredible knew it meant something important, but what?

Mr. Incredible heard the ***click**, click, click* of an **electronic probe**. It was entering the grotto. He quickly **crawl**ed under Gazerbeam's skeleton.

The probe **scan**ned the entire cave and then **fix**ed on Gazerbeam's skeleton. Mr. Incredible **held his breath** and closed his eyes. The probe **chirp**ed and left.

Above the waterfall, the probe returned to Syndrome. "Life **reading**s **negative**," it reported. "Mr. Incredible **terminate**d."

Syndrome **bow**ed his head in respect for his **former idol** and then chuckled **wicked**ly.

E led Helen **downstairs** to her secret **lab**. "This **project** has completely **confiscate**d my life, **darling** . . . **consume**d me as only hero work can," E said with her usual **enthusiasm**. "My best work, I must admit. Simple. **Elegant**, yet **bold**. You will die. I did Robert's suit and it **turn**ed **out** so beautiful I just had to continue!"

"E," Helen said, "I have no idea what you're talking about. I just—"

"Yes, words are **useless**," E **went on**. "That is why I show you my work. That is why you are here!"

E turned to the wall. "Edna . . . Mode," she said into

a microphone, and **rapid**ly **execute**d an **elaborate** series of **security measure**s.

In a **flash**, a **ceiling panel** opened, **reveal**ing an enormous gun with its **sight**s **train**ed **on** Helen. E turned back to the microphone and added **hastily**, "*And* guest."

The gun **retreat**ed into the ceiling. The wall in front of them opened, revealing E's lab for **design**ing and testing Super suits.

"Come, sit," E said, inviting Helen in for coffee. "Cream and sugar?" she asked.

Helen **settle**d into a comfortable chair. She **was about to** ask E about Bob's Super suit when the lights in the lab suddenly **dim**med. "I started with the baby," E said **cheerful**ly.

"Started?" Helen asked.

"*Shhh,* darling, *shhh!*" E said as a small **feature**less baby **mannequin** in a **tiny** red suit **emerge**d in a glass **chamber**, moving slowly from one side to the other.

"I cut it a little **roomy** for the free movement." E smiled.

The inside of the chamber **erupt**ed in **flame**s. Helen

jumped back.

"And," E added, "it can also **withstand** a **temperature** of over one thousand degrees!"

The flames were **replace**d by a **barrage** of **machine-gun fire**.

"Completely **bulletproof** and machine **washable**, darling. That's a new feature!"

Helen was shocked. "What **in heaven's name** do you think the baby will be doing?" she asked.

"Well, I'm sure I don't know, darling. Luck **favor**s the prepared," E answered. "I didn't know the baby's powers, so I **cover**ed the basics."

"Jack-Jack doesn't have any powers," Helen said, **staring** at the little bulletproof suit.

"No? Well, he'll look **fabulous** anyway."

As the mannequin **exit**ed at one end, a mannequin of a young boy running at top speed appeared at the other end. The arms and legs **accelerate**d until they **blur**red. "Your boy's suit," E said proudly. "I designed it to withstand enormous **friction**.

"Your daughter's suit was **tricky**," she continued as

another mannequin entered. "I finally created a **sturdy material** that will disappear completely as she does."

All the red Super suits **match**ed, and each had the letter *I* for *Incredible* **emblazon**ed on the chest. Helen was **stun**ned.

"Your suit can **stretch** as far as you can without **injuring** yourself and still **retain** its shape," E said, as if she was saving the best for last. A suit designed for Helen entered the chamber. Two giant robot arms appeared and **clamp**ed onto the arms of the new red Super suit on the mannequin. Two more clamped onto the pants, pulling and **twist**ing them into every possible shape.

"**Virtual**ly **indestructible**!" E smiled. "Yet it **breathe**s like Egyptian cotton.★ As an extra feature, each suit **contain**s a **homing device**, giving you the **precise** global **location** of the wearer at the touch of a button."

The lights in E's design lab came up as the chamber went dark. "Well, darling? What do you think?" E asked.

"What do I think? Bob is **retire**d! I'm retired! Our

★ Egyptian cotton 면(cotton)은 무명이나 목화솜 등을 원료로 한 실 또는 그 실로 짠 천을 말한다. 섬유가 가늘고 긴 것을 고급으로 여기는데, 이집트 면이 그 대표적인 예이다.

family is **underground**! You helped my husband **resume** secret hero work behind my back?"

"I **assume**d you knew, darling! Why would he keep secrets from you?" E asked.

"He wouldn't! He didn't—doesn't!" Helen **stammer**ed.

"Do you *know* where he is?" E replied, **tilt**ing her head.

Helen hesitated. "Of course."

E picked up her phone and handed it to Helen. "Do you *know* where he is?" she asked again.

Helen dialed Insuricare. "Hello, this is Helen Parr. Bob Parr is my husband. I was wondering if you could give me the number of the hotel he's staying at."

"Mr. Parr no longer works at Insuricare," the **receptionist** answered politely.

"What do you mean? He—he's on a business trip, a company retreat."

"My records say his **employ**ment was **terminate**d almost two months ago."

Helen handed the phone back to E. Her face was **expressionless**.

"So," E said, shaking her head. "You don't know where he is. Would you like to find out?" she asked, holding up the homing device.

Helen hit the button on the homing device.

"I'm such an **idiot**!" Helen cried. "I let this happen, you know. The new sports car, the **get**ting **in shape**!"

"Yes," E **sigh**ed. It was a familiar story. "He attempts to **relive** the past."

It was true. Helen knew Bob was happier when he was Mr. Incredible. "And now I am losing him!" she said. "What will I do? What will I do?"

"What are you talking about?" asked an **impatient** E. "*You are Elastigirl!* My God, **pull yourself together**! You will show him you remember that he is Mr. Incredible, and you will **remind** him who *you* are. You know where he is," she said, placing the homing device in Helen's hand. "Go. **Confront** the problem! *Fight! Win!*"

E walked Helen to the door. "And call me when you get back, darling. I enjoy our visits."

Chapter 17

At that moment on the island of Nomanisan, Mr. Incredible was **calculating** how he could get back into Syndrome's **base unseen** and dis**arm** his **control** center.

Mr. Incredible **caught hold of** the next mono**pod** **streak**ing through the **jungle** and quickly got control of it from the **guard**s. He **zoom**ed to the front gates and entered the **compound**.

As soon as he was deeper inside the **facility**, he headed for the dining hall, the one place he knew held a secret **passage** to Syndrome's control room. Mr. Incredible stood in front of the **lava** falls, not knowing how to open it.

Finally, Mr. Incredible picked up a large stone **statue** at the end of the room and held it above his head. He was about to run into the lava, using the statue as a **shield**, when the falls suddenly **part**ed. He **struggle**d to replace the enormous statue to its original position and **duck**ed behind it.

Mirage stepped out from the lava and walked across the room. The falls began to close. Mr. Incredible **rush**ed into the closing passage and jumped clear as the hot lava closed behind him.

He followed a series of floor lights that led to an **elaborate** chair in front of an enormous screen. He sat down and typed KRONOS into the controls.

Syndrome's plan to un**leash** his new and **improve**d Omnidroid on the world flashed onto the screen, followed by the **status** of all the Supers that Syndrome had **lure**d to the island. They'd all been **do**ne **in** by the **evil mastermind**. He had used them all as test **subject**s to **perfect** his Omnidroid. Mr. Incredible shook his head.

DYNAGUY: **TERMINATE**D. GAZERBEAM: TERMINATED. The list went on and on.

Then Mr. Incredible saw FROZONE: **LOCATION** KNOWN. He suddenly thought of Helen. He searched for her name. ELASTIGIRL: LOCATION UNKNOWN. Mr. Incredible breathed a sigh of **relief**, but it was **short-lived**.

The **homing** device on his Super suit **went off**! An **alarm** sounded. Mr. Incredible tried to run out of the hall, but **turret**s came out of the walls and shot balls of **sticky foam** right at him. As the foam **engulf**ed him, Mr. Incredible saw just one thing—Mirage's **high-heeled** shoes. He was caught!

At the Parr house, Helen was preparing to take a trip.

"There's lots of **leftover**s you can reheat," she told Vi. "Make sure Dash does his homework and both of you get to bed on time. I should be back tonight, late. You can be in **charge** that long, can't you?" Helen asked.

"Yeah . . . but why am I in charge again?" Vi asked.

"Nothing. Just a little trouble with Daddy."

"You mean Dad's in trouble? Or Dad is the trouble?" Vi asked Helen.

"I mean either he's in trouble . . . or he's going to be," said Helen darkly as she walked into her bedroom.

Helen took a small duffel bag★ from the **closet**. She **pack**ed a few things and then held up her Super **suit**. She took a deep breath and **stuff**ed the suit into her bag.

Dash **did a double take** as he passed her door. "Hey, what's *that?*" he asked, seeing the red suit. "Where'd you get that, Mom?"

Helen stretched her arm to the door and closed it. Dash ran and **immediate**ly appeared outside the window. He looked at the matching red suits laid out on the bed.

"Hey, are those for us? We all get cool **outfit**s?" he asked, **intrigue**d.

Helen took her hand off the door and stretched it to shut the **blind**s. Dash zoomed back through the door, **nab**bed his Super suit, and was gone.

"Wait a—Dash! You come back *this moment!*" Helen **yell**ed as the phone rang.

It was her friend Snug, the owner and **pilot** of some of the fastest **jet** planes ever to fly. Helen knew Snug from the old days.

★duffel bag 더플백. 거친 방모 직물로 짠 가방으로 보통 가방의 길이만큼 지퍼가 달려 있고 원통형의 모양을 하고 있다.

"Hey, Snug! Thanks for getting back. Listen, I know this is short **notice**, but I'm **call**ing **in a solid** you owe me," Helen said into the phone.

"Whaddya need?" Snug asked.

"A jet," Helen said calmly. "What can you get that's fast?"

"Let me think," said Snug.

Violet walked into her mom's bedroom.

"What are these?" she asked, staring at the red suits on the bed.

Suddenly, Dash appeared.

"Look!" he said proudly, wearing his Super suit and smiling at himself in the mirror. "I'm 'The Dash'!"

"Just a moment," Helen said to Snug, and placed her hand over the **mouthpiece**. "Take that off, before somebody sees you," she ordered.

"But you're packing one just like it," Vi said, pointing to the red suit in Helen's bag. "Are you hiding something?"

"Please, honey, I'm on the phone," Helen **plead**ed.

Dash picked up Vi's suit and handed it to her. "This is yours!" he told her. "It's specially made."

"What's going on?" Violet asked, dropping her shoulders and turning to her mom. Helen pushed them both into the hall and closed the door.

Vi was still holding her Super suit. "What makes you think it's special?" she asked Dash as they stood in the hall.

"I dunno. Why'd Mom try to hide it?" Dash replied **matter-of-fact**ly before running off.

Vi looked down at her suit and wondered. Then, making her hand in**visible**, she touched a finger to it. The suit disappeared in her hand.

"Whoa," said Vi.

It had been a long time since Helen had flown a jet—but it all came back to her quickly. "Island approach, India Golf Niner Niner★ checking in, VFR✻ on top. Over," she said into her **headset**. She had **track**ed Bob through the **homing device** to the small **volcanic** island below, but the

---

★India Golf Niner Niner 무전 통신에서 쓰이는 코드. 'India'는 알파벳 'I', 'Golf'는 알파벳 'G', 그리고 'Niner'는 숫자 '9'를 나타낸다.

✻VFR 'Visual Flight Rules(유시계 비행 규칙)'의 약어. 항공기 계기에 의존하지 않고 조종사 자신이 시각으로 지형지물을 확인하고 항공기 자세 및 위치를 파악하여 이루어지는 비행에 관한 규칙.

landing tower didn't answer.

Helen tried again. "Island tower. This is India, Golf, Niner, Niner **request**ing **vector**s!" Still no one responded.

Helen began to feel a little nervous. "Easy," she told herself. "You're **overreact**ing. Everything's fine." Five seconds later, she put the jet on **autopilot** and grabbed her Super suit.

As Helen flew toward the island of Nomanisan, Mr. Incredible awoke and found himself in Syndrome's **prison chamber**, his arms and legs **bound** by metal **restraint**s that held him **suspend**ed by Syndrome's immobi-**ray technology**. Syndrome stood **triumphant** over his **capture**d hero.

"You, sir, truly are Mr. Incredible," Syndrome said enthusiastically. "You know, I was right to **idolize** you. I always knew you were tough. But **trick**ing the **probe** by hiding under the **bone**s of another Super? Ohhhh, man! I'm still **geek**ing **out** about it!"

Syndrome's face suddenly **sour**ed. "Then you had to go and just—**ruin** the **ride**." He shook his head. "I mean, Mr. Incredible calling for help? 'Help me!' **Lame**, lame,

lame, lame, *lame!* Who did you **contact**?"

"Contact? What are you talking about?" asked Mr. Incredible.

With a **nod** from Syndrome, a **jolt** of **electricity** went into Mr. Incredible's chest. He **wince**d in pain.

"I'm **refer**ring to last night at 2307 hours,★ while you were **snoop**ing around, you sent out a homing **signal**," Syndrome said impatiently, and jolted Mr. Incredible again.

"I didn't—" said Mr. Incredible **painful**ly.

"And now a **government** plane is requesting **permission** to land here! *Who did you contact?*" Syndrome demanded in a **rage**.

"I didn't send for . . . a plane." Mr. Incredible **grimace**d.

"Play the **transmission**," said Syndrome to Mirage.

"Island approach, India Golf Niner Niner checking in, VFR on top."

Mr. Incredible's head **snap**ped up. "Helen!" he said.

"So you do know these people," Syndrome said,

★2307 hours 시간을 군대식으로 표현한 것으로 오후 11시 7분을 가리킨다.

smiling **malicious**ly. “Well then, I’ll send them a little **greet**ing.” He pressed LAUNCH on the **console** and began to laugh.

“No!” shouted Mr. Incredible, but he was **helpless**.

Helen changed into her Super suit and **toss**ed her duffel bag into a **passenger** seat.

"Ow!"

"Violet!" Helen said angrily as her daughter re**materialize**d.

"It's not my **fault**!" Violet explained as fast as she could. "Dash ran away and I knew I'd get **blame**d for it and—"

"That's not true!" Dash loudly **interrupt**ed, **pop**ping up from behind a seat. Helen threw her arms in the air. They were both in the plane. "*You* said, 'Something's up

with Mom,'" Dash continued hotly, "and, 'We hafta★ find out what,' and it was *your idea, your idea, one hundred percent all yours all the time idea!*"

"I thought he'd try to **sneak** on the plane so I came here and you closed the doors before I could find him and then you **took off**," Violet argued. "It's *not my fault!*"

Helen's expression suddenly changed. "Wait a minute, you left Jack-Jack alone?" she asked them.

"Yes, Mom! I'm completely stupid," Violet said **sarcastic**ally. "Of course we got a **sitter**! Do you think I'm totally ir**responsible**? Thanks a lot!"

"Well, who'd you get?" asked Helen **anxious**ly as she **dial**ed home.

"You don't have to worry about one single thing, Mrs. Parr. I've got this **babysit**ting thing wired,✱" Jack-Jack's new thirteen-year-old babysitter said.

"Kari?" said Helen **uncertain**ly.

"I also brought Mozart❋ to play while he sleeps

★ hafta 'have to'의 줄임말.

✱ wired 여기에서는 'wire'의 일반적인 뜻이 아니라, '처리하다' 또는 '해결하다'라는 뜻으로 사용되었다.

❋ Mozart 모차르트. 오스트리아의 작곡가. 18세기의 빈 고전파를 대표하는 한 사람으로, 고전파의 양식을 확립하였다.

because **leading experts** say Mozart makes babies smarter," Kari continued.

"Kari—" Helen interrupted.

"—and the beauty part is the babies don't even have to listen 'cause they're asleep!"

"Kari, I really don't feel comfortable with this. I'll pay you for your trouble, but I'd really rather call a service."

"There's really no need, Mrs. Parr. I can **handle** anything this baby can **dish out**. Can't I, little boobily boy?" Kari **coo**ed at Jack-Jack.

A warning signal sounded from the **cockpit**. Helen's eyes **widen**ed. She ran to the cockpit. The white **trail** of a **missile**—coming straight for them—was visible above the clouds.

Helen **grab**bed the **headset** as the **rocket roar**ed toward them. "**Friendlies** at two-zero miles★ south-southwest of your position, dis**engage**. Over!" Helen yelled into the headset. "Disengage!"

Dash and Vi exchanged **frantic glances**. The red light

★ mile 거리의 단위 마일. 1마일은 약 1.6킬로미터이다.

above their heads flashed **FASTEN** SEAT BELTS. **Panic**ked, they tried to **buckle** in, but it was too late. The jet took a **dive**, **slam**ming them to the **ceiling**. The missile **smoke**d by as Helen tried to call for help.

The jet was in a dive, the ocean coming straight at them. Helen **yank**ed back on the controls. The **nose** came up enough for the plane to **skim** the **wave**s before it finally turned upward.

Helen saw two more missiles appear on her screen. She **whirl**ed around to Violet.

"Vi! You have to put a **force field** around the plane!" Helen shouted.

"But you said we weren't supposed to use our powers—" Violet **protest**ed.

"I know what I said," Helen told her. "Listen to what I'm saying now!"

In the **prison cell**, Mr. Incredible had heard the entire radio **transmission**.

"I've never done one that big before!" he heard Violet say.

Then he heard Helen shout, *"Violet! Do it now!"*

"**Call off** the missiles! I'll do anything!" Mr. Incredible yelled.

"Too late," Syndrome told him coldly. "Fifteen years too late."

Inside the jet, Helen turned back to the radar screen. The missiles were **closing in** fast. There was no time left.

Helen threw off the headset and **leap**ed out of her seat. She stretched herself around her two children.

Mr. Incredible saw the missile **register** a hit on the radar screen. He closed his eyes in **grief** and **horror**.

Syndrome smiled as Mirage **confirm**ed that the **target** was destroyed. Mr. Incredible was **crush**ed. Helen and the kids were gone. "Ah, you'll **get over** it," Syndrome said to him. "I seem to **recall** you prefer to 'work alone.'"

In a sudden **burst** of **rage**, Mr. Incredible **lunge**d at Syndrome. Mirage pushed Syndrome away, but Mr. Incredible managed to grab her instead.

"**Release** me. Now!" Mr. Incredible **growl**ed as a guard turned up the control **panel**, **suspend**ing Mirage and Mr. Incredible in the chamber.

"Or what?" said Syndrome.

"I'll crush her," Mr. Incredible said, **squeezing** Mirage tightly.

"Sounds a little dark for you." Syndrome laughed. "Go ahead."

"No!" Mirage cried.

"It'll be easy," Mr. Incredible said. "Like breaking a **toothpick**."

"Show me," Syndrome said **smug**ly.

Mr. Incredible **hesitate**d, **grit**ted his teeth, then let Mirage go. Syndrome laughed as Mirage fell to the floor.

"I knew you couldn't do it. Even when you have nothing to lose, you're weak. I've **outgrow**n you," he said in **disgust**, and walked out.

Meanwhile, far out over the ocean, the smoke from the **missile**'s **explosion** began to **disperse**. Then an orange-red ball **emerge**d from the **blast** and began to un**furl**. It was Helen back in action as Elastigirl. Dash and Vi were **plummet**ing fast beneath her. Elastigirl quickly **stretch**ed herself into a human **parachute** as she grabbed both her children in **midair**, **break**ing **their fall** as they **splash**ed into the water below.

Dash and Vi broke the water's **surface**, **sputter**ing and splashing.

"Mom!"

"Everybody calm down," Helen told them as they struggled to stay **afloat**. "We're not going to **panic**!"

But on the ocean, Dash and Vi couldn't help it. Panic began to **overtake** them.

"We're dead! We're dead!" Dash cried, **tread**ing water. "We **survive**d, but we're dead!"

"Stop it!" shouted Helen. "We are not going to die! Now, both of you will **get a grip** or **so help me** I'll **ground** you for a month! Understand?"

Dash and Vi looked at their mom; then both **nod**ded at the same time.

"Those were short-**range** missiles," Helen told them as they **bob**bed in the water. "Land **base**d. That way is our best **bet**." She pointed at the missile trails.

"You want to go toward the people that tried to kill us?" asked Dash.

"If it means land . . . yes."

"Do you expect us to swim there?" asked Violet.

"I expect you to trust me," Helen told them.

Dash and Vi watched, **amaze**d, as their mother stretched her body into the shape of a boat. They both climbed **on board**. Helen had Dash put his legs over the side and kick them at Super speed. The Parr family boat was moving toward the island of Nomanisan.

It was sunset when they reached the beach. "What a **trooper**," Helen said as she reached over to **hug** Dash. He was **exhaust**ed. "I'm so proud of you."

"Thanks, Mom." Dash smiled **wearily**.

Cold and wet, Helen and the kids found a **cave** in the volcanic rock and built a fire to warm themselves as the sun went down.

"I think your father is in trouble," Helen told Dash and Vi as they **huddle**d around the fire. "I'm going to look for him. That means you're in charge until I get back, Violet."

"What?" asked Dash.

"You heard her," Vi said.

Helen reached into the **battered** duffel bag.

"Put these on," she said, handing them their black **mask**s. "Your **identity** is your most **valuable possess**ion. Protect it. If anything goes wrong, use your powers."

"But you said never to use—" began Violet.

Helen **sigh**ed. "Remember the bad guys on those shows you used to watch on Saturday mornings? Well, these guys are not like those guys. They will kill you. Do *not* give them that chance. Vi, I'm **count**ing **on** you."

Helen turned to Dash. "Be strong," she told him. "If anything goes wrong, I want you to run as fast as you can."

"As fast as I can?" Dash asked, making sure.

"As fast as you can," Helen told him. "Stay hidden. Keep each other safe. I'll be back by morning."

Helen gave them both a long hug and turned to leave. Vi ran after her.

"Mom . . . what happened on the plane . . . ," Vi said with **tear**s in her eyes. She knew her force field could have helped if she had just been **confident** enough to try. "I—couldn't—I'm—I didn't—I'm so sorry."

Helen placed a finger over Vi's lips and **tilt**ed her

head.

"Shhh," she told her. "It wasn't fair for me to suddenly ask so much of you. But things are different now. And **doubt** is a **luxury** we can't **afford** anymore, sweetie."

Then Helen smiled. "You have more power than you **realize**. And don't worry. If the time comes, you'll know what to do. It's in your blood."

At the same time that Dash and Vi were watching Helen disappear into the dark jungle, Mirage was outside Mr. Incredible's **cell** door, talking to Syndrome.

"He's not weak, you know," Mirage said.

"What?" snapped Syndrome.

Mirage **rub**bed the back of her neck. "**Valuing** life is not weakness," she said softly.

"Hey, if you're talking about what happened—" Syndrome began as he **wave**d a hand toward Mr. Incredible's cell.

Mirage snapped her head up. "And **disregard**ing it is not strength," she said **accusingly**.

"I called his **bluff**." Syndrome **shrug**ged. "I knew he

wouldn't—"

But Mirage was already walking away. "Next time you **gamble**," she said coldly, "bet your own life."

Elastigirl **fluid**ly moved through the **dense jungle**, **occasional**ly pulling herself from tree to tree with her **outstretched** arms. **Making her way** into a **clearing**, she saw the **glint** of a gray steel monorail★ overhead. Then she heard the **hum** of a mono**pod** approaching in the **distance**.

Elastigirl threw her arms up high as the lights of the monopod **streak**ed above her. Her hands **grip**ped the **vehicle**, and it **yank**ed her feet from the jungle floor.

★monorail 모노레일. 선로가 한 가닥으로 이루어진 철도. 차체가 선로에 매달리는 방식과 선로 위를 구르는 방식 두 가지가 있다.

She **dangle**d from the monopod until she could **swing** herself to its top.

The pod **slice**d through the jungle **canopy** with Elastigirl **determine**d to **hang on**. As she **squint**ed into the wind, she could see that the monopod was **speed**ing toward the base of a **tower**ing volcano. The pod **plunge**d into a dark tunnel and emerged inside a room with a **massive launchpad**. "A rocket?" Elastigirl wondered. She decided it was time to **drop in** and **investigate**.

Finding a **corridor** off the launchpad, Elastigirl stretched her neck and looked around a corner. A **guard** was **sliding** a key card through a **reader**, and ***whoosh***, the door in front of him opened. She needed that key card. It would let her **access** different parts of Syndrome's **lair** to look for her husband.

But as Elastigirl stretched toward the guard holding the key card, the doors behind her snapped shut, **trap**ping her leg. Soon more guards approached, opening more doors, and Elastigirl found herself caught in two **separate** **doorway**s—her **torso** in one, and her leg still in the other. Using her Super **elasticity**, she managed to kick and

punch all the guards till they were un**conscious**.

She grabbed a key card, **free**d herself, and **set off** down the corridor once again. It was time to find her husband.

Chapter 22

Inside the cave, Dash and Vi sat close to the fire. Dash **stare**d into space as Vi practiced **generating** force fields over the fire. Each try was like a little **bubble**.

"Well, not that this isn't fun," Dash finally said, "but I'm gonna go look around."

Vi stood up. "What do you think is going on here? You think we're on vacation or something? Mom and Dad's lives could be in **jeopardy**. Mom said to stay hidden."

Dash **roll**ed **his eyes**. "I'm not gonna leave the cave," he said, **annoy**ed.

He **grumble**d as he took a **flaming** stick and moved

into the darkness. Vi could see the flame getting smaller as Dash moved farther and farther away. "Cool . . . ," she heard him say in the far **distance**. Then suddenly . . . she heard Dash scream.

"Vi! Vi, Vi, Vi, Vi, Vi!" Dash **yell**ed, running back toward her at **warp** speed.

"What?" said Violet as Dash pointed to an orange **glow** at one end of the cave. It was growing brighter and brighter, getting closer and closer. Vi could feel the heat of it on her face. "What did you *do?*" she screamed as they both **race**d out of the cave.

Dash and Vi **outran** the **fireball in time** to see a rocket **roar** into the sky. Looking up, they realized they hadn't been hiding in a cave at all. It was the **exhaust** tunnel for the rocket launch.

That night, they had no choice but to sleep on the jungle floor.

Dash awoke to the **exotic** sounds of the jungle. He stretched his legs, still **stiff** from the day before. Suddenly, he heard the words "**Identification**, please." He **rub**bed his eyes and looked up. The words had come from a **brilliant**ly colored **robotic** bird **perch**ed in a **nearby** tree. Dash watched it, **mesmerize**d.

He was **thrill**ed. "Hey, Violet!" He laughed, **nudging** his sister. "Look! It talks!"

"Huh? What?" Vi answered, still sleepy.

Vi **tilt**ed her head and smiled. They stared at the bird, **enchant**ed, waiting for it to speak again.

"Voice key incorrect," the bird said.

"Voice key?" Vi repeated, and **frown**ed.

The bird's head **mechanical**ly **swivel**ed toward Dash and Vi. Its eyes lit up red as its **beak** dropped open and it let out a **shrill electronic alarm**.

"What do we do?" asked Dash as Vi began to back away.

"Run!" yelled Violet.

"Where are we going?" said Dash, **hesitating**.

"Away from here!" she called back.

Chapter 23

The **silhouette** of a **slender** woman appeared in Mr. Incredible's cell. She walked to the **control** panel and **switch**ed **off** the immobi-**ray**. "There isn't much time," she told Mr. Incredible, who dropped to his **knee**s. It was Mirage.

"No, there isn't," Mr. Incredible said, **grab**bing Mirage's **throat**. "There's no time at all."

"Please . . . ," Mirage **gasp**ed.

In a **fury**, Mr. Incredible **lash**ed out. "Why are you here? How can you possibly bring me lower? What more can you take away from me?"

"F-f-amily . . . **survive**d the **crash** . . . ," Mirage gasped. "They're here—on the island."

"They're alive?" Mr. Incredible said, **astound**ed. **Overjoyed**, he stood up and threw his arms around Mirage.

Mr. Incredible opened his eyes and saw another woman standing in the **doorway**. "Helen!" he cried.

Mirage stepped back. She **was about to** say hello when Elastigirl's **fist** flew across the room. Mirage fell hard.

"She was helping me to escape," Bob said, trying to explain.

"No, that's what I was doing!" Helen replied.

Bob took Helen in his arms.

"Let go of me, you un**faithful creep**," Helen **protest**ed.

"How could I **betray** the perfect woman?" he said. "Where are the kids?"

Mirage sat up and rubbed her **jaw**. "They might have **trigger**ed the **alert**," she told them. "**Security**'s been sent into the jungle. You'd better get going."

Bob and Helen headed for the door. "Now our kids are in danger," Helen said, still **upset** by the whole situation.

“If you **suspect**ed danger, why’d you bring them?” Bob asked as he began to run.

“I didn’t bring them,” Helen said, running right next to him. “They **stow**ed **away**, and I don’t think you’re **striking** the **proper tone** here.”

At that moment, Dash and Vi were running **blind**ly through the jungle. Almost **out of breath**, they **stop**ped dead **in their tracks**. Three high-speed velocipods were in their path. Vi spoke calmly in a low voice as she looked into the faces of the **arm**ed guards. "Dash. Remember what Mom said."

"What?" Dash asked, **terrified**, remembering the part about these guys not being like the bad guys you watched on TV. Then Vi disappeared.

"Dash! *Run!*" Vi shouted.

Right! Dash thought as he **bolt**ed into the jungle.

"They're *Supers!*" one of the guards yelled. *"Get the boy!"*

Dash ran at **lightning** speed, the velocipods hot on his **trail**. The **vine**s and **undergrowth** were so **dense** that Dash was **force**d to **stick to** a **narrow** jungle trail. Suddenly, he **rocket**ed through a thick, dark cloud. It was a **swarm** of black jungle flies. *"Aggcchh!"* Dash **choke**d as the flies hit his face like bugs **smash**ing into a **windshield**. He shook his head and **tumble**d into the undergrowth. He sat up and **rub**bed his bug-**spatter**ed teeth with the back of his **sleeve**.

"Achppt! *Ptthwaaagh! Pthtp!*" **sputter**ed Dash, **spit**ting bits of fly wings and legs from his mouth.

The velocipods suddenly **burst** through the undergrowth, and Dash began **tear**ing through the jungle again. He saw a hanging vine ahead and reached for it as he **zoom**ed by. Dash **swung** around in a wide **arc**, surprising the last velocipod and causing it to **veer** off into the undergrowth. **Immediate**ly, another velocipod was hot on his trail. Dash grabbed another vine and was **propel**led forward. But the vine **snap**ped and he rose into the air, suddenly **realizing** that he was no longer over land. He was falling fast off the **edge** of a **cliff**! Dash screamed.

With a **thud**, he **land**ed on the **hood** of a velocipod. He couldn't believe his luck. He was okay! A guard turned and took a swing at him. But Dash used his Super speed to **duck** every punch. He was beginning to get comfortable with his Super powers. He even managed to get in a few highspeed punches himself.

Dash was feeling pretty proud until he realized that the velocipod was headed straight for a cliff wall. The guard suddenly **sock**ed Dash in the **jaw**, **knock**ing him off the vehicle. Dash watched the velocipod **slam** into the cliff wall, **vaporizing** into a ball of fire.

Dash fell through the trees below the cliff. He hit **branch** after branch as he fell **flail**ing through an **enormous** tree. He tried to grab anything to stop his fall and finally got his hands around a vine. Dash hung from the vine. Then he looked down. He was about three feet off the jungle floor. How had he ever **survive**d that? He dropped to the ground and let out a loud **whoop** in **victory**.

Two **nearby** guards on velocipods turned and headed toward the sound. The velocipods picked up Dash's trail as he ran toward a **lagoon**. Dash **charge**d straight ahead and took a deep breath. He was ready to get wet, but when he looked down, he was surprised. He was running fast enough to **skim** along the water's **surface**.

Dash **blast**ed across the lagoon, **weaving** like a speedboat★ around the **volcanic** rocks **jut**ting out of the water. One velocipod followed as he **dart**ed into a **cave**. Dash realized he was in a tunnel when he saw the second velocipod coming at him from the other side. He **frantic**ally looked for a way out. He was trapped. Dash stopped running and dropped beneath the water's surface. He was **relieve**d when he heard the ***boom!*** of the two velocipods **colliding** overhead.

A guard **scan**ned the area with his **rifle**, looking for any **sign** of Violet. In**visible**, Violet quickly **club**bed the guard, knocking away his rifle and giving herself just

---

★ speedboat 고속 모터보트. 빠른 속도를 내는 것을 목적으로 만들어진 보트.

enough time to run into the jungle.

"Show yourself!" he **command**ed.

He picked up his gun and **fire**d, un**leash**ing a **barrage** of **bullet**s at a series of **footprint**s that streaked toward the river. The guard heard a **splash** and fired at a **rippling mass** under the water's surface.

He reached down, grabbed a **handful** of dirt, and threw it into the river. Violet's **outline** showed clearly in the **murky** water. The guard smiled, raised his rifle, and took **aim**.

But Vi didn't stay still—she splashed out of the river and **made a run for** the jungle. The guard swung his gun toward her. At that moment, Dash darted from the jungle, running full **throttle** toward the guard's legs.

"Don't touch my sister!" Dash shouted as he knocked the guard down. The guard managed to get a punch in as the two tumbled. **Stun**ned for a moment, Dash looked up to see the rifle pointed at his chest. The guard smiled and the **trigger click**ed. Violet **leap**ed between them, throwing a force **field** around her and Dash, protecting them. Dash was **amaze**d. Violet **float**ed in **midair**, **suspend**ed in her own force field.

"How are you doing that?" Dash asked as the bullets from the guard **ricochet**ed off the force field.

"I don't know!" Vi answered.

"Whatever you do—*don't stop!*" Dash said **enthusiastic**ally.

Dash began to run within the force field like a gerbil★ in a **wheel**, causing them to roll into the jungle, **rumbling** past the guards and down a **hillside**.

★gerbil 게르빌루스쥐. 주로 애완용 또는 실험용으로 많이 기르는 소형 쥐.

Mr. Incredible and Elastigirl raced through the **jungle side by side**. "I should have told you I was fired, I admit it," Mr. Incredible said, trying to **apologize**, "but I didn't want you to worry."

"You didn't want me to worry?" Elastigirl **exclaim**ed. "And now we're running for our lives through some **godforsaken** jungle!"

But Mr. Incredible just shook his head and smiled. "You keep trying to **pick a fight**, but I'm still just happy you're alive."

Mr. Incredible and Elastigirl heard an **explosion echo**

through the jungle, followed by a deep rumble that grew louder and louder. Suddenly, the rolling force field with Dash and Vi, having just **barely** escaped two **chasing** veloci**pod**s, **burst** out of the jungle in front of them.

"Mom! Dad!" Dash and Vi yelled.

The force field **flatten**ed Mr. Incredible and Elastigirl like cookie **dough** against a **rolling pin**. "Kids!"

Violet **disintegrate**d the force field, and the family fell to the ground, **hug**ging wildly.

Suddenly, a velocipod blasted out of the jungle. The Incredibles jumped to their feet and faced the fight together.

Elastigirl threw a **stretch**ed scissor kick★ that caught a **guard** in the chest, knocking him out of his velocipod. In perfect **harmony**, Mr. Incredible threw a chop✳ at a second passing velocipod and sent it **plow**ing into the jungle floor. Elastigirl **coil**ed her arm around the pod's **pilot** and **whiplash**ed him into another guard, knocking

---

★scissor kick 가위차기. 뛰어서 두 발을 가위 모양으로 벌리며 두 개의 목표물을 동시에 가격하는 기술.

✳chop 무술에서 손을 펴고 아래쪽을 향해 치는 타법.

them both **out cold**. Mr. Incredible grabbed the crashed velocipod and threw it into another that had just **emerge**d from the trees. Mr. Incredible and Elastigirl looked around at the crashed velocipods that now **litter**ed the jungle floor.

"I love you," they were saying to each other with **admiration** when the jungle suddenly filled with guards. The whole family **react**ed in a **blur** of Super powers. The guards were no **match** for the Incredibles.

"Whoa, whoa, *whoa!*" Syndrome said, stepping out of the jungle. ***"Time out!"*** he shouted, firing his immobi-ray and suspending the Incredibles **motionless** in **midair**.

Syndrome **cross**ed his arms and **assess**ed the **scene**. "What have we here?" he asked, **amuse**d. "Matching uniforms?"

He **narrow**ed his eyes and looked at Elastigirl.

"Oh, no!" He laughed out loud. "Elastigirl? You married Elastigirl? And got *biz-zay!*★" he said to Mr. Incredible. "It's a whole family of Supers! Looks like I've

---

★ biz-zay 'busy(바쁜)'를 강하게 발음한 표현.

hit the **jackpot**! Oh, this is just *too good!*" he exclaimed, **relish**ing the moment.

Inside Syndrome's **prison chamber**, Mr. Incredible, Elastigirl, Dash, and Vi were held **captive** in immobi-**ray**s, **side by side**. On a giant screen in front of them, a **newscast** showed a **crowd gather**ed around a large **smolder**ing **craft** at the base of a building. The Omnidroid had landed in the city. The Incredibles had no choice but to watch.

"Huh?" Syndrome said, seeing their **react**ion to the **destruction** of Metroville. "Oh, come on, you gotta admit this is cool! Just like a movie! The robot will emerge **dramatic**ally, do some **damage**, **throng**s of screaming

people, and just when all hope is lost, Syndrome will **save the day**. I'll be a bigger hero than you ever were!"

"You killed off real heroes so that you could pretend to be one?" Mr. Incredible asked him.

"Oh, I'm real enough to **defeat** you!" Syndrome said **cynical**ly. "And I did it without your **precious** gifts. Your oh-so-special powers."

Syndrome continued excitedly, "I'll give them **heroic**s. I'll give them the most **spectacular** heroics the world has ever seen." Syndrome **cackle**d darkly. "And when I'm old, I'll sell my **invent**ions so that everyone can be Super. And when everyone's Super, no one will be." He **exit**ed in **triumph** as Bob **hung his head**. "I'm sorry," he said to his family. Helen and the kids looked up.

"This is my **fault**," Bob said. "I've been a **lousy** father. **Blind** . . . to what I have."

As Bob spoke, he didn't **notice** Vi moving. She was **suspend**ed in her own force field and no longer in the immobi-rays. She began to roll toward the control **panel**. "So **obsess**ed with being under**value**d that I undervalued all of you," Bob continued, **lost in** his own **confess**ion.

"Dad," Dash said.

"Shhh! Don't **interrupt**," Helen said.

"So **caught up in** the past that I . . . I . . . You are my greatest **adventure**. And I almost missed it," Bob said as Vi **dissipate**d the force field around her. "I **swear** I'm gonna get us out of this safely."

Vi suddenly spoke as she placed her hand on the control panel. "Well, I think Dad has made some excellent **progress** today . . . but I think it's time we **wind down** now." Bob looked at his daughter, stunned.

Vi threw a **switch** and the **beam flicker**ed off, dropping Bob, Helen, and Dash to the floor. Vi had saved the family!

The Incredibles **race**d through an empty **corridor**. "We need to get back to the mainland," Bob said.

"I saw an **aircraft hangar** on my way in," Helen said. "Straight ahead, I think."

They came to the hangar door and Bob quickly **pried** it open, expecting **swarm**s of guards on the other side. But no one was to be found.

"Where are all the guards?" he asked.

Then he heard **cheer**s from inside a **mobile command vehicle** parked in the hangar **bay**. The guards were inside, watching the Omnidroid attack the city on the news and **celebrating**.

Bob entered the vehicle alone. The door closed behind him. When he came out, all of the guards had been knocked out. He **whistle**d to his family, who were hiding behind the vehicle.

"This is the right hangar," Helen said, "but I don't see any **jet**s."

"A jet's not fast enough," Bob said, knowing Syndrome had a good **head start**.

"How about a rocket?" Dash suggested, pointing to a rocket in the **launch**ing bay.

"I can't fly a rocket," Helen said.

"You don't have to," Vi told her. "Use the **coordinate**s from the last launch."

Bob and Helen looked at each other, beaming over their clever daughter.

"I'll **bet** Syndrome's changed the password by now,"

Bob said suddenly. "How do I get into the computer?"

A woman's voice came over the **loudspeaker**. "Say please." The Incredibles looked up. It was Mirage. She stood at the **monitor**ing **station**, smiling.

In Metroville, Lucius Best was dressing for a dinner **engage**ment. He was putting on cologne★ when he thought he heard a series of explosions. Suddenly, Lucius saw a huge six-legged Omnidroid outside his window. He began opening his **dresser drawer**s.

"Honey?" he called to his wife in the other room.

"What?" Honey answered.

"Where's my Super **suit**?"

"What?" Honey asked.

★cologne 콜론. 연한 향수.

"Where is my Super suit?" Lucius demanded.

"I **put** it **away**!" she shouted to him.

"Where?" he said, going through the drawers as the Omnidroid filled the window.

"Why do you need to know?"

"The public is in danger!" Lucius shouted.

"My evening's in danger!" Honey said **firm**ly.

"You tell me where my suit is, woman! We're talking about the **greater good**!"

"Greater good?" she shouted back. "I am your wife! I am the greatest good you are ever going to get!"

Out on the streets of Metroville, the city's new Super, Syndrome, had the situation well **in hand**.

"Stand back!" Syndrome told the crowd. "Someone needs to teach this **hunk** of metal a few manners!"

Syndrome **fake**d a **punch** while he secretly used the **remote** on his **wrist** to send a **signal** to the arm of the Omnidroid, which fell out of its **socket**, **crash**ing into the street. The crowd **went wild**. Syndrome **revel**ed **in** their cheers of **appreciation**. The Omnidroid, however, was still a learning robot.

CONTROL STOLEN BY **EXTERNAL** SIGNAL, the robot began to **process**. It **crunch**ed the numbers and slowly turned toward Syndrome.

SIGNAL SOURCE: REMOTE CONTROL, it **conclude**d. The robot shot a laser at the remote control, knocking it from Syndrome's wrist. Syndrome's eyes grew wide. Then the robot shot a laser at Syndrome's rocket **boot**s. The hot laser blasted the boots, causing Syndrome to lose control and sending him wildly **careen**ing into a building, where he was knocked un**conscious**. The Omnidroid went back to **thrash**ing the city without **interference**.

High above Metroville, another rocket shot across the sky. A **land**ing **craft** broke away from the **rocket**, but it wasn't another Omnidroid. The landing craft was carrying the **mobile command** vehicle from the island. It looked a lot like a family **van**, but this was no vacation. Bob was at the **wheel**.

"Are we there yet?" Dash asked from the backseat.

"We get there when we get there!" Bob said **impatient**ly.

Bob rolled down the window and **lean**ed his head out. Helen was stretched to the **max** on top of the mobile command vehicle. She was using her **elastic** body to keep it **attach**ed to the landing craft. "How you doing, honey?"

"Do I have to answer?" a very stretched-out Helen replied.

"Kids!" Bob shouted. "**Strap** yourselves down like I told you!" he said. "This is going to be **rough**."

He **poke**d his head out the window and shouted to Helen, "Here we go, honey!"

Helen **release**d her hold on the landing craft as the van was dis**engage**d. It now **streak**ed through the sky and was headed for the **freeway**. The van hit the **pavement** in a **shower** of **spark**s, doing two hundred miles an hour. Bob **struggle**d to **maintain** control as he hit the **brake**s. Tires **smoking**, he **steer**ed the van into freeway **traffic**.

"The robot is in the **financial district**," he said, his heart racing. "Which **exit** do I take?"

"Traction **Avenue**," Helen said from the **passenger** seat.

Bob cut across three **lane**s of traffic like a **bullet**, heading for the Seventh Avenue exit. "That'll take me **downtown**! I take Seventh, don't I?"

"Don't take Seventh!" Helen **yell**ed.

"Great!" Bob said, **furious**. "We missed it!"

"You asked me how to get there and I told you: exit at Traction!"

"That'll take me downtown!" Bob **insist**ed.

"It's coming up! Get in the right lane! ***Signal!***" Helen screamed.

Bob changed into the left lane again. "We don't exit at Traction!"

"You're gonna miss it!" Helen warned.

At the last possible second, Bob **swerve**d across the freeway.

"Eeewhyaaaahhhh!" Bob yelled as the van hit the **guardrail**, barely making the exit.

Bob **struggle**d to keep control of the **van** as it **careen**ed down the street. He hit the **brake**s, the tires **blew**, and the **vehicle overturn**ed and **tumble**d down the street, **coming to rest** perfectly in a parking **spot**. "Is everybody all right?"

"**Super-duper**, Dad," Vi said.

"Let's do that again!" Dash laughed.

The family watched the Omnidroid disappear between some buildings. "Wait here and stay hidden," Bob told them. "I'm going in."

"While what?" Helen asked, following him out of the

vehicle. “I watch **helpless**ly from the **sideline**s? I don’t think so.”

“I’m asking you to wait with the kids.”

“And I’m telling you, **not a chance**,” Helen **insist**ed. “You’re my husband. I’m with you. For better or worse.”

“I have to do this alone,” Bob said **stern**ly.

“What is this to you? **Playtime**?” Helen asked.

“No,” Bob said.

“So you can be Mr. Incredible again?”

“No!” Bob **snap**ped.

“Then what?” Helen asked, **confuse**d. “What is it?”

“I’m . . . I’m not . . . not strong enough!” Bob said finally.

“Strong enough?” Helen asked. “And this will make you stronger? *That’s* what this is? Some sort of **workout**?”

“I can’t lose you again!” Bob shouted at Helen. “I can’t,” he **whisper**ed. “Not again . . . I’m not strong enough.”

Helen was **stun**ned. She leaned over and kissed him. “If we work together,” she said, “you won’t have to be.”

“I don’t know what’ll happen,” Bob said.

“Hey, we’re Supers.” Helen smiled. “What could happen?”

Suddenly, the **raging** Omnidroid was **loom**ing over Dash and Violet.

“Vi! Dash! No!” Helen shouted.

But it was too late. The Omnidroid **pounce**d on the kids with its full weight. Helen **froze**. She could **barely** see Dash and Vi beneath the **enormous** robot. But something was keeping the Omnidroid from **crush**ing the kids completely. A **force field**! Vi was keeping her brother and herself safe by **project**ing a **protective** force field around them.

The robot **press**ed hard on Vi’s force field. So hard that she **knock**ed her head on its metal bottom and the force field **vanish**ed.

“Violet!” Dash yelled.

Mr. Incredible went into action. He quickly **wedge**d himself under the robot, holding it off the kids.

“Go! Go!” Mr. Incredible shouted, barely raising the Omnidroid.

Dash and Vi **took off** toward Elastigirl, who told them

to **stay put** as she headed out to help her husband. Just then, the robot picked up Mr. Incredible and threw him into a glass building. Mr. Incredible got up and **lunge**d toward the robot, landing a **powerful punch**.

In the same **instant**, the sun **flash**ed off the **surface** of a blue **bolt** made of ice.

"Frozone!" Mr. Incredible yelled, happy to see his Super **buddy gliding** on a path of ice toward the Omnidroid. Help was on the way!

Mr. Incredible turned back toward his **foe** and landed a powerful punch on the robot, but it **backhand**ed him into the side of a building.

Mr. Incredible **shook off** the **momentary** pain and **notice**d Syndrome's **remote** lying on the ground. He couldn't believe his good luck. The remote controlled everything on the Omnidroid—if only he could **figure out** how to work it. He **grab**bed the **gadget** just as the Omnidroid got its metal **claw** around him and lifted him high into the air.

Mr. Incredible pressed a button on the remote. The Omnidroid's arm instantly dropped into the street and

released Mr. Incredible. The robot was still fighting for the remote when Mr. Incredible got an idea.

"Dash, go long!" he shouted to his son. Dash headed down the street in a **blur** as Mr. Incredible threw the remote like a football.★ The Super-**speed**y kid reached the gadget just **in time**.

But now the Omnidroid went after Dash. The robot used its laser to **trap** Dash in a ring of **burn**ing cars.

"**Take out** its guns!" Mr. Incredible yelled to Elastigirl.

Elastigirl **flung** a **manhole cover** at the robot, destroying its laser **beam**, as Frozone **swoop**ed in to **rescue** Dash. The Omnidroid **thunder**ed down the street after them. The learning robot knew it needed to get the remote back.

Then it was Frozone's **turn** to help out. He cut across the river, freezing a path and taking Dash along. The Omnidroid **vault**ed into the air and nearly landed on them. Ice **chunk**s sent Frozone and Dash tumbling while the remote **spun** out of Dash's hand. Mr. Incredible

---

★football 미식축구 또는 그 경기에서 사용하는 공. 미국에서 발달한, 럭비와 축구를 혼합한 경기로 11명을 한 팀으로 한다.

charged forward to grab it, but the robot **fire**d its claw at him, trapping him down the street in its metal **pincer**s.

Then the remote **seeming**ly moved by itself.

"Mom! I've got it!" Vi shouted, holding it in her **invisible** hand. "I've got the remote!"

"A remote?" Frozone asked. "A remote that controls what? The robot?"

"It's getting closer," Dash warned as the Omnidroid **bore** down upon them.

"It's not working," said Violet, **desperate**ly pushing buttons on the remote. Her mother and Dash soon joined in, all trying various **combination**s of buttons, hoping to destroy the Omnidroid.

"That's not doing anything. Try the one next to it. The red one!" Frozone argued.

The robot kept coming after them, but the remote did open the claw that had Mr. Incredible **pin**ned down the street. He **realize**d that the only thing that could **penetrate** and destroy the robot was itself. Suddenly, a rocket at the end of the claw was **activate**d. That gave Mr. Incredible an idea. He struggled to control the claw and looked down the street toward his family and Frozone. The Omnidroid was bearing down on them.

Mr. Incredible pointed the claw and yelled to his family, "**Duck**!" The rocket fired, and the claw flew right through the center of the Omnidroid. It fell in the river in a **mass** of **spark**s and **explosion**s as the Supers and the **citizen**s of Metroville watched its every **circuit** blow.

The **crowd**s cheered. The Supers were back!

The Incredibles were heroes again. They were driven home first class in the **company** of Rick Dicker, the **government**'s Super **relocation handle**r. "The people of this country owe you all a **debt** of **gratitude**," Rick said. "We'll **make good on** it."

"Does this mean we can come out of hiding?" Bob asked **hopeful**ly.

"Let the **politician**s **figure** that one **out**," Rick said. "But I've been asked to **assure** you we'll **take care of** everything else. You did good, Bob."

Meanwhile, Helen was on the **cell** phone, checking

the messages. The first was from Kari, the **babysit**ter.

"Hello, Mrs. Parr. Everything's fine, but there's something **unusual** about Jack-Jack. Call me, okay?"

Bob sat back, relaxed for the first time in ages. He looked at his daughter.

"You're wearing your hair back," he said to her, smiling.

"Huh? Oh . . . yeah," Vi said, touching her hair. "I just . . . yeah."

"It looks good," he said.

"Thanks, Dad," Violet said, **blush**ing.

"That was so cool when you threw that car," Dash said, remembering the **battle** against Syndrome's **guard**s in the **jungle**.

"Not as cool as you running on water," Bob told Dash.

"And, Mom," Dash **went on**, "that was sweet when you **snag**ged that bad guy with your arm and kinda, like, **whiplash**ed him into the other guy."

Helen smiled. "I'm trying to listen to messages, honey."

Dash fell back in his seat, **exclaim**ing, "That was the

best vacation ever! I love our family!"

Helen **cover**ed her ear, trying to hear the next message. "It's me!" Kari said. "Jack-Jack's fine but I'm really getting **weird**ed **out**! *When are you coming back? Call me, okay?*"

"Bob, listen to this," Helen said, suddenly **concern**ed. Bob **lean**ed in to hear the message: "Hi, this is Kari. Sorry for **freak**ing **out**. But your baby has special needs. Anyway, thanks for sending a **replace**ment **sitter**."

Bob and Helen exchanged worried looks.

Bob and Helen opened their **front door** and saw the **replace**ment **sitter**.

"*Shhh*. The baby's sleeping," Syndrome said, holding Jack-Jack in his arms.

"You took away my future," he said calmly. "I'm simply returning the **favor**. Don't worry. I'll be a good **mentor**: **supportive**, **encouraging**. Everything you weren't."

Jack-Jack woke up and began to cry. "And in time, who knows?" Syndrome smiled. "He might make a good **sidekick**."

Syndrome **blast**ed a hole in the **roof**. A **jet** was

hovering high above the house. Syndrome **activate**d his **rocket boot**s and **zoom**ed upward with Jack-Jack crying in his arms.

As he neared the jet, a **hatch** opened. He **was about to duck** in when Jack-Jack's cries became louder and louder and *louder.* Syndrome **froze** as Jack-Jack suddenly **transform**ed from fire to a **hideous** screaming mini-**monster**.

Horrified, Syndrome tried to drop the baby, but Jack-Jack managed to **cling** to his rocket boots. Syndrome **spun** out of **control** as Jack-Jack began **rip**ping the boots apart. With a **chunk** of rocket boot in each hand, Jack-Jack let go and began to fall.

Bob and Helen watched from the ground, **helpless**. What could they do? Helen quickly **stretch**ed herself into a **javelin**, and with all his Super strength, Bob **flung** her toward the baby. She **soar**ed into the sky but **overshot** the baby and **dove** down like a sky diver. The ground was coming up fast when Helen reached out and **snatch**ed Jack-Jack out of the air. **Billow**ing out like a **parachute**, Helen **drift**ed down with the baby in her arms.

"This isn't the end of it!" Syndrome shouted, having **regain**ed control. He stood in the **dock**ing door of his jet, his **cape blow**ing in the wind. Then Bob reached for his **beloved** new sports car and flung it into the air.

"I will get your son!" Syndrome shouted as the car hit the jet, **knock**ing him off **balance**. *"I'll—"*

Then he felt the **tug** at his neck. He turned **in time** to see the end of his cape **suck**ed into the jet's turbines. It was his last **monologue**.

"Look at Mommy, honey," Helen said to baby Jack-Jack, who had returned to normal in her arms. "Mommy's got you. Everything's all right."

But Jack-Jack saw the **burn**ing **wreckage** of the jet coming toward them. Pointing upward, the **terrified** baby began to **shriek**. Helen **land**ed, and the Incredibles **huddle**d together as the **debris** landed around them, **erupt**ing in a **massive explosion**.

The Parr home was completely destroyed. But inside the wreckage, **inch**es from being **crush**ed, the Incredibles were alive. Vi had created her most **powerful force field** ever. They looked at her from within the **bubble**, **amaze**d by her strength.

"That's my girl," Helen said. The family was saved! They walked out of the **smolder**ing wreckage without a **scratch**.

"Ooohh, man, *that was totally* ***wicked!***" The **neighborhood** boy on the **trike** was **wow**ed.

Things were different for the Parr family from then on. Their Super **identities** were still secret, but their new **confidence** wasn't.

"You're . . . Violet, right?" Tony Rydinger said to Vi at the school **track meet**.

"That's me," Vi answered, holding her head up.

"You look . . . different," Tony said.

"I feel different. Is different okay?"

"Different is great," Tony said, liking the person he saw. "Do you think maybe you and I . . . you know?" Tony **stammer**ed, feeling a little **shy**.

“I like movies.” Vi smiled, putting him at **ease**. “I’ll buy the popcorn, okay?”

“A movie,” Tony answered. “There you go, yeah . . . yeah! So, Friday?”

“Friday,” Violet said with a big smile.

Running in the track meet that day was Dash Parr. His family was in the **stand**s to **cheer** him on.

“Go! Go, Dash, *go!* Run. Run! *Run!*” Bob, Helen, and Vi **yell**ed after the starting **pistol fire**d.

Dash stayed at the back of the **pack** and smiled up at his family.

*“Go, Dash, go! Go bigger, don’t **give up**.”*

Dash **accelerate**d and moved to the front of the pack.

“But not too fast!” Bob and Helen cheered as Dash **held back**, finishing the **race** a **triumphant** second. The Incredible family couldn’t have been prouder.

As they all headed for home, a sudden **rumble** began to shake the **parking lot**. The ground **swell**ed and then **violent**ly broke apart as a **massive drill**ing machine **surface**d. **Dramatic**ally, a super **villain** with giant metal **claws emerge**d, shouting, “**Behold** the Underminer! I am always beneath you, but nothing is beneath me!"

The villain continued to **monologue** as Bob looked over at Helen, shook his head, and smiled. The family already had their **mask**s on. *This one is going to be easy,* Bob thought as he **rip**ped off his shirt, **reveal**ing the *I* for *Incredible* on his Super **suit**. The Incredibles were ready!

롱테일북스

CONTENTS

전직 슈퍼히어로 가장, 미스터 인크레더블!
조용한 삶을 보내던 그와 그의 가족 앞에 펼쳐진 흥미로운 모험!

디즈니•픽사의 〈인크레더블〉은 평범한 일상을 보내던 슈퍼히어로 가족이 겪게 되는 스릴 넘치는 모험을 다룬 애니메이션입니다.
미스터 인크레더블은 세계에서 가장 사랑받는 슈퍼히어로였습니다. 하지만 사회로부터 슈퍼히어로들이 외면당하면서 그는 강제로 은퇴하게 되고, 이제 슈퍼히어로가 아닌 밥 파라는 일반인으로 살아야만 합니다. 15년이라는 세월이 흐른 뒤, 밥은 이제 배불뚝이에 빠지는 머리카락을 걱정해야만 하는 평범한 가장이 되었습니다. 아내 헬렌도 슈퍼히어로 엘라스티 걸로 지내던 과거는 잊고 그들의 세 아이 바이올렛, 대쉬, 그리고 아기 잭잭을 키우면서 평범한 주부로 살고 있습니다.
그러던 어느 날 밥은 실수로 자신의 상사를 다치게 하면서 회사에서 해고되고 맙니다. 그날 저녁, 미라지라는 신비로운 여성이 그에게 다시 슈퍼히어로가 되어 활동해 달라는 비밀 임무를 제안합니다. 언제나 슈퍼히어로로 돌아가는 것을 꿈꿔온 밥은 이를 수락하고, 세월을 이기지 못한 몸을 이끌고 힘겹게 임무를 완수합니다. 이후, 밥은 운동을 해서 몸을 만들고 새로운 스포츠카를 사며 밝은 모습으로 지냅니다. 하지만 활기찬 밥의 모습에 아내 헬렌은 뭔가 수상하다고 생각합니다. 그리고 그의 오래된 슈퍼 슈트에서 수선한 흔적을 발견하면서 그녀의 의심은 더욱 커집니다.
또다시 비밀 임무를 전달받은 미스터 인크레더블! 과연 그는 무사히 이 임무를 마치고 원하는 대로 슈퍼히어로로 복귀할 수 있을까요? 그리고 헬렌은 밥이 감추고 있는 비밀을 알게 될까요?
화려한 과거를 잊고 지내던 전직 슈퍼히어로와 그의 가족의 흥미진진한 모험을 그려낸 〈인크레더블〉을 지금 영어 원서로 읽어 보세요!

한국인을 위한 맞춤형 영어원서!

원서 읽기는 모두가 인정하는 최고의 영어 공부법입니다. 하지만 영어 구사력이 뛰어나지 않은 보통 영어 학습자들에게는 원서 읽기를 선뜻 시작하기가 부담되는 것도 사실이지요.
이 책은 영어 초보자들도 쉽게 원서 읽기를 시작하고, 꾸준한 읽기를 통해 '영어원서 읽기 습관'을 형성할 수 있도록 만들어진 책입니다. 남녀노소 누구나 좋아할 만한 내용의 원서를 기반으로 내용 이해와 영어 실력 향상을 위한 다양한 콘텐츠를 덧붙였고, 리스닝과 낭독 훈련에 활용할 수 있는 오디오북까지 함께 제공하여, 원서를 부담 없이 읽으면서 자연스럽게 영어 실력이 향상되도록 도와줍니다.

특히 원서와 워크북을 분권하여 휴대와 학습이 효과적으로 이루어지도록 배려했습니다. 일반 원서에서 찾아볼 수 없는 특장점으로, 워크북과 오디오북을 적절히 활용하면 더욱 쉽고 재미있게 영어 실력을 향상시킬 수 있습니다. ('원서'와 '워크북' 및 '오디오북 MP3 CD'의 3가지 패키지가 이상 없이 갖추어져 있는지 다시 한 번 확인해보세요!)

이런 분들께 강력 추천합니다!

- 영어원서 읽기를 처음 시작하는 독자
- 쉽고 재미있는 원서를 찾고 있는 영어 학습자
- 영화 『인크레더블』을 재미있게 보신 분
- 특목고 입시를 준비하는 초·중학생
- 토익 600~750점, 고등학교 상위권 수준의 영어 학습자
- 엄마표 영어를 위한 교재를 찾고 있는 부모님

본문 텍스트

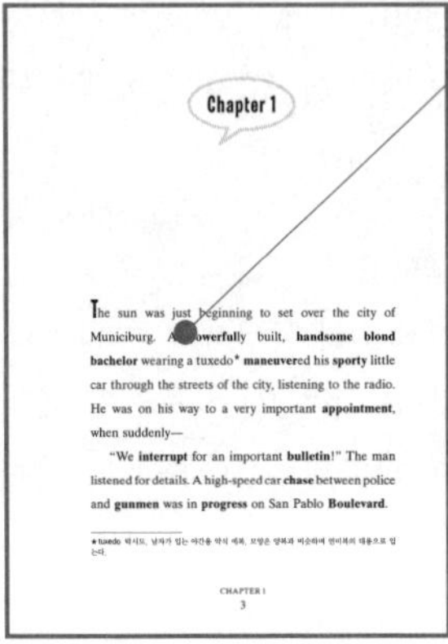
Chapter 1

The sun was just beginning to set over the city of Municiburg. A **powerfully** built, **handsome blond bachelor** wearing a tuxedo* **maneuvere**d his **sporty** little car through the streets of the city, listening to the radio. He was on his way to a very important **appointment**, when suddenly—

"We **interrupt** for an important **bulletin**!" The man listened for details. A high-speed car **chase** between police and **gunmen** was in **progress** on San Pablo **Boulevard**.

CHAPTER 1
3

내용이 담긴 본문입니다.

원어민이 읽는 일반 원서와 같은 텍스트지만, 암기해야 할 중요 어휘들은 볼드체로 표시되어 있습니다. 이 어휘들은 지금 들고 계신 워크북에 챕터별로 정리되어 있습니다.

학습 심리학 연구 결과에 따르면, 한 단어씩 따로 외우는 단어 암기는 거의 효과가 없다고 합니다. 대신 단어를 제대로 외우기 위해서는 문맥(Context) 속에서 단어를 암기해야 하며, 한 단어 당 문맥 속에서 15번 이상 마주칠 때 완벽하게 암기할 수 있다고 합니다.
이 책의 본문은 중요 어휘를 볼드로 강조하여, 문맥 속의 단어들을 더 확실히 인지(Word Cognition in Context)하도록 돕고 있습니다. 또한 대부분의 중요한 단어들은 다른 챕터에서도 반복해서 등장하기 때문에 이 책을 읽는 것만으로도 자연스럽게 어휘력을 향상시킬 수 있습니다.

또한 본문에는 내용 이해를 돕기 위해 '각주'가 첨가되어 있습니다. 각주는 굳이 암기할 필요는 없지만, 알아두면 내용을 더 깊이 있게 이해할 수 있어 원서를 읽는 재미가 배가됩니다.

Without **hesitation**, the man **punch**ed a button on the **dash**. The radio **immediate**ly **convert**ed into an **electronic aerial** map. The map's **sophisticate**d radar* system **locked on** two red **dots speed**ing through the city. "Yeah, I've got time," the man decided, giving his watch a **glance**. He could still make his appointment.

He hit another button, marked AUTODRIVE, and the car began to drive itself. Then he typed MERGE PURSUIT into the **controls**. The autodrive immediately began to **plot** a course to **intercept** the trouble.

Next, the seat backs of the car **snap**ped down **flat**. Two steel bands suddenly **wrap**ped around the man's **waist** and **slid** over his body in **opposing** directions, removing his clothes to **reveal** a **slick** Super **suit** underneath. He wore a dark **mask** over his eyes.

The seat backs returned to an **upright** position. The man in the driver's seat was **none other than** Mr. Incredible. And he was ready for action!

Mr. Incredible smiled as his **vehicle** converted into

THE INCREDIBLES
4

워크북(Workbook)의 구성

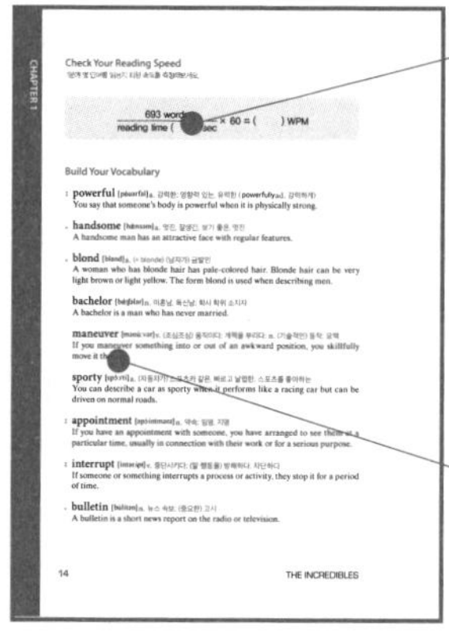
CHAPTER 1

Check Your Reading Speed

693 words / reading time (sec × 60 = ( ) WPM

Build Your Vocabulary

powerful You say that someone's body is powerful when it is physically strong.

handsome A handsome man has an attractive face with regular features.

blond A woman who has blonde hair has pale-colored hair. Blonde hair can be very light brown or light yellow. The form blond is used when describing men.

bachelor A bachelor is a man who has never married.

maneuver If you maneuver something into or out of an awkward position, you skillfully move it th...

sporty You can describe a car as sporty when it performs like a racing car but can be driven on normal roads.

appointment If you have an appointment with someone, you have arranged to see them at a particular time, usually in connection with their work or for a serious purpose.

interrupt If someone or something interrupts a process or activity, they stop it for a period of time.

bulletin A bulletin is a short news report on the radio or television.

14 THE INCREDIBLES

Check Your Reading Speed

해당 챕터의 단어 수가 기록되어 있어, 리딩 속도를 측정할 수 있습니다. 특히 리딩 속도를 중시하는 독자들이 유용하게 사용할 수 있습니다.

Build Your Vocabulary

본문에 볼드 표시되어 있는 단어들이 정리되어 있습니다. 리딩 전, 후에 반복해서 보면 원서를 더욱 쉽게 읽을 수 있고, 어휘력도 빠르게 향상됩니다.

단어는 〈빈도 – 스펠링 – 발음기호 – 품사 – 한글 뜻 – 영문 뜻〉 순서로 표기되어 있으며 빈도 표시(★)가 많을수록 필수 어휘입니다. 반복 등장하는 단어는 빈도 대신 '복습'으로 표기되어 있습니다. 품사는 아래와 같이 표기했습니다.

n. 명사 | **a.** 형용사 | **ad.** 부사 | **v.** 동사

conj. 접속사 | **prep.** 전치사 | **int.** 감탄사 | **idiom** 숙어 및 관용구

Comprehension Quiz

간단한 퀴즈를 통해 읽은 내용에 대한 이해력을 점검해 볼 수 있습니다.

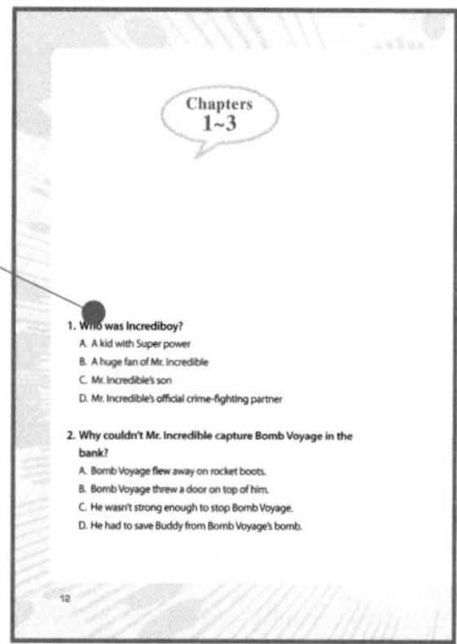
Chapters 1~3

1. Who was Incrediboy?
   A. A kid with Super power
   B. A huge fan of Mr. Incredible
   C. Mr. Incredible's son
   D. Mr. Incredible's official crime-fighting partner

2. Why couldn't Mr. Incredible capture Bomb Voyage in the bank?
   A. Bomb Voyage flew away on rocket boots.
   B. Bomb Voyage threw a door on top of him.
   C. He wasn't strong enough to stop Bomb Voyage.
   D. He had to save Buddy from Bomb Voyage's bomb.

12

영어원서 읽기, 이렇게 시작해보세요!!

아래와 같이 프리뷰(Preview) → 리딩(Reading) → 리뷰(Review) 세 단계를 거치면서 원서를 읽으면, 더욱 효과적으로 영어실력을 향상할 수 있습니다!

1. 프리뷰(Preview) : 오늘 읽을 내용을 먼저 점검한다!

- 워크북을 통해 오늘 읽을 Chapter에 나와 있는 단어들을 쭉 훑어봅니다. 어떤 단어들이 나오는지, 내가 아는 단어와 모르는 단어가 어떤 것들이 있는지 가벼운 마음으로 살펴봅니다.
- 평소처럼 하나하나 쓰면서 암기하려고 하지는 마세요! 그렇게 해서는 원서를 읽기도 전에 지쳐 쓰러져버릴 것입니다. 익숙하지 않은 단어들을 주의 깊게 보되, 어차피 리딩을 하면서 점차 익숙해질 단어라는 것을 잊지 말고 빠르게 훑어봅니다.
- 뒤 Chapter로 갈수록 '복습'이라고 표시된 단어들이 늘어나는 것을 알 수 있습니다. '복습' 단어인데도 여전히 익숙하지 않다면 더욱 신경을 써서 봐야겠죠? 매일매일 꾸준히 읽는다면, 익숙한 단어들이 점점 많아진다는 것을 몸으로 느낄 수 있습니다.

2. 리딩(Reading) : 내용에 집중하며 빠르게 읽어가자!

- 프리뷰를 마친 후 바로 리딩을 시작합니다. 방금 살펴봤던 어휘들을 문장 속에서 다시 만나게 되는데 이 과정에서 단어의 쓰임새와 어감을 자연스럽게 익히게 됩니다.
- 모르는 단어, 이해 가지 않는 문장이 나오더라도 멈추지 말고 전체적인 맥락을 잡아가면서 스피디하게 읽어가세요. 특히 영화를 먼저 보고 책을 읽으면 맥락을 통해 읽을 수 있어 훨씬 수월합니다.
- 이해 가지 않는 문장들은 따로 표시를 하되, 일단 넘어가서 계속 읽는 것이 좋습니다. 뒷부분을 읽다 보면 자연히 이해가 되는 경우도 있고, 정 이해가 되지 않는 부분은 리딩을 마친 이후에 따로 리뷰하는 시간을 가지면 됩니다. 문제집을 풀듯이 모든 문장을 분석하면서 원서를 읽는 것이 아니라, 리딩할 때는 리딩에만, 리뷰할 때는 리뷰에만 집중하는 것이 필요합니다.
- 볼드 처리된 단어의 의미가 궁금하더라도, 워크북을 바로 펼치지 마세요. 정 궁금하다면 한 번씩 참고하는 것도 나쁘진 않지만, 워크북과 원서를 번갈아

보면서 읽는 것은 리딩의 흐름을 끊고 단어 하나하나에 집착하는 좋지 않은 리딩 습관을 만들 수 있습니다.

- 초보자라면 분당 150단어의 리딩 속도를 목표로 잡아서 리딩을 합니다. 분당 150단어는 원어민이 말하는 속도로, 영어 학습자들이 리스닝과 스피킹으로 넘어가기 위해 가장 기초적으로 달성해야 하는 단계입니다. 분당 50~80단어 정도의 낮은 리딩 속도를 가지고 있는 경우는 대부분 영어 실력이 부족해서라기보다 '잘못된 리딩 습관'을 가지고 있어서 그렇습니다. 이해력이 조금 떨어진다고 하더라도 분당 150단어까지는 속도에 대한 긴장감을 놓치지 말고 스피디하게 읽어나가도록 하세요.
- 이미 150단어 이상의 리딩 속도에 도달한 상태라면, 각자의 상황에 맞게 원서를 보다 다양한 방식으로 활용해보세요. 이에 대한 자세한 조언이 워크북 말미에 실려 있습니다.

3. 리뷰(Review) : 이해력을 점검하고 꼼꼼하게 다시 살펴보자!

- 해당 Chapter의 Comprehension Quiz를 통해 이해력을 점검해봅니다.
- 오늘 만난 어휘도 다시 한 번 복습합니다. 읽으면서 중요하다고 생각했던 단어를 연습장에 써보면서 꼼꼼하게 외우는 것도 좋습니다.
- 이해가 되지 않는다고 표시해뒀던 부분도 주의 깊게 분석해봅니다. 다시 한 번 문장을 꼼꼼히 읽고, 어떤 이유에서 이해가 되질 않았는지 생각해봅니다. 따로 메모를 남기거나 노트를 작성하는 것도 좋은 방법입니다.
- 사실 꼼꼼히 리뷰하는 것은 매우 고된 과정입니다. 원서를 읽고 리뷰하는 시간을 가지는 것은 영어 실력 향상에 많은 도움이 되긴 하나, 이 과정을 철저히 지키려다가 원서 읽기의 재미를 반감시키는 것은 바람직하지 않습니다. 그럴 때는 차라리 리뷰를 가볍게 하는 것이 좋을 수 있습니다. '내용에 빠져서 재미있게', 문제집에서는 상상도 못할 '많은 양'을 읽으면서, 매일매일 조금씩 꾸준히 실력을 향상하는 것이 원서를 활용하는 기본적인 방법이며, 영어 공부의 왕도입니다. 문제집 풀듯이 원서 읽기를 시도하고 접근해서는 실패할 수 밖에 없습니다.

1. Who was Incrediboy?

A. A kid with Super power

B. A huge fan of Mr. Incredible

C. Mr. Incredible's son

D. Mr. Incredible's official crime-fighting partner

2. Why couldn't Mr. Incredible capture Bomb Voyage in the bank?

A. Bomb Voyage flew away on rocket boots.

B. Bomb Voyage threw a door on top of him.

C. He wasn't strong enough to stop Bomb Voyage.

D. He had to save Buddy from Bomb Voyage's bomb.

3. What was true about Elastigirl?

A. She was best friends with Frozone.

B. She was not close to Mr. Incredible.

C. She became Mr. Incredible's wife.

D. She had more power than the other Supers.

4. Why did the man who jumped from a building sue Mr. Incredible?

A. He had not wanted Mr. Incredible to save his life.

B. He was upset that Mr. Incredible got him injured.

C. He thought Mr. Incredible should have helped him more.

D. He believed Mr. Incredible should pay for the window he broke.

5. What was part of the Super Relocation Program?

A. Supers had to tell the public their real identities.

B. Supers had to pay the government millions of dollars.

C. Supers were expected to protect society more carefully.

D. Supers were no longer allowed to use their powers.

Check Your Reading Speed

1분에 몇 단어를 읽는지 리딩 속도를 측정해보세요.

$$\frac{\text{693 words}}{\text{reading time (\qquad) sec}} \times 60 = (\qquad) \text{ WPM}$$

Build Your Vocabulary

* **powerful** [páuərfəl] a. 강력한; 영향력 있는, 유력한 (powerfully ad. 강력하게)
You say that someone's body is powerful when it is physically strong.

* **handsome** [hǽnsəm] a. 멋진, 잘생긴; 보기 좋은, 멋진
A handsome man has an attractive face with regular features.

* **blond** [bland] a. (= blonde) (남자가) 금발인
A woman who has blonde hair has pale-colored hair. Blonde hair can be very light brown or light yellow. The form blond is used when describing men.

bachelor [bǽtʃələr] n. 미혼남, 독신남; 학사 학위 소지자
A bachelor is a man who has never married.

maneuver [mənú:vər] v. (조심조심) 움직이다; 계책을 부리다; n. (기술적인) 동작; 묘책
If you maneuver something into or out of an awkward position, you skillfully move it there.

sporty [spɔ́:rti] a. (자동차가) 스포츠카 같은, 빠르고 날렵한; 스포츠를 좋아하는
You can describe a car as sporty when it performs like a racing car but can be driven on normal roads.

* **appointment** [əpɔ́intmənt] n. 약속; 임명, 지명
If you have an appointment with someone, you have arranged to see them at a particular time, usually in connection with their work or for a serious purpose.

* **interrupt** [ìntərʌ́pt] v. 중단시키다; (말·행동을) 방해하다; 차단하다
If someone or something interrupts a process or activity, they stop it for a period of time.

* **bulletin** [búlitən] n. 뉴스 속보; (중요한) 고시
A bulletin is a short news report on the radio or television.

chase [ʧeis] **n.** 추적, 추격; 추구함; **v.** 뒤쫓다, 추적하다; 추구하다
A chase is the action of following someone or something quickly because you want to catch them.

gunman [gʌ́nmən] **n.** (pl. gunmen) 무장 범인, 총기를 소지한 사람
A gunman is a man who uses a gun to commit a crime such as murder or robbery.

progress [prágres] **n.** 진행; 진전; 나아감; **v.** 진전을 보이다; (앞으로) 나아가다
(in progress **idiom** 진행 중인)
If something is in progress, it has started and is still continuing.

boulevard [búləvà:rd] **n.** (거리 이름) 대로
A boulevard is a wide street in a city, usually with trees along each side.

hesitate [hézətèit] **v.** 망설이다, 주저하다; 거리끼다 (hesitation **n.** 주저, 망설임)
Hesitation is an unwillingness to do something, or a delay in doing it, because you are uncertain, worried, or embarrassed about it.

punch [pʌnʧ] **v.** (자판 · 번호판 등을) 치다; 주먹으로 치다; **n.** 주먹으로 한 대 침
If you punch something such as the buttons on a keyboard, you touch them in order to store information on a machine such as a computer or to give the machine a command to do something.

dash [dæʃ] **n.** (= dashboard) (승용차의) 계기판; 돌진, 질주; **v.** (급히) 서둘러 가다; 내동댕이치다
The dash of a car is its dashboard which is the panel facing the driver's seat where most of the instruments and switches are.

immediate [imí:diət] **a.** 즉각적인; 당면한; 아주 가까이에 있는 (immediately **ad.** 즉시, 즉각)
If something happens immediately, it happens without any delay.

convert [kənvə́:rt] **v.** 전환시키다, 개조하다; (의견 · 습관 등을) 바꾸다
If one thing is converted or converts into another, it is changed into a different form.

electronic [ilektránik] **a.** 전자의, 전자 장비와 관련된
An electronic device has transistors or silicon chips which control and change the electric current passing through the device.

aerial [ɛ́əriəl] **a.** 항공기에 의한; 공중의, 대기의 (aerial map **n.** 항공지도)
You talk about aerial attacks and aerial photographs to indicate that people or things on the ground are attacked or photographed by people in airplanes.

sophisticated [səfístəkèitid] **a.** 정교한, 복잡한; 세련된, 교양 있는
A sophisticated machine, device, or method is more advanced or complex than others.

lock on idiom 자동 추적하다
To lock on means to aim something at a moving target so as to follow it automatically.

* **dot** [dat] n. 점; v. 여기저기 흩어져 있다, 산재하다; 점을 찍다
A dot is a very small round mark, for example one that is used as the top part of the letter 'i,' as a full stop, or as a decimal point.

** **speed** [spi:d] v. 빨리 가다; 더 빠르게 하다; n. 속도
If you speed somewhere, you move or travel there quickly, usually in a vehicle.

* **glance** [glæns] n. 흘낏 봄; v. 흘낏 보다; 대충 훑어보다
A glance is a quick look at someone or something.

* **merge** [məːrdʒ] v. 합치다; 어우러지다
If one thing merges with another, or is merged with another, they combine or come together to make one whole thing.

* **pursue** [pərsúː] v. 뒤쫓다, 추적하다; 추구하다 (pursuit n. 추적, 추격)
Someone who is in pursuit of a person, vehicle, or animal is chasing them.

** **control** [kəntróul] n. (기계 · 차량의) 제어 장치; 통제, 제어; v. 지배하다; 조정하다
A control is a device such as a switch or lever which you use in order to operate a machine or other piece of equipment.

* **plot** [plat] v. (위치 · 항로 등을 지도에) 표시하다; 음모하다; n. (소설 · 영화 등의) 구성; 음모
When someone plots the position or course of a plane or ship, they mark it on a map using instruments to obtain accurate information.

intercept [ìntərsépt] v. (중간에) 가로막다, 가로채다
If you intercept someone or something that is traveling from one place to another, you stop them before they get to their destination.

* **snap** [snæp] v. 탁 하고 움직이다; 급히 움직이다; 날카롭게 말하다; 툭 부러지다; n. 탁 하는 소리
If you snap something into a particular position, or if it snaps into that position, it moves quickly into that position, with a sharp sound.

** **flat** [flæt] ad. 평평하게, 반듯이; a. 평평한, 편평한; 납작한; 단호한
Flat means horizontal and not upright.

** **wrap** [ræp] v. (무엇의 둘레를) 두르다; 포장하다; 둘러싸다; n. 포장지; 랩
When you wrap something such as a piece of paper or cloth round another thing, you put it around it.

⁑ **waist** [weist] n. 허리
Your waist is the middle part of your body where it narrows slightly above your hips.

* **slide** [slaid] v. (slid-slid/slidden) 미끄러지듯이 움직이다; 슬며시 넣다; n. 떨어짐; 미끄러짐
When something slides somewhere or when you slide it there, it moves there smoothly over or against something.

opposing [əpóuziŋ] a. 정반대의; 서로 대립하는
The opposing side or part of something is the side or part that is furthest away from you.

* **reveal** [riví:l] v. (보이지 않던 것을) 드러내 보이다; (비밀 등을) 밝히다
If you reveal something that has been out of sight, you uncover it so that people can see it.

slick [slik] a. 매끈한; (겉만) 번드르르한; 교활한; v. 매끈하게 하다
If you describe something as slick, you mean that it is smooth and slippery.

⁑ **suit** [su:t] n. (특정한 활동 때 입는) 옷; 정장; 소송; v. ~에게 편리하다; 어울리다
A particular type of suit is a piece of clothing that you wear for a particular activity.

* **mask** [mæsk] n. 마스크; 가면; v. 가면을 쓰다; (감정 · 냄새 · 사실 등을) 가리다
A mask is a piece of cloth or other material, which you wear over your face so that people cannot see who you are, or so that you look like someone or something else.

* **upright** [ʌ́prait] a. 수직으로 세워 둔; (자세가) 똑바른
If you are sitting or standing upright, you are sitting or standing with your back straight, rather than bending or lying down.

none other than idiom 다름 아닌 바로 ~인
You use none other than and no other than to emphasize the name of a person or thing when something about that person or thing is surprising in a particular situation.

⁑ **vehicle** [ví:ikl] n. 차량, 운송 수단; 수단, 매개체
A vehicle is a machine such as a car, bus, or truck which has an engine and is used to carry people from place to place.

sleek [sli:k] a. (모양이) 매끈한; 윤이 나는
Sleek vehicles, furniture, or other objects look smooth, shiny, and expensive.

futuristic [fjù:ʧərístik] **a.** 초현대적인; 미래를 상상하는
Something that is futuristic looks or seems very modern and unusual, like something from the future.

⁑ **flame** [fleim] **v.** 활활 타오르다; 시뻘게지다; **n.** 불길, 불꽃; 격정
If something flames or flames up, it burns more brightly.

* **rocket** [rákit] **v.** 로켓처럼 가다, 돌진하다; 급증하다; **n.** 로켓; 로켓 추진 미사일
If something such as a vehicle rockets somewhere, it moves there very quickly.

catch one's eye **idiom** 눈에 띄다; 눈길을 끌다
If something catches your eye, you suddenly notice it.

* **frantic** [fræ̀ntik] **a.** (두려움 · 걱정으로) 제정신이 아닌; 정신없이 서두는
(frantically **ad.** 미친 듯이)
If you are frantic, you are behaving in a wild and uncontrolled way because you are frightened or worried.

⁑ **wave** [weiv] **v.** (손 · 팔을) 흔들다; 손짓하다; **n.** 물결; (손 · 팔을) 흔들기; (열 · 소리 · 빛 등의) -파
If you wave or wave your hand, you move your hand from side to side in the air, usually in order to say hello or goodbye to someone.

* **brake** [breik] **n.** 브레이크, 제동 장치; 제동; **v.** 브레이크를 밟다; 속도를 줄이다
(hit the brakes **idiom** 브레이크를 걸다)
Brakes are devices in a vehicle that make it go slower or stop.

* **reverse** [rivə́:rs] **a.** 반대의; **v.** 후진하다; 뒤바꾸다; **n.** (정)반대; (자동차의) 후진 기어
Reverse means opposite to what you expect or to what has just been described.

retro [rétrou] **a.** 역추진의; 복고풍의
Retro is used to form adjectives and nouns which indicate that something goes back or goes backward.

⁂ **fire** [faiər] **v.** (엔진이) 점화되다; 해고하다; 발사하다; **n.** 화재, 불; 발사, 총격
When the engine of a motor vehicle fires, an electrical spark is produced which causes the fuel to burn and the engine to work.

stop on a dime **idiom** 갑자기 멈추다
If someone or something stops on a dime, they are able to stop almost immediately, even when moving very quickly.

tint [tint] **v.** (약간의) 색깔을 넣다; **n.** 엷은 색, 색조
If something is tinted, it has a small amount of a particular color or dye in it.

wild-eyed [wáild-àid] a. 눈빛이 날카로운
Someone who is wild-eyed looks very angry or frightened.

⋆ **stubborn** [stʌ́bərn] a. 완고한, 고집 센 (stubbornly ad. 완고하게)
Someone who is stubborn or who behaves in a stubborn way is determined to do what they want and is very unwilling to change their mind.

⁑ **grip** [grip] v. 꽉 잡다, 움켜잡다; (마음 · 흥미 · 시선을) 끌다; n. 꽉 붙잡음, 움켜쥠; 통제, 지배
If you grip something, you take hold of it with your hand and continue to hold it firmly.

⋆ **blaze** [bleiz] v. (총이) 불을 뿜다; 활활 타다; n. 불길; 휘황찬란한 빛
If guns blaze, or blaze away, they fire continuously, making a lot of noise.

⁑ **battle** [bætl] n. 싸움; 전투; v. 싸우다, 투쟁하다
A battle is a violent fight between groups of people, especially one between military forces during a war.

⋆ **rip** [rip] v. 빠른 속도로 돌진하다; (거칠게) 떼어 내다, 뜯어 내다; (갑자기) 찢다; n. (길게) 찢어진 곳
To rip somewhere means to move forcefully and rapidly.

stand clear idiom (안전 등을 위하여) 떨어져 있다
If you stand clear of something, you move a short distance away from it so that you are safe.

squeal [skwi:l] n. 끼익 하는 소리; v. 꽥액 소리를 지르다; 끼익 하는 소리를 내다
A squeal is a long, very high sound or cry.

⋆ **screech** [skri:ʧ] v. 끼익 하는 소리를 내다; n. 끼익, 꽥 (하는 날카로운 소리)
If a vehicle screeches somewhere or if its tires screech, its tires make an unpleasant high-pitched noise on the road.

⋆ **headlight** [hédlait] n. 전조등, 헤드라이트
A vehicle's headlights are the large powerful lights at the front.

⁑ **sweep** [swi:p] v. 휩쓸고 가다; (빗자루로) 쓸다; 훑다; n. 쓸기, 비질하기
If your arm or hand sweeps in a particular direction, or if you sweep it there, it moves quickly and smoothly in that direction.

⋆ **motion** [móuʃən] n. 동작, 몸짓; 운동, 움직임; v. (손 · 머리로) 몸짓을 해 보이다
A motion is an action, gesture, or movement.

⁑ **tear** [tɛər] ① v. (tore-torn) 뜯어 내다; 찢다, 뜯다; 부리나케 가다; n. 찢어진 곳, 구멍 ② n. 눈물
To tear something from somewhere means to remove it roughly and violently.

★ **enormous** [inɔ́:rməs] a. 막대한, 거대한
Something that is enormous is extremely large in size or amount.

outstretched [àutstréʧt] a. 쭉 뻗은
If a part of the body of a person or animal is outstretched, it is stretched out as far as possible.

★ **slam** [slæm] v. 세게 치다, 놓다; 쾅 닫다; n. 쾅 하고 닫기; 탕 하는 소리
If you slam something down, you put it there quickly and with great force.

★ **hood** [hud] n. (자동차 등의) 덮개; (외투 등에 달린) 모자
The hood of a car is the metal cover over the engine at the front.

oncoming [ɔ́nkʌmiŋ] a. 다가오는
Oncoming means moving toward you.

stop in one's tracks idiom 갑자기 딱 멈추다
If you stop in your tracks or stop dead in your tracks, you suddenly stop moving because you are very surprised, impressed, or frightened.

★★ **criminal** [krímənl] n. 범인, 범죄자; a. 범죄의; 형사상의
A criminal is a person who regularly commits crimes.

replant [riplǽnt] v. 다시 심다; 이식하다
To replant a tree or plant which has been dug up means to plant it again, especially in a larger pot or new site.

★★ **nod** [nad] n. (고개를) 끄덕임; v. (고개를) 끄덕이다, 까딱하다
A nod is a movement up and down with the head.

★ **officer** [ɔ́:fisər] n. 경찰관; 순경; 장교
Members of the police force can be referred to as officers.

be about to idiom 막 ~하려는 참이다
If you are about to do something, you are going to do it immediately.

★★ **scene** [si:n] n. 현장; 장면, 광경; 풍경
The scene of an event is the place where it happened.

blare [blɛər] v. (소리를) 요란하게 울리다; n. 요란한 소리
If something such as a siren or radio blares or if you blare it, it makes a loud, unpleasant noise.

* **rob** [rab] v. (사람 · 장소를) 도둑질하다 (robbery n. 강도 사건)
Robbery is the crime of stealing money or property from a bank, shop, or vehicle, often by using force or threats.

* **vicinity** [visínəti] n. (~의) 부근, 인근
If something is in the vicinity of a particular place, it is near it.

pull out idiom (차가) 옆으로 빠져나가다
If a vehicle or driver pulls out, they move onto a road or onto a part of a road where the traffic is moving faster.

* **takeoff** [téikɔ̀:f] n. 이륙, 도약; 제거, 분리
Takeoff is the beginning of a flight, when an aircraft leaves the ground.

pudgy [pʌ́dʒi] a. 땅딸막한, 통통한
If you describe someone as pudgy, you mean that they are rather fat in an unattractive way.

* **passenger** [pǽsəndʒər] n. 승객 (passenger seat n. (자동차의) 조수석)
A passenger in a vehicle such as a bus, boat, or plane is a person who is traveling in it, but who is not driving it or working on it.

* **enthusiastic** [inθù:ziǽstik] a. 열렬한, 열광적인 (enthusiastically ad. 열광적으로)
If you are enthusiastic about something, you show how much you like or enjoy it by the way that you behave and talk.

* **homemade** [hoummféid] a. 집에서 만든, 손수 만든
Something that is homemade has been made in someone's home, rather than in a shop or factory.

* **recognize** [rékəgnàiz] v. 알아보다; 인식하다; 공인하다
If you recognize someone or something, you know who that person is or what that thing is.

* **president** [prézədənt] n. 회장; 대통령
The president of an organization is the person who has the highest position in it.

* **frown** [fraun] n. 찡그림, 찌푸림; v. 얼굴을 찡그리다; 눈살을 찌푸리다
A frown is an expression on your face made by moving your eyebrows down and closer together that shows you are annoyed, worried, or thinking hard.

* **patient** [péiʃənt] a. 참을성 있는, 인내심 있는; n. 환자
If you are patient, you stay calm and do not get annoyed, for example when something takes a long time, or when someone is not doing what you want them to do.

★★★ **sign** [sain] v. 서명하다; 신호를 보내다; n. 표지판; 몸짓; 기색, 흔적
When you sign a document, you write your name on it, usually at the end or in a special space.

★ **scrap** [skræp] n. (종이 · 옷감 등의) 조각; 폐품; v. 폐기하다, 버리다
A scrap of something is a very small piece or amount of it.

★★ **crime** [kraim] n. 범죄, 죄
A crime is an illegal action or activity for which a person can be punished by law.

crank up idiom (음악 등의) 소리를 높이다; (기계 등을) 돌리다
To crank up means to make the sound of something, especially music, louder.

★ **yell** [jel] v. 고함치다, 소리 지르다; n. 고함, 외침
If you yell, you shout loudly, usually because you are excited, angry, or in pain.

whoosh [hwu:ʃ] v. (아주 빠르게) 휙 하고 움직이다; n. 쉭 하는 소리
If something whooshes somewhere, it moves there quickly or suddenly.

eject [idʒékt] v. 쫓아내다, 내쫓다; 튀어나오게 하다
If you eject someone from a place, you force them to leave.

peel out idiom 쌩 하고 떠나다
If you peel out, you suddenly make a car start moving very quickly so that it makes a lot of noise.

Check Your Reading Speed

1분에 몇 단어를 읽는지 리딩 속도를 측정해보세요.

$$\frac{\text{855 words}}{\text{reading time (\quad\quad) sec}} \times 60 = (\quad\quad) \text{ WPM}$$

Build Your Vocabulary

복습 **rob** [rab] v. (사람 · 장소를) 도둑질하다 (robber n. 강도)
A robber is someone who steals money or property from a bank, a shop, or a vehicle, often by using force or threats.

rooftop [rú:ftap] n. (건물의) 옥상
A rooftop is the outside part of the roof of a building.

root [ru:t] v. 뒤지다; (식물이) 뿌리를 내리다; n. (식물의) 뿌리; (문제의) 근원
If you root through or in something, you search for something by moving other things around.

crook [kruk] n. 사기꾼, 도둑; 구부러진 곳; v. (손가락 · 팔을) 구부리다
A crook is a dishonest person or a criminal.

⋆ **loom** [lu:m] v. (무섭게) 흐릿하게 보이다; (일이) 곧 닥칠 것처럼 보이다
If something looms over you, it appears as a large or unclear shape, often in a frightening way.

⋆ **content** [kántent] ① n. (pl.) 내용물; 내용 ② a. 만족하는; v. 만족시키다
The contents of a container such as a bottle, box, or room are the things that are inside it.

formidable [fɔ́:rmidəbl] a. 어마어마한
If you describe something or someone as formidable, you mean that you feel slightly frightened by them because they are very great or impressive.

whack [wæk] n. 퍽, 철썩 (하는 소리); 강타; v. 세게 치다, 후려치다
A whack is the act of hitting someone or something with a lot of force, or the sound that it makes.

복습 **punch** [pʌntʃ] n. 주먹으로 한 대 침; v. (자판 · 번호판 등을) 치다; 주먹으로 치다
A punch is the action of hitting someone or something with your fist.

⁑ **thief** [θi:f] n. 도둑, 절도범
A thief is a person who steals something from another person.

⁑ **dazzle** [dæzl] v. 황홀하게 하다; 눈부시게 하다; n. 눈부심 (dazzling a. 현혹적인)
Something that is dazzling is very impressive or beautiful.

복습 **mask** [mæsk] v. 가면을 쓰다; (감정 · 냄새 · 사실 등을) 가리다; n. 마스크; 가면 (masked a. 가면을 쓴)
If someone is masked, they are wearing a mask.

knowingly [nóuiŋli] ad. 다 알고 있다는 듯이; 고의로
If you do something knowingly, you do it in a way that suggests you have secret knowledge or awareness.

⁑ **stretch** [stretʃ] v. (길이 · 폭 등을) 늘이다; 펼쳐지다; 기지개를 켜다; n. (길게) 뻗은 구간; 기간
When something soft or elastic stretches or is stretched, it becomes longer or bigger as well as thinner, usually because it is pulled.

thug [θʌg] n. 폭력배
You can refer to a violent person or criminal as a thug.

복습 **snap** [snæp] v. 탁 하고 움직이다; 급히 움직이다; 날카롭게 말하다; 툭 부러지다; n. 탁 하는 소리
If you snap something into a particular position, or if it snaps into that position, it moves quickly into that position, with a sharp sound.

take out idiom ~을 죽이다, 없애다
If you take out someone or something, you kill or destroy them, or injure or damage them so that they cannot work or be used.

⁑ **playful** [pleifl] a. 장난으로 한; 장난기 많은 (playfully ad. 농담으로)
A playful gesture or person is friendly or humorous.

take in idiom 체포하다
If the police take someone in, they take them to a police station to question them about a crime.

⁑ **graceful** [gréisfəl] a. 우아한, 기품 있는
Someone or something that is graceful moves in a smooth and controlled way which is attractive to watch.

⁑ **ease** [i:z] n. 쉬움, 용이함; (근심 · 걱정 없이) 편안함; v. 편해지다
If you do something with ease, you do it easily, without difficulty or effort.

★ **loop** [lu:p] v. 고리 모양을 만들다; (필름 · 테이프 등이) 끊임없이 반복되다; n. 고리
If you loop something such as a piece of rope around an object, you tie a length of it in a loop around the object, for example in order to fasten it to the object.

★ **fluid** [flu:id] a. 부드러운, 우아한; 가변적인; n. 유체(流體), 유동체
Fluid movements or lines or designs are smooth and graceful.

복습 **motion** [móuʃən] n. 동작, 몸짓; 운동, 움직임; v. (손 · 머리로) 몸짓을 해 보이다
A motion is an action, gesture, or movement.

★★ **flexible** [fléksəbl] a. 융통성 있는; 잘 구부러지는, 유연한
Something or someone that is flexible is able to change easily and adapt to different conditions and circumstances as they occur.

★ **eyebrow** [áibràu] n. 눈썹
Your eyebrows are the lines of hair which grow above your eyes.

★★ **previous** [prí:viəs] a. 앞의, 이전의
A previous event or thing is one that happened or existed before the one that you are talking about.

★★ **engage** [ingéidʒ] v. 약속하다; 교전을 시작하다; 관여하다; 기계 부품이 맞물리다
(engagement n. 약속)
An engagement is an arrangement that you have made to do something at a particular time.

★ **whisper** [hwíspər] v. 속삭이다, 소곤거리다; n. 속삭임, 소곤거리는 소리
When you whisper, you say something very quietly, using your breath rather than your throat, so that only one person can hear you.

★ **pointed** [pɔ́intid] a. (말 등이) 날카로운; (끝이) 뾰족한 (pointedly ad. 비난하듯이)
Pointed comments or behavior express criticism in a clear and direct way.

★★ **admire** [ædmáiər] v. 감탄하며 바라보다; 존경하다, 칭찬하다 (admiration n. 감탄, 존경)
Admiration is a feeling of great liking and respect for a person or thing.

handcuff [hǽndkʌ̀f] v. 수갑을 채우다; n. 수갑
If you handcuff someone, you put handcuffs around their wrists.

★★ **crack** [kræk] n. 날카로운 소리; 금; (좁은) 틈; v. 깨지다, 부서지다; 날카로운 소리가 나다
A crack is a sharp sound, like the sound of a piece of wood breaking.

gunfire [gʌ́nfàiər] n. 총소리; 발포, 총격
Gunfire is the repeated shooting of guns.

armed to the teeth idiom 완전 무장을 한
If you describe someone is armed to the teeth, you are saying that they are heavily or formidably armed.

★ **buzz** [bʌz] v. ~의 위를 낮게 날다; 윙윙거리다; 활기가 넘치다; n. 윙윙거리는 소리
If an aircraft buzzes a place, it flies low over it, usually in a threatening way.

zoom [zu:m] v. 쌩 하고 가다; 급등하다; n. (빠르게) 쌩 하고 지나가는 소리
If you zoom somewhere, you go there very quickly.

swoop [swu:p] v. 급강하하다, 위에서 덮치다; 급습하다; n. 급강하; 급습
When a bird or airplane swoops, it suddenly moves downward through the air in a smooth curving movement.

★★ **sheet** [ʃi:t] n. (물 · 얼음 · 불 등의) 넓은 층; (종이) 한 장; 얇은 천
A sheet of something is a thin wide layer of it over the surface of something else.

★★ **fellow** [félou] a. 동료의; n. 녀석, 친구; 동료
You use fellow to describe people who are in the same situation as you, or people you feel you have something in common with.

★ **moisture** [mɔ́isʧər] n. 습기, 수분
Moisture is tiny drops of water in the air, on a surface, or in the ground.

★ **bolt** [boult] n. (물 등의) 분출; 볼트; v. 달아나다; 빗장을 지르다
A bolt of some liquid is a jet or column of it.

★ **palm** [pa:m] n. 손바닥; v. 쓰다듬다, 손으로 만지다
The palm of your hand is the inside part.

복습 **chase** [ʧeis] v. 뒤쫓다, 추적하다; 추구하다; n. 추적, 추격; 추구함
If you chase someone, or chase after them, you run after them or follow them quickly in order to catch or reach them.

★ **flee** [fli:] v. 달아나다, 도망하다
If you flee from something or someone, or flee a person or thing, you escape from them.

★★★ **notice** [nóutis] v. 알아채다, 인지하다; 주의하다; n. 신경 씀, 알아챔; 통지, 예고
If you notice something or someone, you become aware of them.

복습 **yell** [jel] v. 고함치다, 소리 지르다; n. 고함, 외침
If you yell, you shout loudly, usually because you are excited, angry, or in pain.

⋆ **skyscraper** [skáiskrèipər] n. 고층 건물
A skyscraper is a very tall building in a city.

⋆ **ledge** [ledʒ] n. (벽에서 튀어나온) 선반; 절벽에서 튀어나온 바위
A ledge is a narrow shelf along the bottom edge of a window.

복습 **be about to** idiom 막 ~하려는 참이다
If you are about to do something, you are going to do it immediately.

⋆⋆ **crowd** [kraud] n. 사람들, 군중; v. 가득 메우다; 바싹 붙어 서다
A crowd is a large group of people who have gathered together, for example to watch or listen to something interesting, or to protest about something.

⋆ **gasp** [gæsp] v. 헉 하고 숨을 쉬다; 숨을 제대로 못 쉬다; n. 헉 하는 소리를 냄
When you gasp, you take a short quick breath through your mouth, especially when you are surprised, shocked, or in pain.

⋆ **tumble** [tʌmbl] v. 굴러떨어지다; 폭삭 무너지다; n. (갑자기) 굴러떨어짐; 폭락
If someone or something tumbles somewhere, they fall there with a rolling or bouncing movement.

⋆ **pavement** [péivmənt] n. 인도, 보도; 노면
A pavement is a path with a hard surface, usually by the side of a road.

⋆⋆ **burst** [bəːrst] v. (burst-burst) 갑자기 ~하다; 불쑥 움직이다; n. (갑자기) ~을 함; 파열, 폭발
To burst into something means to suddenly start doing it.

⋆⋆ **calculate** [kǽlkjulèit] v. 추정하다, 추산하다; 계산하다, 산출하다 (calculated a. 계산된)
You can describe a clever or dishonest action as calculated when it is very carefully planned or arranged.

⋆⋆ **roof** [ruːf] n. 지붕; (터널 · 동굴 등의) 천장; v. 지붕을 씌우다
The roof of a building is the covering on top of it that protects the people and things inside from the weather.

⋆ **tackle** [tækl] v. 달려들다; (힘든 문제 · 상황과) 씨름하다; n. 태클
If you tackle someone, you attack them and fight them.

midair [midέər] n. 공중, 상공
If something happens in midair, it happens in the air, rather than on the ground.

⋆⋆ **sail** [seil] v. 미끄러지듯 나아가다; 항해하다; n. 돛
If a person or thing sails somewhere, they move there smoothly and fairly quickly.

* **crash** [kræʃ] v. 부딪치다; 충돌하다; 굉음을 내다; n. (자동차 · 항공기) 사고; 요란한 소리
If something crashes somewhere, it moves and hits something else violently, making a loud noise.

* **shower** [ʃáuər] n. 빗발침, 쏟아짐; 소나기; v. (작은 조각들을) 쏟아 붓다; 샤워를 하다
You can refer to a lot of things that are falling as a shower of them.

* **land** [lænd] v. (땅 · 표면에) 내려앉다, 착륙하다; 놓다, 두다; n. 육지, 땅; 지역
When someone or something lands, they come down to the ground after moving through the air or falling.

* **moan** [moun] v. 신음하다; 투덜거리다; n. 신음; 투덜거림
If you moan, you make a low sound, usually because you are unhappy or in pain.

* **counsel** [káunsəl] v. 상담을 하다; n. 변호인; 조언, 충고 (counseling n. 상담)
Counseling is advice which a therapist or other expert gives to someone about a particular problem.

복습 **crime** [kraim] n. 범죄, 죄
A crime is an illegal action or activity for which a person can be punished by law.

kick in idiom 효과가 나타나기 시작하다
If something kicks in, it starts to have an effect.

* **boom** [bu:m] v. 쾅 하는 소리를 내다; 굵은 목소리로 말하다; n. 쾅 (하는 소리)
When something such as someone's voice, a cannon, or a big drum booms, it makes a loud, deep sound that lasts for several seconds.

* **explode** [iksplóud] v. 폭발하다; (갑자기 강한 감정을) 터뜨리다 (explosion n. 폭발)
An explosion is a sudden, violent burst of energy, for example one caused by a bomb.

* **pin** [pin] v. 꼼짝 못하게 하다; (핀으로) 고정시키다; n. 핀
If someone pins you to something, they press you against a surface so that you cannot move.

* **smoke** [smouk] n. 연기; v. (담배를) 피우다; 연기를 내뿜다; 질주하다
Smoke consists of gas and small bits of solid material that are sent into the air when something burns.

rubble [rʌbl] n. (허물어진 건물의) 돌무더기, 잔해
When a building is destroyed, the pieces of brick, stone, or other materials that remain are referred to as rubble.

* **bomb** [bam] **n.** 폭탄; **v.** 폭탄으로 공격하다, 폭격하다
A bomb is a device which explodes and damages or destroys a large area.

villain [vílən] **n.** 악인, 악한; (이야기 · 연극 등의) 악당
A villain is someone who deliberately harms other people or breaks the law in order to get what they wants.

stumble into **idiom** 우연히 ~에 관여하게 되다
If you stumble into something, you become involved in it by chance.

복습 **progress** [prágres] **n.** 진행; 진전; 나아감; **v.** 진전을 보이다; (앞으로) 나아가다
(in progress **idiom** 진행 중인)
If something is in progress, it has started and is still continuing.

notorious [noutɔ́:riəs] **a.** 악명 높은
To be notorious means to be well-known for something bad.

* **mock** [mak] **v.** 놀리다, 조롱하다; 무시하다; **a.** 거짓된, 가짜의
If someone mocks you, they show or pretend that they think you are foolish or inferior, for example by saying something funny about you, or by imitating your behavior.

* **flash** [flæʃ] **v.** 획 내보이다; 획 움직이다; (잠깐) 번쩍이다; **n.** (잠깐) 반짝임; 뉴스 속보; 순간
If you flash something such as an identity card, you show it to people quickly and then put it away again.

복습 **homemade** [hoummeíd] **a.** 집에서 만든, 손수 만든
Something that is homemade has been made in someone's home, rather than in a shop or factory.

복습 **rocket** [rákit] **n.** 로켓; 로켓 추진 미사일; **v.** 로켓처럼 가다, 돌진하다; 급증하다
A rocket is an engine that operates by the combustion of its contents, providing thrust as in a jet engine but without depending on the intake of air for combustion.

* **boot** [bu:t] **n.** 목이 긴 신발, 부츠; **v.** 세게 차다; (컴퓨터를) 부팅하다
Boots are shoes that cover your whole foot and the lower part of your leg.

* **curious** [kjúəriəs] **a.** 궁금한, 호기심이 많은; 별난, 특이한
If you are curious about something, you are interested in it and want to know more about it.

* **invent** [invént] **v.** 발명하다; (사실이 아닌 것을) 지어내다
If you invent something such as a machine or process, you are the first person to think of it or make it.

★ **insist** [insíst] v. 고집하다, 주장하다, 우기다
If you insist that something should be done, you say so very firmly and refuse to give in about it.

★ **ruin** [ru:in] v. 엉망으로 만들다; 폐허로 만들다; n. 붕괴, 몰락; 파멸
To ruin something means to severely harm, damage, or spoil it.

복습 **dash** [dæʃ] v. (급히) 서둘러 가다; 내동댕이치다; n. (= dashboard) (승용차의) 계기판; 돌진, 질주
If you dash somewhere, you run or go there quickly and suddenly.

★ **shatter** [ʃǽtər] v. 산산이 부수다, 산산조각 내다; 엄청난 충격을 주다
If something shatters or is shattered, it breaks into a lot of small pieces.

★ **clip** [klip] v. 핀으로 고정하다; 깎다, 자르다; n. 핀, 클립
When you clip things together or when things clip together, you fasten them together using a clip or clips.

★ **cape** [keip] n. 망토
A cape is a short cloak.

★ **spot** [spat] v. 발견하다, 찾다, 알아채다; n. (특정한) 곳; (작은) 점
If you spot something or someone, you notice them.

★ **race** [reis] v. 쏜살같이 가다; 경주하다; n. 경주; 경쟁; 인종, 종족
If you race somewhere, you go there as quickly as possible.

★ **grab** [græb] v. (와락 · 단단히) 붙잡다; 급히 ~하다; n. 와락 잡아채려고 함
If you grab something, you take it or pick it up suddenly and roughly.

activate [ǽktəvèit] v. 작동시키다; 활성화시키다
If a device or process is activated, something causes it to start working.

★ **spark** [spa:rk] n. 불꽃, 불똥; (전류의) 스파크; v. 촉발시키다; 불꽃을 일으키다
A spark is a tiny bright piece of burning material that flies up from something that is burning.

get hold of idiom ~을 잡다
If you get hold of an object or information, you obtain it, usually after some difficulty.

★ **streak** [stri:k] v. 전속력으로 가다; 줄무늬를 넣다; n. 줄무늬
If something or someone streaks somewhere, they move there very quickly.

★ **wreck** [rek] v. 엉망으로 만들다; 파괴하다; n. 충돌; 사고 잔해
To wreck something means to completely destroy or ruin it.

* **flight** [flait] **n.** 비행; 항공기; 계단, 층계
Flight is the action of flying, or the ability to fly.

복습 **tear** [tɛər] ① **v.** (tore-torn) 뜯어 내다; 찢다, 뜯다; 부리나케 가다; **n.** 찢어진 곳, 구멍 ② **n.** 눈물
To tear something from somewhere means to remove it roughly and violently.

* **track** [træk] **n.** (기차) 선로; 경주로, 트랙; 자국; **v.** 추적하다, 뒤쫓다
Railway tracks are the rails that a train travels along.

* **elevate** [éləvèit] **v.** (들어)올리다; (정도를) 높이다 (elevated train **n.** 고가 철도 열차)
If you elevate something, you raise it above a horizontal level.

* **blast** [blæst] **n.** 폭발; (한 줄기의) 강한 바람; **v.** 확 뿌리다; 폭발시키다; 빠르게 가다
A blast is a big explosion, especially one caused by a bomb.

복습 **rip** [rip] **v.** (거칠게) 떼어 내다, 뜯어 내다; (갑자기) 찢다; 빠른 속도로 돌진하다; **n.** (길게) 찢어진 곳
If something rips into someone or something or rips through them, it enters that person or thing so quickly and forcefully that it often goes completely through them.

* **section** [sékʃən] **n.** 구역; 부분; (조직의) 부서; **v.** 구분하다, 구획하다
A section of something is one of the parts into which it is divided or from which it is formed.

복습 **oncoming** [ánkʌmiŋ] **a.** 다가오는
Oncoming means moving toward you.

복습 **screech** [skriːʧ] **v.** 끼익 하는 소리를 내다; **n.** 끼익, 꽥 (하는 날카로운 소리)
If a vehicle screeches somewhere or if its tires screech, its tires make an unpleasant high-pitched noise on the road.

* **ounce** [auns] **n.** 아주 적은 양; 온스
You can refer to a very small amount of something, such as a quality or characteristic, as an ounce.

* **halt** [hɔːlt] **v.** 멈추다, 서다; 중단시키다; **n.** 멈춤, 중단
When a person or a vehicle halts or when something halts them, they stop moving in the direction they were going and stand still.

CHAPTER 3

Check Your Reading Speed

1분에 몇 단어를 읽는지 리딩 속도를 측정해보세요.

$$\frac{\text{676 words}}{\text{reading time (} \qquad \text{) sec}} \times 60 = (\qquad) \text{ WPM}$$

Build Your Vocabulary

thanks to idiom ~의 덕분에, 때문에
If you say that something happens thanks to a particular person or thing, you mean that they are responsible for it happening or caused it to happen.

복습 **officer** [ɔ́:fisər] n. 경찰관; 순경; 장교
Members of the police force can be referred to as officers.

☆ **protest** [próutest] v. 항의하다, 이의를 제기하다; n. 항의; 시위
If you protest against something or about something, you say or show publicly that you object to it.

☆ **injure** [índʒər] v. 부상을 입히다; (평판 · 자존심 등을) 해치다
If you injure a person or animal, you damage some part of their body.

복습 **blast** [blæst] n. 폭발; (한 줄기의) 강한 바람; v. 확 뿌리다; 폭발시키다; 빠르게 가다
A blast is a big explosion, especially one caused by a bomb.

복습 **bomb** [bam] n. 폭탄; v. 폭탄으로 공격하다, 폭격하다
A bomb is a device which explodes and damages or destroys a large area.

nab [næb] v. 붙잡다, 체포하다; 움켜쥐다
If people in authority such as the police nab someone who they think has done something wrong, they catch them or arrest them.

set up idiom ~을 세우다; 준비하다; (기계 · 장비를) 설치하다
If you set up something, you build it or put it somewhere.

⋆ **perimeter** [pərímitər] n. 방어선; (어떤 구역의) 주위, 주변
A perimeter is a defended boundary protecting a military position.

get away idiom 도망치다; ~로부터 벗어나다
If you get away from someone or somewhere, you escape from them or there.

복습 **nod** [nad] v. (고개를) 끄덕이다, 까딱하다; n. (고개를) 끄덕임
If you nod in a particular direction, you bend your head once in that direction in order to indicate something or to give someone a signal.

affiliate [əfílièit] v. 제휴하다; 가입하다
If an organization affiliates to or with another larger organization, it forms a close connection with the larger organization or becomes a member of it.

⁑ **tiny** [táini] a. 아주 작은
Something or someone that is tiny is extremely small.

* **alarm** [əlá:rm] n. 자명종; 경보 장치; 불안, 공포; v. 불안하게 하다; 경보장치를 달다
An alarm is the same as an alarm clock which is a clock that you can set to make a noise so that it wakes you up at a particular time.

⁑ **signal** [sígnəl] v. (동작 · 소리로) 신호를 보내다; 암시하다; n. 신호; 징조
If you signal to someone, you make a gesture or sound in order to send them a particular message.

복습 **futuristic** [fjù:ʧərístik] a. 초현대적인; 미래를 상상하는
Something that is futuristic looks or seems very modern and unusual, like something from the future.

복습 **vehicle** [ví:ikl] n. 차량, 운송 수단; 수단, 매개체
A vehicle is a machine such as a car, bus, or truck which has an engine and is used to carry people from place to place.

* **roar** [rɔ:r] v. 굉음을 내며 질주하다; 고함치다; 웅웅거리다; n. 함성; 울부짖는 듯한 소리
If something, usually a vehicle, roars somewhere, it goes there very fast, making a loud noise.

⁑ **eventually** [ivénʧuəli] ad. 결국, 마침내
Eventually means at the end of a situation or process or as the final result of it.

복습 **fire** [faiər] v. (엔진이) 점화되다; 해고하다; 발사하다; n. 화재, 불; 발사, 총격
When the engine of a motor vehicle fires, an electrical spark is produced which causes the fuel to burn and the engine to work.

복습 **speed** [spi:d] v. (sped-sped) 빨리 가다; 더 빠르게 하다; n. 속도
If you speed somewhere, you move or travel there quickly, usually in a vehicle.

복습 **flat** [flæt] a. 단호한; 평평한, 편평한; 납작한; ad. 평평하게, 반듯이 (flatly ad. 단호히, 딱 잘라서)
A flat denial or refusal is definite and firm, and is unlikely to be changed.

fumble [fʌmbl] v. (손으로) 더듬거리다; (말을) 더듬거리다; n. (손으로) 더듬거리기
If you fumble for something or fumble with something, you try and reach for it or hold it in a clumsy way.

⋆ **bow** [bou] ① n. 나비 모양 (매듭 · 리본) ② v. (고개를) 숙이다; 절하다; n. (고개 숙여 하는) 인사
A bow is a knot with two loops and two loose ends that is used in tying shoelaces and ribbons.

⋆ **chapel** [ʧǽpəl] n. 채플, 예배당
A chapel is a part of a church which has its own altar and which is used for private prayer.

⁑ **smart** [sma:rt] a. 깔끔한, 맵시 있는; 똑똑한, 영리한 (smartly ad. 말쑥하게)
Smart people and things are pleasantly neat and clean in appearance.

⋆ **aisle** [ail] n. 통로
An aisle is a long narrow gap that people can walk along between rows of seats in a public building.

⋆ **cathedral** [kəθí:drəl] n. 대성당, 큰 교회당
A cathedral is a very large and important church which has a bishop in charge of it.

best man [best mǽn] n. (신랑의) 들러리
The best man at a wedding is the man who assists the bridegroom.

⋆ **altar** [ɔ́:ltər] n. 제단
An altar is a holy table in a church or temple.

⋆ **bride** [braid] n. 신부
A bride is a woman who is getting married or who has just got married.

⁑ **ceremony** [sérəmòuni] n. 의식, 의례
A ceremony is a formal event such as a wedding.

⋆ **lawful** [lɔ́:fəl] a. 합법적인 (lawfully ad. 합법적으로)
If an activity, organization, or product is lawful, it is allowed by law.

wed [wed] v. 결혼하다 (wedded a. 결혼한)
If one person weds another or if two people wed or are wed, they get married.

복습 **whisper** [hwíspər] v. 속삭이다, 소곤거리다; n. 속삭임, 소곤거리는 소리
When you whisper, you say something very quietly, using your breath rather than your throat, so that only one person can hear you.

cut it close idiom 시간이 촉박하다
To cut it close means to give yourself only a very short amount of time to do something.

복습 **flexible** [fléksəbl] a. 융통성 있는; 잘 구부러지는, 유연한
Something or someone that is flexible is able to change easily and adapt to different conditions and circumstances as they occur.

* **wink** [wiŋk] n. 윙크; v. 윙크하다; (빛이) 깜박거리다
A wink is the action of quickly closing and opening one eye as a sign to someone.

** **conclude** [kənklúːd] v. 끝내다, 마치다; 결론을 내리다
When something concludes, or when you conclude it, you end it.

복습 **crowd** [kraud] n. 사람들, 군중; v. 가득 메우다; 바싹 붙어 서다
A crowd is a large group of people who have gathered together, for example to watch or listen to something interesting, or to protest about something.

** **cheer** [ʧiər] v. 환호성을 지르다, 환호하다; n. 환호(성), 응원
When people cheer, they shout loudly to show their approval or to encourage someone who is doing something such as taking part in a game.

** **confident** [kánfədənt] a. 자신감 있는; 확신하는 (confidently ad. 자신 있게)
If a person or their manner is confident, they feel sure about their own abilities, qualities, or ideas.

복습 **flash** [flæʃ] n. 뉴스 속보; (잠깐) 반짝임; 순간; v. 휙 내보이다; 휙 움직이다; (잠깐) 번쩍이다
A flash is an important item of news that television or radio companies broadcast as soon as they receive it, often interrupting other programs to do so.

* **stun** [stʌn] v. 깜짝 놀라게 하다; 어리벙벙하게 하다; 기절시키다 (stunning a. 깜짝 놀랄)
A stunning event is extremely unusual or unexpected.

*** **turn** [təːrn] n. 전환; 차례, 순번; 돌기, 돌리기; v. 돌다; 변하다
If a situation or trend takes a particular kind of turn, it changes so that it starts developing in a different or opposite way.

sue [suː] v. 고소하다, 소송을 제기하다
If you sue someone, you start a legal case against them, usually in order to claim money from them because they have harmed you in some way.

* **apparent** [əpǽrənt] a. ~인 것처럼 보이는; 분명한 (apparently ad. 보아하니)
You use apparently to refer to something that seems to be true, although you are not sure whether it is or not.

plaintiff [pléintif] **n.** (민사 소송의) 원고, 고소인
A plaintiff is a person who brings a legal case against someone in a court of law.

foil [fɔil] **v.** 좌절시키다, 저지하다; **n.** (알루미늄) 포장지, 포일
If you foil someone's plan or attempt to do something, for example to commit a crime, you succeed in stopping them from doing what they want.

⋆ **suicide** [sjúːəsàid] **n.** 자살; 자살 행위(나 다름없는 것)
People who commit suicide deliberately kill themselves because they do not want to continue living.

⋆ **file** [fail] **v.** (소송 등을) 제기하다; (문서 등을) 보관하다; **n.** 파일, 서류철; 정보
If you file a formal or legal accusation, complaint, or request, you make it officially.

복습 **suit** [suːt] **n.** 소송; (특정한 활동 때 입는) 옷; 정장; **v.** ~에게 편리하다; 어울리다
In a court of law, a suit is a case in which someone tries to get a legal decision against a person or company, often so that the person or company will have to pay them money for having done something wrong to them.

⋆ **fame** [feim] **n.** 명성 (famed **a.** 아주 유명한, 저명한)
If people, places, or things are famed for a particular thing, they are very well known for it.

⋆ **superior** [səpíəriər] **a.** 상급의; 우수한; **n.** 상급자, 상관
A superior person or thing is more important than another person or thing in the same organization or system.

⋆⋆ **court** [kɔːrt] **n.** 법정, 법원; (테니스 등을 하는) 코트 (superior court **n.** 상급 법원)
A court is a place where legal matters are decided by a judge and jury or by a magistrate.

courthouse [kɔ́ːrthaus] **n.** 법원 청사
A courthouse is a building in which a court of law meets.

⋆⋆ **lawyer** [lɔ́ːjər] **n.** 변호사
A lawyer is a person who is qualified to advise people about the law and represent them in court.

⋆⋆ **media** [míːdiə] **n.** (신문 · 텔레비전 등의) 매체
You can refer to television, radio, newspapers, and magazines as the media.

⋆ **client** [kláiənt] **n.** 의뢰인, 고객
A client of a professional person or organization is a person or company that receives a service from them in return for payment.

⋆ **accuse** [əkjúːz] v. 비난하다, 고발하다 (accuser n. 고소인; 비난자)
An accuser is a person who says that another person has done something wrong, especially that he or she has committed a crime.

복습 **ruin** [ruːin] v. 엉망으로 만들다; 폐허로 만들다; n. 붕괴, 몰락; 파멸
To ruin something means to severely harm, damage, or spoil it.

⋆ **victim** [víktim] n. (범죄 · 질병 · 사고 등의) 피해자
A victim is someone who has been hurt or killed.

⋆⋆ **government** [gʌ́vərnmənt] n. 정부, 정권; 행정, 통치
The government of a country is the group of people who are responsible for governing it.

open season [óupən siːzn] n. (특정 집단을) 마음대로 비판할 수 있는 시간
Open season refers to a time when a lot of people are criticizing someone or something.

⋆ **headline** [hédlain] n. (신문 기사의) 표제; v. (기사에) 표제를 달다
A headline is the title of a newspaper story, printed in large letters at the top of the story, especially on the front page.

⋆⋆ **pile** [pail] v. 쌓다; 집어 넣다; 우르르 가다; n. 무더기; 쌓아 놓은 것, 더미
If you pile things somewhere, you put them there so that they form a pile.

turn against idiom ~에게 등을 돌리다
If you turn against someone, you stop being friendly toward them or supporting them.

⋆⋆ **identity** [aidéntəti] n. 신원, 신분, 정체; 독자성
Your identity is who you are.

congresswoman [káŋgrəswùmən] n. 여자 국회의원
A Congresswoman is a female member of the US Congress.

⋆⋆⋆ **favor** [féivər] n. 지지, 인정; 호의, 친절; v. 편들다; 선호하다
If you are in favor of something, you support it and think that it is a good thing.

⋆ **tremendous** [triméndəs] a. 엄청난; 굉장한, 대단한
You use tremendous to emphasize how strong a feeling or quality is, or how large an amount is.

⋆⋆ **pressure** [préʃər] n. 압박, 스트레스; 압력; v. 강요하다; 압력을 가하다
If you are experiencing pressure, you feel that you must do a lot of tasks or make a lot of decisions in very little time, or that people expect a lot from you.

initiate [iníʃièit] v. 개시하다, 착수시키다; 가입시키다; n. 가입자
If you initiate something, you start it or cause it to happen.

relocate [riːlóukeit] v. 이전하다, 이동하다 (relocation n. 재배치)
If people or businesses relocate or if someone relocates them, they move to a different place.

anonymous [ənánəməs] a. 익명인; 익명으로 된 (anonymity n. 익명)
If you remain anonymous when you do something, you do not let people know that you were the person who did it.

⁑ **average** [ǽvəridʒ] a. 평범한; 보통의, 일반적인; 평균의; n. 평균; v. 평균을 내다
An average person or thing is typical or normal.

blend in idiom 조화를 이루다; (주위 환경에) 섞여들다
If someone blends in with other people, they become similar to the people around them.

golden age [góuldən eidʒ] n. 황금기, 전성기
A golden age is a period of time during which a very high level of achievement is reached in a particular field of activity, especially in art or literature.

Chapters 4~6

1. What did Bob do at the insurance company?

A. He quietly tried to help Mrs. Hogenson.

B. He acted disrespectfully toward Mrs. Hogenson.

C. He refused to listen to his boss.

D. He apologized to his boss for not working harder.

2. Why wasn't Dash caught putting thumbtacks on his teacher's chair?

A. He threw the thumbtacks onto the chair when no one was looking.

B. He put the thumbtacks there before school started.

C. He erased all the video footage of the classroom.

D. He moved too quickly to be seen.

3. When did Violet tend to turn herself invisible?

A. When she wanted to play tricks

B. When she wanted to fit in with other kids

C. When she was around boys that she liked

D. When she was excited about something

4. Why was Bob so distracted by the newspaper?

A. There was news about major crime in the city.

B. There was news about a missing Super.

C. There was news about the future rights of Supers.

D. There was news about a new villain.

5. What was true about Jack-Jack?

A. He seemed to be an ordinary baby.

B. He was proud of his family's Super powers.

C. He did not want to be normal.

D. He thought everyone in his family was special.

CHAPTER 4

Check Your Reading Speed

1분에 몇 단어를 읽는지 리딩 속도를 측정해보세요.

$$\frac{500 \text{ words}}{\text{reading time (}\quad\text{) sec}} \times 60 = (\qquad) \text{ WPM}$$

Build Your Vocabulary

cubicle [kjú:bikl] **n.** 칸막이한 작은 방
A cubicle is a very small enclosed area.

⁑ **insurance** [inʃúərəns] **n.** 보험, 보증
Insurance is an arrangement in which you pay money to a company, and they pay money to you if something unpleasant happens to you, for example if your property is stolen or damaged, or if you get a serious illness.

⁑ **stamp** [stæmp] **v.** (도장 · 스탬프 등을) 찍다; 밟다; **n.** 도장; (발을) 쿵쾅거리기
If you stamp a mark or word on an object, you press the mark or word onto the object using a stamp or other device.

⁂ **deny** [dinái] **v.** 거부하다, 허락하지 않다; 부정하다
If you deny someone something that they need or want, you refuse to let them have it.

⁑ **collar** [kálər] **n.** (윗옷의) 칼라, 깃; (개 등의 목에 거는) 목걸이
The collar of a shirt or coat is the part which fits round the neck and is usually folded over.

adjuster [ədʒʌ́stər] **n.** (보험 회사의) 손해 사정인
An adjuster is someone whose job is to get information about an accident or theft in order to decide how much money to pay an insurance customer.

overweight [òuvərwéit] **a.** 과체중의, 비만의; 중량 초과의
Someone who is overweight weighs more than is considered healthy or attractive.

* **frail** [freil] **a.** 노쇠한; 약한; 부서지기 쉬운
Someone who is frail is not very strong or healthy.

* **elderly** [éldərli] **a.** 나이가 지긋한
You use elderly as a polite way of saying that someone is old.

* **confuse** [kənfjúːz] v. (사람을) 혼란시키다; 혼동하다 (confused a. 혼란스러워하는)
If you are confused, you do not know exactly what is happening or what to do.

* **upset** [ʌpsét] a. 속상한, 마음이 상한; v. 속상하게 하다; (계획 · 상황 등이) 잘못되게 하다
If you are upset, you are unhappy or disappointed because something unpleasant has happened to you.

* **claim** [kleim] n. 청구; 주장; v. (~이 사실이라고) 주장하다; 요구하다
A claim is a demand for something that you think you have a right to.

liability [làiəbíləti] n. 법적 책임; 골칫거리
A company's or organization's liabilities are the sums of money which it owes.

spell out idiom ~을 설명하다
To spell out means to say or explain something very clearly because someone has not understood something.

* **paragraph** [pǽrəgræ̀f] n. 단락, 절
A paragraph is a section of a piece of writing. A paragraph always begins on a new line and contains at least one sentence.

복습 **interrupt** [ìntərʌ́pt] v. (말 · 행동을) 방해하다; 중단시키다; 차단하다
If you interrupt someone who is speaking, you say or do something that causes them to stop.

복습 **crook** [kruk] n. 구부러진 곳; 사기꾼, 도둑; v. (손가락 · 팔을) 구부리다
The crook of your arm or leg is the soft inside part where you bend your elbow or knee.

* **thigh** [θai] n. 허벅지 (thigh-high a. 허벅지까지 오는)
Your thighs are the top parts of your legs, between your knees and your hips.

복습 **boot** [buːt] n. 목이 긴 신발, 부츠; v. 세게 차다; (컴퓨터를) 부팅하다
Boots are shoes that cover your whole foot and the lower part of your leg.

* **replace** [ripléis] v. 대신하다, 대체하다; 교체하다
If you replace one thing or person with another, you put something or someone else in their place to do their job.

* **sensible** [sénsəbl] a. 실용적인; 상식적인, 분별 있는; 느낄 수 있는
Sensible shoes or clothes are practical and strong rather than fashionable and attractive.

★ **celebrate** [séləbrèit] v. 기념하다, 축하하다
If you celebrate, you do something enjoyable because of a special occasion or to mark someone's success.

momentous [mouméntəs] a. 중대한, 중요한
If you refer to a decision, event, or change as momentous, you mean that it is very important, often because of the effects that it will have in the future.

★★ **occasion** [əkéiʒən] n. 경우, 기회; 특별한 일, 행사
An occasion is a time when something happens, or a case of it happening.

squirm [skwə:rm] v. (몸을) 꼼지락대다; 몹시 당혹해하다
If you squirm, you move your body from side to side, usually because you are nervous or uncomfortable.

★ **official** [əfíʃəl] a. 공식적인; n. 공무원 (officially ad. 공식적으로)
Official activities are carried out by a person in authority as part of their job.

move in idiom 이사를 오다
To move in means to start living in a different house or flat.

★ **pack** [pæk] v. (짐을) 싸다; 가득 채우다; n. 무리, 집단; 묶음 (unpack v. (짐을) 풀다)
When you unpack a suitcase, box, or similar container, or you unpack the things inside it, you take the things out of the container.

have high hopes idiom 큰 기대를 하다
If you have high hopes or great hopes that something will happen, you are confident that it will happen.

★ **stick** [stik] v. (장소 · 지위 등에) 계속 있다; 찌르다; 붙이다; n. 나뭇가지
To stick means to continue to the end of a difficult or unpleasant situation.

복습 **client** [kláiənt] n. 의뢰인, 고객
A client of a professional person or organization is a person or company that receives a service from them in return for payment.

★ **policy** [páləsi] n. 보험 증권; 정책, 방침
An insurance policy is a document which shows the agreement that you have made with an insurance company.

pick up idiom ~를 (차에) 태우러 가다; 더 강해지다
If you pick up someone or something, you go and meet them to take somewhere in a vehicle.

⁑ **desperate** [déspərət] a. 간절히 원하는; 필사적인, 극단적인 (desperately ad. 간절히)
If you are desperate for something or desperate to do something, you want or need it very much indeed.

the coast is clear idiom 들킬 위험이 없다
When you say that the coast is clear, you mean that it is safe to do something because there is no one to see or catch you.

loophole [lú:phoul] n. (법률 · 계약서 등의 허술한) 구멍
A loophole in the law is a small mistake which allows people to do something that would otherwise be illegal.

⁑ **grateful** [gréitfəl] a. 고마워하는, 감사하는 (gratefully ad. 감사하여)
If you are grateful for something that someone has given you or done for you, you have warm, friendly feelings toward them and wish to thank them.

in case idiom (~할) 경우에 대비해서
If you do something in case or just in case a particular thing happens, you do it because that thing might happen.

eavesdrop [í:vzdràp] v. 엿듣다, 도청하다
If you eavesdrop on someone, you listen secretly to what they are saying.

* **pat** [pæt] v. 쓰다듬다; 가볍게 두드리다; n. 쓰다듬기, 토닥거리기
If you pat something or someone, you tap them lightly, usually with your hand held flat.

mean-spirited [mi:n-spíritid] a. 비열한, 천한, 옹졸한
If you describe someone or something as mean-spirited, you mean that they are unkind, motivated by cruelty or intended to be hurtful.

* **barge** [ba:rdʒ] v. 밀치고 가다; n. 바지선
If you barge into a place or barge through it, you rush or push into it in a rough and rude way.

* **authorize** [ɔ́:θəràiz] v. 정식으로 허가하다, 권한을 부여하다
If someone in a position of authority authorizes something, they give their official permission for it to happen.

⁑ **payment** [péimənt] n. 지불, 납입
A payment is an amount of money that is paid to someone, or the act of paying this money.

cover [kʌ́vər] v. (보험으로) 보장하다; 다루다; 가리다; 덮다; n. 위장, 속임수; 몸을 숨길 곳; 덮개 (coverage n. (보험의) 보장)
An insurance policy that covers a person or thing guarantees that money will be paid by the insurance company in relation to that person or thing.

in the black idiom 흑자인
If a bank account is in the black, it contains some money, and if a person or business is in the black, they have money in the bank and are not in debt.

check [ʧek] n. 수표; 확인, 점검; v. 살피다, 점검하다; 확인하다
A check is a printed form on which you write an amount of money and who it is to be paid to. Your bank then pays the money to that person from your account.

storm [stɔːrm] v. 쿵쾅대며 가다, 뛰쳐나가다; 기습하다; n. 폭풍, 폭풍우
If you storm into or out of a place, you enter or leave it quickly and noisily, because you are angry.

mute [mjuːt] a. 무언의, 말없는; v. 소리를 줄이다; 약화하다
Someone who is mute is silent for a particular reason and does not speak.

typical [típikəl] a. 보통의, 일반적인; 전형적인, 대표적인
You use typical to describe someone or something that shows the most usual characteristics of a particular type of person or thing, and is therefore a good example of that type.

Check Your Reading Speed

1분에 몇 단어를 읽는지 리딩 속도를 측정해보세요.

$$\frac{\text{535 words}}{\text{reading time (}\quad\text{) sec}} \times 60 = (\quad) \text{ WPM}$$

Build Your Vocabulary

복습 **pile** [pail] v. 집어 넣다; 쌓다; 우르르 가다; n. 무더기; 쌓아 놓은 것, 더미
If a group of people pile into or out of a vehicle, they all get into it or out of it in a disorganized way.

in time idiom 제때에, 시간 맞춰, 늦지 않게
If you are in time for a particular event, you are not too late for it.

* **principal** [prínsəpəl] n. 교장; a. 주요한, 주된
The principal of a school or college is the person in charge of the school or college.

* **lightning** [láitniŋ] a. 아주 빨리; 급작스럽게; n. 번개, 번갯불
Lightning describes things that happen very quickly or last for only a short time.

thumbtack [θʌ́mtæk] n. 압정
A thumbtack is a short pin with a broad flat top which is used for fastening papers or pictures to a board, wall, or other surface.

* **stool** [stu:l] n. (등받이와 팔걸이가 없는) 의자, 스툴
A stool is a seat with legs but no support for your arms or back.

** **grade** [greid] n. 학년; (상품의) 품질; 등급; v. (등급을) 나누다; 성적을 매기다
In the United States, a grade is a group of classes in which all the children are of a similar age.

triumphant [traiʌ́mfənt] a. 의기양양한; 크게 성공한, 큰 승리를 거둔
(triumphantly ad. 의기양양하여)
Someone who is triumphant has gained a victory or succeeded in something and feels very happy about it.

hold one's breath idiom (흥분 · 공포 등으로) 숨을 죽이다
If you say that someone is holding their breath, you mean that they are waiting anxiously or excitedly for something to happen.

★ **stare** [stɛər] v. 빤히 쳐다보다, 응시하다; n. 빤히 쳐다보기, 응시
If you stare at someone or something, you look at them for a long time.

복습 **sign** [sain] n. 기색, 흔적; 표지판; 몸짓; v. 서명하다; 신호를 보내다
If there is a sign of something, there is something which shows that it exists or is happening.

nuts [nʌts] a. 미친, 제정신이 아닌; ~에 열광하는
If someone goes nuts, they become extremely angry or insane.

★ **sigh** [sai] n. 한숨; v. 한숨을 쉬다, 한숨짓다; 탄식하듯 말하다
A sigh is a slow breath out that makes a long soft sound, especially because you are disappointed, tired, annoyed, or relaxed.

★ **relieve** [rilíːv] v. 안도하다; (불쾌감 · 고통 등을) 없애 주다; 완화하다 (relief n. 안도, 안심)
If you feel a sense of relief, you feel happy because something unpleasant has not happened or is no longer happening.

복습 **protest** [próutest] v. 항의하다, 이의를 제기하다; n. 항의; 시위
If you protest against something or about something, you say or show publicly that you object to it.

★★ **guilty** [gílti] a. 유죄의; 책임이 있는; 죄책감이 드는
If someone is guilty of doing something wrong, they have done that thing.

smug [smʌg] a. 의기양양한, 우쭐해하는
If you say that someone is smug, you are criticizing the fact they seem very pleased with how good, clever, or lucky they are.

★ **exclaim** [ikskléim] v. 소리치다, 외치다
If you exclaim, you cry out suddenly in surprise, strong emotion, or pain.

★ **outlet** [áutlet] n. (감정 · 생각 · 에너지의) 발산 수단; (액체 · 기체의) 배출구
If someone has an outlet for their feelings or ideas, they have a means of expressing and releasing them.

slump [slʌmp] v. 털썩 앉다; (가치 · 수량 등이) 급감하다; n. 부진, 슬럼프; 급감; 불황
If you slump somewhere, you fall or sit down there heavily, for example because you are very tired or you feel ill.

★ **mutter** [mʌ́tər] v. 중얼거리다; 투덜거리다; n. 중얼거림
If you mutter, you speak very quietly so that you cannot easily be heard, often because you are complaining about something.

glum [glʌm] a. 침울한 (glumly ad. 무뚝뚝하게, 침울하게)
Someone who is glum is sad and quiet because they are disappointed or unhappy about something.

복습 **tiny** [táini] a. 아주 작은
Something or someone that is tiny is extremely small.

★★★ **fit** [fit] v. 어울리게 하다; (모양 · 크기가) 맞다; 적절하다; a. 건강한; 적합한, 알맞은
(fit in idiom 어울리다)
To fit in means to be accepted by a group of people because you are similar to them.

★★ **ashamed** [əʃéimd] a. (~여서) 부끄러운, 창피한
If someone is ashamed, they feel embarrassed or guilty because of something they do or they have done, or because of their appearance.

★ **weary** [wíəri] a. 지친, 피곤한; ~에 싫증난; v. 지치게 하다; ~에 싫증나다 (wearily ad. 지쳐서)
If you are weary, you are very tired.

sulk [sʌlk] v. 부루퉁하다, 샐쭉하다; n. 부루퉁함
If you sulk, you are silent and bad-tempered for a while because you are annoyed about something.

복습 **pick up** idiom ~를 (차에) 태우러 가다; 더 강해지다
If you pick up someone or something, you go and meet them to take somewhere in a vehicle.

★ **talent** [tǽlənt] n. 재주, (타고난) 재능; 재능 있는 사람
Talent is the natural ability to do something well.

★ **visible** [vízəbl] a. (눈에) 보이는, 알아볼 수 있는; 뚜렷한 (invisible a. 보이지 않는)
If you describe something as invisible, you mean that it cannot be seen, for example because it is transparent, hidden, or very small.

★ **handy** [hǽndi] a. 편리한, 유용한 (come in handy idiom 여러 모로 편리하다)
If something comes in handy, it is useful in a particular situation.

★ **shy** [ʃai] a. 수줍음을 많이 타는, 수줍어하는
A shy person is nervous and uncomfortable in the company of other people.

★ **generate** [dʒénərèit] v. 발생시키다, 만들어 내다
To generate a form of energy or power means to produce it.

★★★ **force** [fɔːrs] n. 작용력; 힘; 영향력; v. 억지로 ~하다; ~를 강요하다
Force is the power or strength which something has.

⁑ **field** [fi:ld] **n.** ~장; 경기장; 들판, 밭
A magnetic, gravitational, or electric field is the area in which that particular force is strong enough to have an effect.

peek [pi:k] **v.** (재빨리) 훔쳐보다; 살짝 보이다; **n.** 엿보기
If you peek at something or someone, you have a quick look at them, often secretly.

⁑ **bush** [buʃ] **n.** 관목, 덤불; 우거진 것
A bush is a large plant which is smaller than a tree and has a lot of branches.

materialize [mətíəriəlàiz] **v.** (갑자기) 나타나다; (예상 · 계획대로) 실현되다
(rematerialize **v.** 다시 나타나다)
If a person or thing materializes, they suddenly appear, after they have been invisible or in another place.

* **blush** [blʌʃ] **v.** 얼굴을 붉히다; ~에 부끄러워하다; **n.** 얼굴이 붉어짐
When you blush, your face becomes redder than usual because you are ashamed or embarrassed.

scamper [skǽmpər] **v.** 날쌔게 움직이다
When people or small animals scamper somewhere, they move there quickly with small, light steps.

Check Your Reading Speed

1분에 몇 단어를 읽는지 리딩 속도를 측정해보세요.

$$\frac{\text{911 words}}{\text{reading time (\quad) sec}} \times 60 = (\quad) \text{ WPM}$$

Build Your Vocabulary

scoop [sku:p] v. (큰 숟갈 같은 것으로) 뜨다; 재빨리 들어올리다; n. 한 숟갈(의 양)
If you scoop something from a container, you remove it with something such as a spoon.

dribble [dribl] v. 질질 흘리다; n. (액체가) 조금씩 흘러내리는 것
If a liquid dribbles somewhere, or if you dribble it, it drops down slowly or flows in a thin stream.

be lost in idiom ~에 빠져 있다
If you are lost in something, you are too interested in it, or concentrating so hard on it, that you do not notice other things around you.

⋆ **distract** [distrǽkt] v. (주의를) 딴 데로 돌리다, 집중이 안 되게 하다
(distractedly ad. 주의가 산만해서)
If you are distracted, you are not concentrating on something because you are worried or are thinking about something else.

복습 **sigh** [sai] v. 한숨을 쉬다, 한숨짓다; 탄식하듯 말하다; n. 한숨
When you sigh, you let out a deep breath, as a way of expressing feelings such as disappointment, tiredness, or pleasure.

⋆⋆ **bite** [bait] n. 한 입; 물기; 소량; v. (이빨로) 물다; 베어 물다
A bite of something, especially food, is the action of biting it.

carnivore [ká:rnəvɔ̀:r] n. 육식 동물
A carnivore is an animal that eats meat.

⋆⋆ **meat** [mi:t] n. 고기; 골자, 알맹이
Meat is flesh taken from a dead animal that people cook and eat.

⋆⋆ **plate** [pleit] n. 접시, 그릇; (자동차) 번호판; 판
A plate is a round or oval flat dish that is used to hold food.

dissect [daisékt] v. 해부하다; 분석하다
If someone dissects the body of a dead person or animal, they carefully cut it up in order to examine it scientifically.

★ **divert** [divə́:rt] v. (생각 · 관심을) 다른 데로 돌리다; 방향을 바꾸게 하다
If you say that someone diverts your attention from something important or serious, you disapprove of them behaving or talking in a way that stops you thinking about it.

복습 **eyebrow** [áibràu] n. 눈썹
Your eyebrows are the lines of hair which grow above your eyes.

matter-of-fact [mætər-əv-fǽkt] a. 사무적인; 사실의, 실제적인
(matter-of-factly ad. 무미건조하게; 사무적으로)
If you describe a person as matter-of-fact, you mean that they show no emotions such as enthusiasm, anger, or surprise, especially in a situation where you would expect them to be emotional.

out of the corner of one's eye idiom 곁눈질로; 흘낏 보고
If you see something out of the corner of your eye, you see it but not clearly because it happens to the side of you.

복습 **thumbtack** [θʌ́mtæk] n. 압정
A thumbtack is a short pin with a broad flat top which is used for fastening papers or pictures to a board, wall, or other surface.

★ **barely** [bέərli] ad. 거의 ~아니게; 간신히, 가까스로
You use barely to say that something is only just true or only just the case.

get away with idiom (나쁜 짓을 하고도) 처벌을 모면하다
If someone gets away with something wrong, they do it and they are not punished or criticized for it.

★★ **pride** [praid] n. 자랑스러움, 자부심; 자존심
Pride is a feeling of satisfaction which you have because you or people close to you have done something good or possess something good.

★★★ **book** [buk] v. 재빨리 움직이다; 예약하다; n. 책
To book means to move quickly or hurry.

★★ **encourage** [inkə́:ridʒ] v. 부추기다; 격려하다, 용기를 북돋우다
If you encourage someone to do something, you try to persuade them to do it, for example by telling them that it would be a pleasant thing to do, or by trying to make it easier for them to do it. You can also encourage an activity.

복습 **crack** [kræk] **n.** 날카로운 소리; 금; (좁은) 틈; **v.** 깨지다, 부서지다; 날카로운 소리가 나다
A crack is a sharp sound, like the sound of a piece of wood breaking.

inadvertent [ìnədvə́:rtnt] **a.** 고의가 아닌, 우연의; 의도하지 않은
(inadvertently **ad.** 무심코, 우연히)
An inadvertent action is one that you do without realizing what you are doing.

★ **poke** [pouk] **v.** (손가락 등으로) 쿡 찌르다; 쑥 내밀다; **n.** (손가락 등으로) 찌르기
If you poke someone or something, you quickly push them with your finger or with a sharp object.

복습 **cover** [kʌ́vər] **v.** 가리다; (보험으로) 보장하다; 다루다; 덮다; **n.** 위장, 속임수; 몸을 숨길 곳; 덮개
If one thing covers another, it has been placed over it in order to protect it, hide it, or close it.

★ **shrug** [ʃrʌg] **v.** (어깨를) 으쓱하다; **n.** 어깨를 으쓱하기
If you shrug, you raise your shoulders to show that you are not interested in something or that you do not know or care about something.

★★★ **hardly** [há:rdli] **ad.** 거의 ~아니다; ~하자마자; 거의 ~할 수가 없다
You use hardly to modify a statement when you want to emphasize that it is only a small amount or detail which makes it true, and that therefore it is best to consider the opposite statement as being true.

★ **tease** [ti:z] **v.** 놀리다, 장난하다; (동물을) 못 살게 굴다; **n.** 장난, 놀림
To tease someone means to laugh at them or make jokes about them in order to embarrass, annoy, or upset them.

★★ **insect** [ínsekt] **n.** 벌레 같은 놈; 곤충
You can use insect to refer to an unimportant or trivial person.

★★★ **firm** [fə:rm] **a.** 단호한, 확고한; 단단한 (firmly **ad.** 단호히)
If you describe someone as firm, you mean they behave in a way that shows that they are not going to change their mind, or that they are the person who is in control.

★ **giggle** [gigl] **v.** 피식 웃다, 킥킥거리다; **n.** 피식 웃음, 킥킥거림
If someone giggles, they laugh in a childlike way, because they are amused, nervous, or embarrassed.

that's it **idiom** 그만해라; 바로 그거야!
You can use 'that's it' when a series of situations has made you angry, so that you decide to leave or to stop what you are doing.

★ **frustrate** [frʌ́streit] **v.** 좌절감을 주다, 불만스럽게 하다; 방해하다
(frustration **n.** 불만, 좌절감)
If something frustrates you, it upsets or angers you because you are unable to do anything about the problems it creates.

lunge [lʌndʒ] **v.** 달려들다, 돌진하다; **n.** 돌진
If you lunge in a particular direction, you move in that direction suddenly and clumsily.

★ **vanish** [vǽniʃ] **v.** 사라지다, 없어지다; 모습을 감추다
If someone or something vanishes, they disappear suddenly or in a way that cannot be explained.

★ **wrestle** [resl] **v.** 몸싸움을 벌이다, 맞붙어 싸우다; (힘든 문제와) 씨름하다
If you wrestle with someone, you fight them by forcing them into painful positions or throwing them to the ground, rather than by hitting them.

blur [bləːr] **n.** 흐릿한 형체; **v.** 흐릿해지다; 모호해지다
A blur is a shape or area which you cannot see clearly because it has no distinct outline or because it is moving very fast.

복습 **force** [fɔːrs] **n.** 작용력; 힘; 영향력; **v.** 억지로 ~하다; ~를 강요하다
Force is the power or strength which something has.

복습 **field** [fiːld] **n.** ~장; 경기장; 들판, 밭
A magnetic, gravitational, or electric field is the area in which that particular force is strong enough to have an effect.

복습 **stretch** [stretʃ] **v.** (길이 · 폭 등을) 늘이다; 펼쳐지다; 기지개를 켜다; **n.** (길게) 뻗은 구간; 기간
When something soft or elastic stretches or is stretched, it becomes longer or bigger as well as thinner, usually because it is pulled.

★★ **dive** [daiv] **v.** (dove/dived-dived) 급히 움직이다; (물속으로) 뛰어들다; 급강하하다;
n. 급강하; (물속으로) 뛰어들기
If you dive in a particular direction or into a particular place, you jump or move there quickly.

fixated [fíkseitid] **a.** (~에) 집착하는
If you accuse someone of being fixated on a particular thing, you mean that they think about it to an extreme and excessive degree.

복습 **headline** [hédlain] **n.** (신문 기사의) 표제; **v.** (기사에) 표제를 달다
A headline is the title of a newspaper story, printed in large letters at the top of the story, especially on the front page.

outspoken [autspóukən] a. 거침없이 말하는
Someone who is outspoken gives their opinions about things openly and honestly, even if they are likely to shock or offend people.

⋆ **advocate** [ǽdvəkèit] n. 옹호자, 지지자; v. 지지하다
An advocate of a particular action or plan is someone who recommends it publicly.

복습 **identity** [aidéntəti] n. 신원, 신분, 정체; 독자성
Your identity is who you are.

⋆⋆ **former** [fɔ́:rmər] a. (시간적으로) 이전의, 먼저의; n. 전자
Former is used to describe someone who used to have a particular job, position, or role, but no longer has it.

복습 **desperate** [déspərət] a. 간절히 원하는; 필사적인, 극단적인 (desperately ad. 간절히)
If you are desperate for something or desperate to do something, you want or need it very much indeed.

복습 **engage** [ingéidʒ] v. 관여하다; 약속하다; 교전을 시작하다; 기계 부품이 맞물리다
If you engage in an activity, you do it or are actively involved with it.

복습 **snap** [snæp] v. 급히 움직이다; 탁 하고 움직이다; 날카롭게 말하다; 툭 부러지다; n. 탁 하는 소리 (snap out of idiom (기분 · 습관에서) 재빨리 벗어나다)
To snap out of something means to become suddenly freed from a condition such as an illness, bad mood, or memory.

hoist [hɔist] v. 들어올리다, 끌어올리다; n. 끌어올리기
If you hoist something heavy somewhere, you lift it or pull it up there.

dangle [dæŋgl] v. 매달리다; (무엇을 들고) 달랑거리다
If something dangles from somewhere or if you dangle it somewhere, it hangs or swings loosely.

⋆⋆ **twist** [twist] v. 휘다, 구부리다; (고개 · 몸 등을) 돌리다; n. (손으로) 돌리기; (고개 · 몸 등을) 돌리기
If you twist something, you turn it to make a spiral shape, for example by turning the two ends of it in opposite directions.

⋆ **hopeless** [hóuplis] a. 엉망인; 가망 없는, 절망적인 (hopelessly ad. 엉망으로)
You use hopeless to emphasize how bad or inadequate something or someone is.

⋆ **tangle** [tæŋgl] v. 헝클어지다, 얽히다; n. (실 등이) 엉킨 것; (혼란스럽게) 꼬인 상태
If something is tangled or tangles, it becomes twisted together in an untidy way.

⁑ **knot** [nat] **n.** 매듭; (긴장 · 화 등으로) 뻣뻣한 느낌; **v.** 매듭을 묶다
If you tie a knot in a piece of string, rope, cloth, or other material, you pass one end or part of it through a loop and pull it tight.

* **shriek** [ʃri:k] **v.** (날카롭게) 비명을 지르다; 악을 쓰며 말하다; **n.** (날카로운) 비명
When someone shrieks, they make a short, very loud cry, for example because they are suddenly surprised, are in pain, or are laughing.

⁑ **freeze** [fri:z] **v.** (froze-frozen) (두려움 등으로 몸이) 얼어붙다; 얼다; **n.** 동결; 한파
If someone who is moving freezes, they suddenly stop and become completely still and quiet.

* **resume** [rizú:m] **v.** 자기 위치로 돌아가다; 재개하다
If you resume your seat or position, you return to the seat or position you were in before you moved.

* **doorway** [dɔ́:rwèi] **n.** 출입구
A doorway is a space in a wall where a door opens and closes.

drop by **idiom** 잠깐 들르다, 불시에 찾아가다
If you drop by somewhere, you pay a short, informal visit to someone, often without arranging this in advance.

write the book **idiom** ~의 전형이다, ~의 선구자가 되다
To write the book on something means to be the embodiment of it.

* **chill** [ʧil] **v.** 아주 춥게 하다; 오싹하게 하다; **n.** 오싹한 느낌; 냉기, 한기
When you chill something or when it chills, you lower its temperature so that it becomes colder but does not freeze.

* **closet** [klázit] **n.** 벽장
A closet is a piece of furniture with doors at the front and shelves inside, which is used for storing things.

복습 **grab** [græb] **v.** (와락 · 단단히) 붙잡다; 급히 ~하다; **n.** 와락 잡아채려고 함
If you grab something, you take it or pick it up suddenly and roughly.

bowling [bóuliŋ] **n.** 볼링
Bowling is a game in which you roll a heavy ball down a narrow track toward a group of wooden objects and try to knock down as many of them as possible.

복습 **confuse** [kənfjú:z] **v.** (사람을) 혼란시키다; 혼동하다 (confused **a.** 혼란스러워하는)
If you are confused, you do not know exactly what is happening or what to do.

★ **remind** [rimáind] v. 상기시키다, 다시 한 번 알려 주다
If someone reminds you of a fact or event that you already know about, they say something which makes you think about it.

go at idiom 맹렬히 ~을 하다
To go at something means to use all of your energy and effort to succeed.

복습 **principal** [prínsəpəl] n. 교장; a. 주요한, 주된
The principal of a school or college is the person in charge of the school or college.

복습 **patient** [péiʃənt] a. 참을성 있는, 인내심 있는; n. 환자
If you are patient, you stay calm and do not get annoyed, for example when something takes a long time, or when someone is not doing what you want them to do.

gleeful [glí:fəl] a. 신이 난; 고소해하는 (gleefully ad. 유쾌하게)
Someone who is gleeful is happy and excited, often because of someone else's bad luck.

★ **spit** [spit] v. (spit/spat-spit/spat) (~을) 뱉다; ~에서 나오다; n. 침; (침 등을) 뱉기
If you spit liquid or food somewhere, you force a small amount of it out of your mouth.

★ **mouthful** [máuθfùl] n. (음식) 한 입, 한 모금; 길고 복잡한 말
A mouthful of drink or food is the amount that you put or have in your mouth.

★ **chin** [ʧin] n. 턱
Your chin is the part of your face that is below your mouth and above your neck.

Chapters 7~9

1. What did Lucius and Bob do in the car?

A. They drove toward a bowling alley.

B. They looked for a place to eat.

C. They listened to police dispatch calls.

D. They told stories about their families.

2. How did they escape from the burning building?

A. Lucius used his power to put out the fire.

B. Bob knocked down a brick wall.

C. They ran down the stairs and out the front entrance.

D. They jumped off the roof and into a jewelry store.

3. Why didn't Helen want Bob to use his Super strength to save people?

A. It was uncontrollable and dangerous.

B. It could end up hurting innocent people.

C. It would make their children want to use their powers as well.

D. It would cause their family to have to move again.

4. Why was Huph unhappy?

A. Insuricare stockholders wanted to fire him.

B. Bob was giving Insuricare customers illegal advice.

C. Insuricare customers knew too much about the company's system.

D. Insuricare customers were making a lot of unreasonable complaints.

5. What happened after Bob said that someone was being mugged outside?

A. Huph accused Bob of lying.

B. Huph ordered Bob not to leave.

C. Huph told Bob to rescue the victim.

D. Huph demanded that Bob give the victim insurance.

Check Your Reading Speed

1분에 몇 단어를 읽는지 리딩 속도를 측정해보세요.

$$\frac{\text{844 words}}{\text{reading time (} \quad \text{) sec}} \times 60 = (\quad) \text{ WPM}$$

Build Your Vocabulary

run-down [rʌn-dáun] a. 황폐한; 쇠퇴한; 건강을 해친
A run-down building or area is in very poor condition.

alleyway [ǽliwèi] n. 골목, 좁은 길
An alleyway is the same as an alley which is a narrow passage or street with buildings or walls on both sides.

복습 **bowling** [bóuliŋ] n. 볼링
Bowling is a game in which you roll a heavy ball down a narrow track toward a group of wooden objects and try to knock down as many of them as possible.

reminisce [rèmənís] v. 추억에 잠기다, 추억담을 나누다
If you reminisce about something from your past, you write or talk about it, often with pleasure.

★ **portable** [pɔ́:rtəbl] a. 휴대가 쉬운, 휴대용의
A portable machine or device is designed to be easily carried or moved.

★ **scan** [skæn] v. 정밀 촬영하다; (유심히) 살피다; (빛 · 레이더 등이) 훑다; n. 정밀 검사
(scanner n. 경찰 · 소방의 무선기)
A police scanner is a device that is used for listening to the police as they talk to each other over the radio.

★ **hiss** [his] v. 쉿 하는 소리를 내다; (화난 어조로) 낮게 말하다; n. 쉭쉭거리는 소리
To hiss means to make a sound like a long 's.'

★ **dispatch** [dispǽtʃ] n. 파견; 발송; 긴급 공문; v. 파견하다; 신속히 해치우다
Dispatch is the act of sending someone or something somewhere.

jolt [dʒoult] n. 충격; 덜컥 하고 움직임; v. 갑자기 거칠게 움직이다; (~하도록) 충격을 주다
A jolt is an abrupt, sharp, jerky blow or movement.

★ **ray** [rei] **n.** 광선; 약간, 소량
Rays of light are narrow beams of light.

epitaph [épitæf] **n.** 묘비명
An epitaph is a short piece of writing about someone who is dead, often carved on their grave.

monologue [mánəlɔ̀:g] **v.** 독백하다; **n.** 독백
If you monologue, you deliver a monologue or long speech.

crack up **idiom** 마구 웃기 시작하다; ~를 몹시 웃기다
If you crack up, you start laughing a lot.

★ **feeble** [fi:bl] **a.** 아주 약한
If you describe someone or something as feeble, you mean that they are weak.

★ **inevitable** [inévətəbl] **a.** 불가피한, 필연적인
If something is inevitable, it is certain to happen and cannot be prevented or avoided.

★★ **defeat** [difí:t] **n.** 패배; **v.** 좌절시키다; 물리치다; 이해가 안 되다
Defeat is the experience of being beaten in a battle, game, or contest, or of failing to achieve what you wanted to.

yammer [jǽmər] **v.** 지껄여대다; 투덜대다; **n.** 불평; 수다
If someone yammers, they talk a lot.

platter [plǽtər] **n.** (큰 서빙용) 접시 (on a platter **idiom** 전혀 애쓰지 않고)
If something is given to you on a silver platter, you do not have to do much in order to get it.

crackle [krækl] **v.** 치직 소리를 내다; **n.** 탁탁 하는 소리
If something crackles, it makes a rapid series of short, harsh noises.

복습 **progress** [prágres] **n.** 진행; 진전; 나아감; **v.** 진전을 보이다; (앞으로) 나아가다 (in progress **idiom** 진행 중인)
If something is in progress, it has started and is still continuing.

복습 **rob** [rab] **v.** (사람 · 장소를) 도둑질하다 (robbery **n.** 강도 사건)
Robbery is the crime of stealing money or property from a bank, shop, or vehicle, often by using force or threats.

복습 **former** [fɔ́:rmər] **a.** (시간적으로) 이전의, 먼저의; **n.** 전자
Former is used to describe someone who used to have a particular job, position, or role, but no longer has it.

★★ **realize** [ríːəlàiz] **v.** 깨닫다, 알아차리다; 실현하다, 달성하다
If you realize that something is true, you become aware of that fact or understand it.

복습 **blonde** [bland] **n.** 금발 머리 여자; **a.** (여자가) 금발인
A blonde is a woman who has fair or pale-yellow hair.

headset [hédsèt] **n.** (마이크가 붙은) 헤드폰
A headset is a small pair of headphones that you can use for listening to a radio or recorded music, or for using a telephone.

★ **bulb** [bʌlb] **n.** 전구
A bulb is the glass part of an electric lamp, which gives out light when electricity passes through it.

복습 **mask** [mæsk] **n.** 마스크; 가면; **v.** 가면을 쓰다; (감정 · 냄새 · 사실 등을) 가리다
A mask is a piece of cloth or other material, which you wear over your face so that people cannot see who you are, or so that you look like someone or something else.

복습 **tear** [tɛər] ① **v.** (tore-torn) 부리나케 가다; 뜯어 내다; 찢다, 뜯다; **n.** 찢어진 곳, 구멍 ② **n.** 눈물
If you tear somewhere, you move there very quickly, often in an uncontrolled or dangerous way.

★ **glow** [glou] **n.** (은은한) 불빛; 홍조; **v.** 빛나다, 타다; (얼굴이) 상기되다
A glow is a dull, steady light, for example the light produced by a fire when there are no flames.

★★★ **burn** [bəːrn] **v.** 불에 타다; 태우다; 상기되다; **n.** 화상
If something is burning, it is on fire.

★★★ **block** [blak] **n.** 구역, 블록; 사각형 덩어리; **v.** 막다, 차단하다; 방해하다
A block in a town is an area of land with streets on all its sides.

복습 **scene** [siːn] **n.** 현장; 장면, 광경; 풍경
The scene of an event is the place where it happened.

★★ **conscious** [kánʃəs] **a.** 의식이 있는; 자각하는; 의도적인 (unconscious **a.** 의식을 잃은)
Someone who is unconscious is in a state similar to sleep, usually as the result of a serious injury or a lack of oxygen.

★ **dwell** [dwel] **v.** 살다, 거주하다 (dweller **n.** 거주자)
A dweller is a person or animal that lives in or at a specified place.

★ **stack** [stæk] v. (깔끔하게 정돈하여) 쌓다; **n.** 무더기, 더미
If you stack a number of things, you arrange them in neat piles.

복습 **smoke** [smouk] **n.** 연기; **v.** (담배를) 피우다; 연기를 내뿜다; 질주하다
Smoke consists of gas and small bits of solid material that are sent into the air when something burns.

make one's way idiom 나아가다, 가다
When you make your way somewhere, you walk or travel there.

put out idiom (불을) 끄다; 내쫓다, 해고하다
If you put out something, especially a fire, you make it stop burning.

복습 **flame** [fleim] **n.** 불길, 불꽃; 격정; **v.** 활활 타오르다; 시뻘게지다
A flame is a hot bright stream of burning gas that comes from something that is burning.

★ **layer** [léiər] **n.** 층, 막; **v.** 층층이 놓다
A layer of a material or substance is a quantity or piece of it that covers a surface or that is between two other things.

★ **evaporate** [ivǽpərèit] v. 증발하다; 사라지다
When a liquid evaporates, or is evaporated, it changes from a liquid state to a gas, because its temperature has increased.

dehydrate [di:háidreit] v. 탈수 상태가 되다; 건조시키다
If you dehydrate or if something dehydrates you, you lose too much water from your body so that you feel weak or ill.

복습 **yell** [jel] v. 고함치다, 소리 지르다; **n.** 고함, 외침
If you yell, you shout loudly, usually because you are excited, angry, or in pain.

be out of idiom ~이 떨어지다, 바닥나다
If you are out of something, you no longer have any of it.

★★★ **excuse** [ikskjú:z] **n.** 변명, 이유; 핑계 거리; **v.** 용서하다; 변명하다
An excuse is a reason which you give in order to explain why something has been done or has not been done, or in order to avoid doing something.

run out of idiom ~을 다 써버리다; ~이 없어지다
If you run out of something like money or time, you use up all of them.

★★ **muscle** [mʌsl] **n.** 근육
A muscle is a piece of tissue inside your body which connects two bones and which you use when you make a movement.

⋆ **incredible** [inkrédəbl] **a.** 믿을 수 없는, 믿기 힘든
If you describe something or someone as incredible, you like them very much or are impressed by them, because they are extremely or unusually good.

복습 **roar** [rɔːr] **n.** 울부짖는 듯한 소리; 함성; **v.** 굉음을 내며 질주하다; 고함치다; 웅웅거리다
A roar is a loud noise made by something such as an engine or a storm.

복습 **roof** [ruːf] **n.** 지붕; (터널 · 동굴 등의) 천장; **v.** 지붕을 씌우다
The roof of a building is the covering on top of it that protects the people and things inside from the weather.

복습 **be about to** **idiom** 막 ~하려는 참이다
If you are about to do something, you are going to do it immediately.

⋆ **collapse** [kəlǽps] **v.** 붕괴되다, 무너지다; 쓰러지다; **n.** 실패; (건물의) 붕괴
If a building or other structure collapses, it falls down very suddenly.

⋆ **trap** [træp] **v.** (위험한 장소에) 가두다; (함정으로) 몰아넣다; **n.** 함정; 덫
If you are trapped somewhere, something falls onto you or blocks your way and prevents you from moving or escaping.

scowl [skaul] **v.** 노려보다, 쏘아보다; **n.** 노려봄, 쏘아봄
When someone scowls, an angry or hostile expression appears on their face.

⋆ **chunk** [ʧʌŋk] **n.** 덩어리; 상당히 많은 양; **v.** 덩어리로 나누다
Chunks of something are thick solid pieces of it.

⋆⋆ **ceiling** [síːliŋ] **n.** 천장
A ceiling is the horizontal surface that forms the top part or roof inside a room.

⋆ **smash** [smæʃ] **v.** 박살내다; (세게) 부딪치다; 부서지다; **n.** 박살내기; 요란한 소리
If you smash something or if it smashes, it breaks into many pieces, for example when it is hit or dropped.

⋆ **heap** [hiːp] **n.** 더미, 무더기; 많음; **v.** (아무렇게나) 쌓다; 쌓아올리다
A heap of things is a pile of them, especially a pile arranged in a rather untidy way.

복습 **spot** [spat] **v.** 발견하다, 찾다, 알아채다; **n.** (특정한) 곳; (작은) 점
If you spot something or someone, you notice them.

⋆ **shift** [ʃift] **v.** (장소를) 옮기다; (견해 · 방식을) 바꾸다; **n.** 교대 근무 (시간); 변화
If you shift something or if it shifts, it moves slightly.

복습 **victim** [víktim] n. (범죄 · 질병 · 사고 등의) 피해자
A victim is someone who has been hurt or killed.

⁑ **charge** [ʧa:rdʒ] n. 책임, 담당; 요금; v. 급히 가다, 달려가다; (요금 · 값을) 청구하다
If you take charge of someone or something, you make yourself responsible for them and take control over them.

* **tail** [teil] n. 끝부분; (동물의) 꼬리; v. 미행하다 (on one's tail idiom ~를 바짝 뒤따라가는)
If you are on someone's tail, you follow them closely.

hallway [hɔ́:lwèi] n. 복도; 통로; 현관
A hallway in a building is a long passage with doors into rooms on both sides of it.

⁑ **brick** [brik] n. 벽돌
Bricks are rectangular blocks of baked clay used for building walls, which are usually red or brown.

복습 **pick up** idiom 더 강해지다; ~를 (차에) 태우러 가다
If your speed picks up, you start to go faster.

* **rescue** [réskju:] v. 구하다, 구출하다; n. 구출, 구조, 구제
If you rescue someone, you get them out of a dangerous or unpleasant situation.

* **instant** [ínstənt] n. 순간, 아주 짧은 동안; a. 즉각적인
An instant is an extremely short period of time.

복습 **alarm** [əlá:rm] n. 경보 장치; 자명종; 불안, 공포; v. 불안하게 하다; 경보장치를 달다
An alarm is an automatic device that warns you of danger, for example by ringing a bell.

go off idiom (경보기 등이) 울리다; 폭발하다; 발사되다
If something like an alarm goes off, it starts making a noise as a signal or warning.

* **jewelry** [dʒú:əlri] n. 보석류, 장신구
Jewelry is ornaments that people wear, for example rings, bracelets, and necklaces.

rookie [rúki] n. 초보자; (스포츠 팀의) 신인 선수
A rookie is someone who has just started doing a job and does not have much experience, especially someone who has just joined the army or police force.

복습 **officer** [ɔ́:fisər] n. 경찰관; 순경; 장교
Members of the police force can be referred to as officers.

★ **spy** [spai] v. (갑자기) 보다, 알아채다; n. 스파이, 정보원
If you spy someone or something, you notice them.

★★ **draw** [drɔ:] v. (drew-drawn) (총·칼 등을 꺼내서) 겨누다; 그리다; 끌어당기다; n. 추첨, 제비뽑기
If someone draws a gun, knife, or other weapon, they pull it out of its container and threaten you with it.

★ **pistol** [pístəl] n. 권총, 피스톨
A pistol is a small gun which is held in and fired from one hand.

복습 **freeze** [fri:z] v. (두려움 등으로 몸이) 얼어붙다; 얼다; n. 동결; 한파
If someone who is moving freezes, they suddenly stop and become completely still and quiet.

복습 **notice** [nóutis] v. 알아채다, 인지하다; 주의하다; n. 신경 씀, 알아챔; 통지, 예고
If you notice something or someone, you become aware of them.

watercooler [wɔ́:tərku:lər] n. 음료수 냉각기
A watercooler is a machine that dispenses drinking water, especially in an office.

★ **convince** [kənvíns] v. 설득하다; 납득시키다, 확신시키다
If someone or something convinces you to do something, they persuade you to do it.

frigid [frídʒid] a. 몹시 추운; 냉랭한
Frigid means extremely cold.

복습 **blast** [blæst] n. (한 줄기의) 강한 바람; 폭발; v. 확 뿌리다; 폭발시키다; 빠르게 가다
A blast can be a strong current of air, wind, or heat.

★★ **split** [split] v. (split-split) 찢어지다, 쪼개지다; 분열되다; n. (길게 찢어진) 틈; 분열
If something such as wood or a piece of clothing splits or is split, a long crack or tear appears in it.

firefighter [fáiərfàitər] n. 소방관
Firefighters are people whose job is to put out fires.

★ **tend** [tend] v. 관리하다; 돌보다, 보살피다; (~하는) 경향이 있다
If you tend to someone or something, you pay attention to them and deal with their problems and needs.

gunshot [gʌ́nʃat] n. 총소리; 발사된 탄환; 발사, 발포
A gunshot is the firing of a gun or the sound of a gun being fired.

bewilder [biwíldər] v. 어리둥절하게 하다, 혼란스럽게 하다 (bewildered a. 당혹한)
If you are bewildered, you are very confused and cannot understand something or decide what you should do.

enormous [inɔ́:rməs] a. 막대한, 거대한
Something that is enormous is extremely large in size or amount.

nearby [nìərbái] ad. 가까운 곳에; a. 인근의, 가까운 곳의
If something is nearby, it is only a short distance away.

stun [stʌn] v. 어리벙벙하게 하다; 깜짝 놀라게 하다; 기절시키다
If you are stunned by something, you are extremely shocked or surprised by it and are therefore unable to speak or do anything.

blink [bliŋk] v. 눈을 깜박이다; (불빛이) 깜박거리다; n. 눈을 깜박거림
When you blink or when you blink your eyes, you shut your eyes and very quickly open them again.

bullet [búlit] n. 총알
A bullet is a small piece of metal with a pointed or rounded end, which is fired out of a gun.

vapor [véipər] n. 증기, 수증기
Vapor consists of tiny drops of water or other liquids in the air, which appear as mist.

trail [treil] n. 자국, 흔적; 자취; v. 끌다; 뒤쫓다, 추적하다
A trail is a series of marks or other signs of movement or other activities left by someone or something.

midair [midέər] n. 공중, 상공
If something happens in midair, it happens in the air, rather than on the ground.

hit the gas idiom 가속 페달을 세게 밟다
If you hit the gas, you push down on the accelerator in a vehicle in a sudden and forceful way.

taillight [téillait] n. (자동차 · 자전거의) 미등
The taillights on a car or other vehicle are the two red lights at the back.

speed [spi:d] v. (sped-sped) 빨리 가다; 더 빠르게 하다; n. 속도
If you speed somewhere, you move or travel there quickly, usually in a vehicle.

radio [réidiòu] v. 무선 연락을 하다, 무전을 보내다; n. 라디오; 무전
If you radio someone, you send a message to them by radio.

headquarter [hédkwɔ:rtər] **n.** (pl.) 본사, 본부; **v.** ~에 본부를 두다
The headquarters of an organization are its main offices.

verify [vérəfài] **v.** 확인하다; 확인해 주다
If you verify something, you state or confirm that it is true.

* **switch** [switʃ] **v.** 전환하다, 바꾸다; **n.** 스위치; 전환
If you switch to something different, for example to a different system, task, or subject of conversation, you change to it from what you were doing or saying before.

* **target** [tá:rgit] **n.** (공격의) 표적; 목표; **v.** (공격 · 비판의) 목표로 삼다
A target is something at which someone is aiming a weapon or other object.

Check Your Reading Speed

1분에 몇 단어를 읽는지 리딩 속도를 측정해보세요.

$$\frac{\text{360 words}}{\text{reading time (\qquad) sec}} \times 60 = (\qquad) \text{ WPM}$$

Build Your Vocabulary

tiptoe [típtòu] v. (발끝으로) 살금살금 걷다
If you tiptoe somewhere, you walk there very quietly without putting your heels on the floor when you walk.

복습 **chunk** [ʧʌŋk] n. 덩어리; 상당히 많은 양; v. 덩어리로 나누다
Chunks of something are thick solid pieces of it.

복습 **plate** [pleit] n. 접시, 그릇; (자동차) 번호판; 판
A plate is a round or oval flat dish that is used to hold food.

* **counter** [káuntər] n. (부엌의) 조리대; 계산대; 반작용; v. 대응하다; 반박하다
A counter is a flat surface in a kitchen which is easy to clean and on which you can prepare food.

복습 **make one's way** idiom 나아가다, 가다
When you make your way somewhere, you walk or travel there.

bathrobe [bǽθròub] n. 목욕 가운
A bathrobe is a loose piece of clothing made of the same material as towels. You wear it before or after you have a bath or a swim.

** **assume** [əsú:m] v. (사실일 것으로) 추정하다; (특질 · 양상을) 띠다
If you assume that something is true, you imagine that it is true, sometimes wrongly.

peeved [pi:vd] a. 짜증이 난
If you are peeved about something, you are annoyed about it.

복습 **rubble** [rʌbl] n. (허물어진 건물의) 돌무더기, 잔해
When a building is destroyed, the pieces of brick, stone, or other materials that remain are referred to as rubble.

CHAPTER 8

복습 **accuse** [əkjú:z] **v.** 비난하다, 고발하다 (accusingly **ad.** 비난하듯)
If you look at someone with an accusing expression or speak to them in an accusing tone of voice, you are showing that you think they have done something wrong.

* **workout** [wə́:rkàut] **n.** 운동
A workout is a period of physical exercise or training.

stay loose **idiom** 긴장을 풀다
To stay loose means to be calm and relaxed.

** **blow** [blou] **v.** (비밀을) 누설하다; (바람 · 입김에) 날리다; (타이어가 터지다); **n.** 강타
To blow someone's cover means to cause their true identity or the true nature of their work to be revealed.

singe [sindʒ] **v.** (겉을) 태우다, 그슬리다
If you singe something or if it singes, it burns very slightly and changes color but does not catch fire.

come down **idiom** 무너져 내리다
If a building or part of it comes down, it is destroyed and falls to the ground.

** **knock** [nak] **v.** 치다, 부딪치다; (문 등을) 두드리다; **n.** 문 두드리는 소리; 부딪침
(knock down **idiom** (건물을) 때려 부수다)
To knock down something means to destroy it and make it fall down.

* **structural** [strʌ́ktʃərəl] **a.** 구조상의, 구조적인 (structurally **ad.** 구조상, 구조적으로)
Structural means relating to or affecting the structure of something.

unsound [ʌnsáund] **a.** 견고하지 못한, 불안정한; 부적절한
If a building or other structure is unsound, it is in poor condition and is likely to collapse.

uproot [ʌ̀prú:t] **v.** 오래 살던 곳에서 떠나다; (나무 · 화초 등을) 뿌리째 뽑다
If you uproot yourself or if you are uprooted, you leave, or are made to leave, a place where you have lived for a long time.

relive [ri:lív] **v.** (특히 상상 속에서) 다시 체험하다
If you relive something that has happened to you in the past, you remember it and imagine that you are experiencing it again.

* **glory** [glɔ́:ri] **n.** 영광, 영예; 자랑스러운 것
A person's glories are the occasions when they have done something people greatly admire which makes them famous.

✲ **loose** [lu:s] **a.** 흩어진; 마음대로 돌아다니는; 꽉 죄지 않는
Something that is loose is not attached to anything, or held or contained in anything.

⋆ **rustle** [rʌsl] **v.** 바스락거리다; **n.** 바스락거리는 소리
When something thin and dry rustles or when you rustle it, it makes soft sounds as it moves.

⋆ **breeze** [bri:z] **n.** 산들바람, 미풍; 식은 죽 먹기; **v.** 경쾌하게 움직이다
A breeze is a gentle wind.

복습 **materialize** [mətíəriəlàiz] **v.** (갑자기) 나타나다; (예상·계획대로) 실현되다
(rematerialize **v.** 다시 나타나다)
If a person or thing materializes, they suddenly appear, after they have been invisible or in another place.

⋆ **couch** [kautʃ] **n.** 긴 의자, 소파
A couch is a long, comfortable seat for two or three people.

upbeat [ʌ́pbì:t] **a.** 긍정적인, 낙관적인
If people or their opinions are upbeat, they are cheerful and hopeful about a situation.

✲ **unite** [ju:náit] **v.** 통합시키다, 결속시키다; 연합하다
If a group of people or things unite or if something unites them, they join together and act as a group.

pigheaded [pighédid] **a.** 고집 센, 황소고집의 (pigheadedness **n.** 완고함)
If you describe someone as pigheaded, you are critical of them because they refuse to change their mind about things, and you think they are unreasonable.

복습 **hesitate** [hézətèit] **v.** 망설이다, 주저하다; 거리끼다
If you hesitate, you do not speak or act for a short time, usually because you are uncertain, embarrassed, or worried about what you are going to say or do.

✲ **evil** [í:vəl] **n.** 악; **a.** 사악한, 악랄한; 유해한; 악마의
Evil is used to refer to all the wicked and bad things that happen in the world.

Check Your Reading Speed

1분에 몇 단어를 읽는지 리딩 속도를 측정해보세요.

$$\frac{\text{567 words}}{\text{reading time (} \quad \text{) sec}} \times 60 = (\quad) \text{ WPM}$$

Build Your Vocabulary

복습 **tiny** [táini] a. 아주 작은
Something or someone that is tiny is extremely small.

복습 **cubicle** [kjú:bikl] n. 칸막이한 작은 방
A cubicle is a very small enclosed area.

intercom [íntərkam] n. 내부 통화 장치, 인터콤
An intercom is a small box with a microphone which is connected to a loudspeaker in another room.

beep [bi:p] v. 삑 소리를 내다; (경적을) 울리다; n. 삑 (하는 소리)
If something such as a horn beeps, or you beep it, it makes a short, harsh sound.

복습 **flat** [flæt] a. 단호한; 평평한, 편평한; 납작한; ad. 평평하게, 반듯이 (flatly ad. 단호히, 딱 잘라서)
A flat denial or refusal is definite and firm, and is unlikely to be changed.

roll one's eyes idiom 눈을 굴리다
If you roll your eyes or if your eyes roll, they move round and upward to show you are bored or annoyed.

★★ **mysterious** [mistíəriəs] a. 신비한; 비밀스러운; 기이한
Someone or something that is mysterious is strange and is not known about or understood.

★★ **attractive** [ətrǽktiv] a. 매력적인; 멋진; 마음을 끄는
A person who is attractive is pleasant to look at.

★ **slip** [slip] v. 슬며시 가다; 미끄러지다; (옷 등을) 재빨리 벗다; n. (작은) 실수; 미끄러짐
If you slip somewhere, you go there quickly and quietly.

★★ **painful** [péinfəl] a. (마음이) 괴로운; 고통스러운 (painfully ad. 극도로; 아플 정도로)
You use painfully to emphasize a quality or situation that is undesirable.

★ **tidy** [táidi] a. 단정한, 말쑥한, 깔끔한; v. 치우다, 정돈하다
Something that is tidy is neat and is arranged in an organized way.

joyless [dʒɔ́ilis] a. 기쁨이 없는
Something that is joyless produces no happiness or pleasure.

★ **announce** [ənáuns] v. 선언하다; 발표하다, 알리다
If you announce something, you tell people about it publicly or officially.

복습 **blink** [bliŋk] v. 눈을 깜박이다; (불빛이) 깜박거리다; n. 눈을 깜박거림
When you blink or when you blink your eyes, you shut your eyes and very quickly open them again.

★ **specific** [spisífik] a. 구체적인, 명확한; 특정한
If someone is specific, they give a description that is precise and exact.

★ **cross** [krɔːs] v. 서로 겹치게 놓다; 반대하다; (가로질러) 건너다; n. 십자 기호
If you cross your arms, legs, or fingers, you put one of them on top of the other.

★ **glare** [glɛər] v. 노려보다; 환하다, 눈부시다; n. 노려봄; 환한 빛, 눈부심
If you glare at someone, you look at them with an angry expression on your face.

복습 **patient** [péiʃənt] a. 참을성 있는, 인내심 있는; n. 환자 (patience n. 인내심, 참을성)
If you have patience, you are able to stay calm and not get annoyed, for example when something takes a long time, or when someone is not doing what you want them to do.

stocky [stáki] a. 땅딸막한, 작고 다부진
A stocky person has a body that is broad, solid, and often short.

★ **suspicious** [səspíʃəs] a. 의심스러운; 의심스러워하는; 의혹을 갖는 (suspiciously ad. 수상쩍게)
You can use suspiciously when you are describing something that you think is slightly strange or not as it should be.

hang around idiom (~에서) 서성거리다
If you hang around, you spend time in a place waiting or doing nothing.

★ **alley** [ǽli] n. 골목, 샛길; 통로
An alley is a narrow passage or street with buildings or walls on both sides.

keep an eye on idiom ~을 계속 지켜보다
If you keep an eye on someone or something, you watch or check them to make sure that they are safe.

★ **customer** [kʌ́stəmər] **n.** 손님, 고객
A customer is someone who buys goods or services, especially from a shop.

★ **complaint** [kəmpléint] **n.** 불평
A complaint is a statement in which you express your dissatisfaction with a particular situation.

★★ **handle** [hændl] **v.** (사람 · 작업 등을) 처리하다; 들다, 옮기다; **n.** 손잡이
If you say that someone can handle a problem or situation, you mean that they have the ability to deal with it successfully.

explicable [iksplíkəbl] **a.** 설명할 수 있는, 납득이 가는 (inexplicable **a.** 설명할 수 없는)
If something is inexplicable, you cannot explain why it happens or why it is true.

★★ **working** [wə́:rkiŋ] **n.** (pl.) (기계 · 시스템 · 조직 등의) 작용 (방식); **a.** 직장이 있는, 일을 하고 있는
The workings of a piece of equipment, an organization, or a system are the ways in which it operates and the processes which are involved in it.

★ **expert** [ékspə:rt] **n.** 전문가; **a.** 숙련된; 전문가의, 전문적인
An expert is a person who is very skilled at doing something or who knows a lot about a particular subject.

★ **exploit** [iksplɔ́it] **v.** 활용하다; (부당하게) 이용하다
If you exploit something, you use it well, and achieve something or gain an advantage from it.

복습 **loophole** [lú:phoul] **n.** (법률 · 계약서 등의 허술한) 구멍
A loophole in the law is a small mistake which allows people to do something that would otherwise be illegal.

★ **dodge** [dadʒ] **v.** 기피하다; (몸을) 재빨리 움직이다; **n.** 몸을 홱 피함
If you dodge something, you deliberately avoid thinking about it or dealing with it, often by being deceitful.

★ **obstacle** [ábstəkl] **n.** 장애; 장애물
You can refer to anything that makes it difficult for you to do something as an obstacle.

★ **penetrate** [pénətrèit] **v.** 간파하다; 뚫고 들어가다; 침투하다
If someone penetrates an organization, a group, or a profession, they succeed in entering it although it is difficult to do so.

⋆ **bureaucracy** [bjuərákrəsi] **n.** 관료 (체제)
Bureaucracy refers to all the rules and procedures followed by government departments and similar organizations, especially when you think that these are complicated and cause long delays.

⋆ **illegal** [ilíːgəl] **a.** 불법적인; 비합법적인
If something is illegal, the law says that it is not allowed.

⋆ **irritate** [írətèit] **v.** 짜증나게 하다, 거슬리다; 자극하다 (irritated **a.** 짜증이 난)
If something irritates you, it keeps annoying you.

grit [grit] **v.** 이를 갈다; 잔모래를 뿌리다; **n.** 투지, 기개; 모래
If you grit your teeth, you press your upper and lower teeth tightly together, usually because you are angry about something.

복습 **explode** [iksplóud] **v.** (갑자기 강한 감정을) 터뜨리다; 폭발하다
If someone explodes, they express strong feelings suddenly and violently.

stockholder [stákhòuldər] **n.** 주주(株主)
A stockholder is a person who owns shares in a company.

go on **idiom** 말을 계속하다; (어떤 상황이) 계속되다; 자자, 어서
To go on means to continue speaking after a short pause.

⋆ **compose** [kəmpóuz] **v.** (감정 · 표정 등을) 가다듬다; 구성하다
If you compose yourself or if you compose your features, you succeed in becoming calm after you have been angry, excited, or upset.

⋆⋆ **dull** [dʌl] **a.** 단조롭고 지루한; 재미없는; 흐릿한 (dully **ad.** 단조롭게)
Someone or something that is dull is not very lively or energetic.

⋆ **lecture** [léktʃər] **n.** 잔소리, 설교; 강의, 강연; **v.** 잔소리를 하다; 강의하다
A lecture is a long serious talk that criticizes you or warns you about something, especially when this is annoying.

drone [droun] **v.** 웅얼거리는 소리를 내다; **n.** (낮게) 웅웅거리는 소리; 저음
If you say that someone drones, you mean that they keep talking about something in a boring way.

cog [kag] **n.** (톱니바퀴의) 톱니
A cog is a wheel with square or triangular teeth around the edge, which is used in a machine to turn another wheel or part.

☆ **wheel** [hwi:l] **n.** 바퀴; (자동차 등의) 핸들; **v.** (바퀴 달린 것을) 밀다
A wheel is a circular object which forms a part of a machine, usually a moving part.

복습 **fit** [fit] **v.** (모양 · 크기가) 맞다; 어울리게 하다; 적절하다; **a.** 건강한; 적합한, 알맞은
If something fits, it is the right size and shape to go onto a person's body or onto a particular object.

★ **cooperative** [kouápərətiv] **a.** 협력하는, 협동하는
If you say that someone is cooperative, you mean that they do what you ask them to without complaining or arguing.

복습 **thug** [θʌg] **n.** 폭력배
You can refer to a violent person or criminal as a thug.

mug [mʌg] **v.** 강도짓을 하다; **n.** (큰) 잔; 머그잔
If someone mugs you, they attack you in order to steal your money.

☆ **citizen** [sítəzən] **n.** 시민; 주민
The citizens of a town or city are the people who live there.

복습 **muscle** [mʌsl] **n.** 근육
A muscle is a piece of tissue inside your body which connects two bones and which you use when you make a movement.

☆ **tense** [tens] **v.** 긴장하다; **a.** 긴장한, 신경이 날카로운
If your muscles tense, if you tense, or if you tense your muscles, your muscles become tight and stiff, often because you are anxious or frightened.

mesh [meʃ] **v.** 맞물리다; 꼭 들어맞게 하다; **n.** 그물망, 철망
If two things or ideas mesh or are meshed, they go together well or fit together closely.

복습 **victim** [víktim] **n.** (범죄 · 질병 · 사고 등의) 피해자
A victim is someone who has been hurt or killed.

복습 **bolt** [boult] **v.** 달아나다; 빗장을 지르다; **n.** (물 등의) 분출; 볼트
If a person or animal bolts, they suddenly start to run very fast, often because something has frightened them.

복습 **fire** [faiər] **v.** 해고하다; (엔진이) 점화되다; 발사하다; **n.** 화재, 불; 발사, 총격
If an employer fires you, they dismiss you from your job.

⁑ **threaten** [θretn] **v.** 위협하다; 협박하다; (나쁜 일이 있을) 조짐을 보이다
If a person threatens to do something unpleasant to you, or if they threaten you, they say or imply that they will do something unpleasant to you, especially if you do not do what they want.

⁂ **narrow** [nǽrou] **v.** (눈을) 찌푸리다; 좁히다; **a.** 좁은
If your eyes narrow or if you narrow your eyes, you almost close them, for example because you are angry or because you are trying to concentrate on something.

⁑ **advantage** [ædvǽntidʒ] **n.** 이점; 장점; **v.** (~에게) 유리하게 하다
If you take advantage of something, you make good use of it while you can.

복습 **confident** [kánfədənt] **a.** 자신감 있는; 확신하는 (confidently **ad.** 자신 있게)
If a person or their manner is confident, they feel sure about their own abilities, qualities, or ideas.

* **knob** [nab] **n.** (동그란) 손잡이; 혹, 마디 (doorknob **n.** 문의 손잡이)
A knob is a round handle on a door or drawer which you use in order to open or close it.

⁑ **crush** [krʌʃ] **v.** 으스러뜨리다; 밀어 넣다; 좌절시키다; **n.** 홀딱 반함
To crush something means to press it very hard so that its shape is destroyed or so that it breaks into pieces.

복습 **powerful** [páuərfəl] **a.** 강력한; 영향력 있는, 유력한
You say that someone's body is powerful when it is physically strong.

* **helpless** [hélplis] **a.** 무력한, 속수무책인
If you are helpless, you do not have the strength or power to do anything useful or to control or protect yourself.

복습 **crime** [kraim] **n.** 범죄, 죄
A crime is an illegal action or activity for which a person can be punished by law.

복습 **get away** **idiom** 도망치다; ~로부터 벗어나다
If you get away from someone or somewhere, you escape from them or there.

blood pressure [blʌ́d prèʃər] **n.** 혈압
Your blood pressure is the amount of force with which your blood flows around your body.

복습 **flash** [flæʃ] **v.** 휙 움직이다; 휙 내보이다; (잠깐) 번쩍이다; **n.** (잠깐) 반짝임; 뉴스 속보; 순간
If something flashes past or by, it moves past you so fast that you cannot see it properly.

⋆ **clamp** [klæmp] **v.** 꽉 잡다; 죔쇠로 고정시키다; **n.** 죔쇠
To clamp something in a particular place means to put it or hold it there firmly and tightly.

scrawny [skrɔ́:ni] **a.** 뼈만 앙상한, 거죽만 남은
If you describe a person or animal as scrawny, you mean that they look unattractive because they are so thin.

⋆ **squeak** [skwi:k] **n.** 찍 하는 소리; **v.** 꽥 소리치다; 끽 하는 소리를 내다
A squeak is a short, high-pitched sound or cry.

⋆⋆ **staff** [stæf] **n.** 직원; 지팡이
The staff of an organization are the people who work for it.

복습 **crash** [kræʃ] **v.** 부딪치다; 충돌하다; 굉음을 내다; **n.** (자동차 · 항공기) 사고; 요란한 소리
If something crashes somewhere, it moves and hits something else violently, making a loud noise.

복습 **slam** [slæm] **v.** 세게 치다, 놓다; 쾅 닫다; **n.** 쾅 하고 닫기; 탕 하는 소리
If one thing slams into or against another, it crashes into it with great force.

복습 **file** [fail] **n.** 파일, 서류철; 정보; **v.** (소송 등을) 제기하다; (문서 등을) 보관하다
A file is a box or a folded piece of heavy paper or plastic in which letters or documents are kept.

⋆ **cabinet** [kǽbənit] **n.** 캐비닛, 보관장; (정부의) 내각
A filing cabinet is a piece of office furniture, usually made of metal, which has drawers in which files are kept.

⋆⋆ **document** [dákjumənt] **n.** 서류, 문서; **v.** 기록하다
A document is one or more official pieces of paper with writing on them.

mumble [mʌmbl] **v.** 중얼거리다, 웅얼거리다; **n.** 중얼거림
If you mumble, you speak very quietly and not at all clearly with the result that the words are difficult to understand.

Chapters 10~12

1. What did Mirage say in her video message?

A. She was a Super just like Mr. Incredible.

B. She wanted Mr. Incredible to test some new technology.

C. Mr. Incredible was needed to design an experimental robot.

D. Mr. Incredible would receive a lot of money for his assistance.

2. What did Bob say to Helen about work?

A. He was almost fired by his boss.

B. He was being sent to a conference.

C. He was going to look for a new job.

D. He was about to receive a promotion.

3. What was wrong with the Omnidroid?

A. It no longer followed instructions.

B. It accidentally got stuck in the jungle.

C. It was not intelligent enough to solve problems.

D. It could not distinguish friends from enemies.

4. What did Bob do after he completed the mission?

A. He went back to Insuricare.

B. He told Helen that he lost his job.

C. He started exercising again.

D. He bought a new house for his family.

5. Why did Bob visit E?

A. To tell her about his recent mission

B. To buy a cape for his Mr. Incredible suit

C. To get his Mr. Incredible suit fixed

D. To ask for a new suit design

Check Your Reading Speed

1분에 몇 단어를 읽는지 리딩 속도를 측정해보세요.

$$\frac{\text{969 words}}{\text{reading time (}\quad\text{) sec}} \times 60 = (\quad) \text{ WPM}$$

Build Your Vocabulary

복습 **government** [gʌ́vərnmənt] n. 정부, 정권; 행정, 통치
The government of a country is the group of people who are responsible for governing it.

* **agent** [éidʒənt] n. 요원, 첩보원; 대리인, 중개상
An agent is a person who is employed by a government to find out the secrets of other governments.

* **appreciate** [əprí:ʃièit] v. 고마워하다; 진가를 알아보다
If you appreciate something that someone has done for you or is going to do for you, you are grateful for it.

복습 **nod** [nad] v. (고개를) 끄덕이다, 까딱하다; n. (고개를) 끄덕임
If you nod, you move your head downward and upward to show that you are answering 'yes' to a question, or to show agreement, understanding, or approval.

* **complicated** [kámpləkèitid] a. 복잡한, 이해하기 어려운
If you say that something is complicated, you mean it has so many parts or aspects that it is difficult to understand or deal with.

복습 **relocate** [ri:lóukeit] v. 이전하다, 이동하다
If people or businesses relocate or if someone relocates them, they move to a different place.

복습 **cover** [kʌ́vər] n. 위장, 속임수; 몸을 숨길 곳; 덮개; v. 가리다; (보험으로) 보장하다; 다루다; 덮다
A cover is a false story that is used for hiding who someone really is.

복습 **blow** [blou] v. (blew-blown) (비밀을) 누설하다; (바람·입김에) 날리다; (타이어가) 터지다; n. 강타
To blow someone's cover means to cause their true identity or the true nature of their work to be revealed.

★ **sake** [seik] **n.** 목적; 원인, 이유
If you do something for the sake of something, you do it for that purpose or in order to achieve that result.

★★★ **settle** [setl] **v.** 자리를 잡다; (서서히) 가라앉다; 결정하다
When people settle a place or in a place, or when a government settles them there, they start living there permanently.

pull into **idiom** ~에 도착하다, ~에 들어오다
If a vehicle or a driver pulls into, they move to the side of the road and stop.

driveway [dráivwèi] **n.** (주택의) 진입로
A driveway is a piece of hard ground that leads from the road to the front of a house or other building.

★ **neighborhood** [néibərhùd] **n.** 인근, 근처; (도시의) 지역, 구역; 이웃 사람들
A neighborhood is one of the parts of a town where people live.

trike [traik] **n.** 세발자전거
A trike is a child's tricycle.

복습 **stare** [stɛər] **v.** 빤히 쳐다보다, 응시하다; **n.** 빤히 쳐다보기, 응시
If you stare at someone or something, you look at them for a long time.

복습 **spy** [spai] **v.** (갑자기) 보다, 알아채다; **n.** 스파이, 정보원
If you spy someone or something, you notice them.

★ **amaze** [əméiz] **v.** (대단히) 놀라게 하다; 경악하게 하다 (amazing **a.** 놀라운)
You say that something is amazing when it is very surprising and makes you feel pleasure, approval, or wonder.

★ **fade** [feid] **v.** 서서히 사라지다; (색깔이) 바래다, 희미해지다
When something that you are looking at fades, it slowly becomes less bright or clear until it disappears.

★★★ **fix** [fiks] **v.** 준비하다; 수리하다; 고정시키다; **n.** 해결책; 곤경
If you fix something for someone, you arrange for it to happen or you organize it for them.

den [den] **n.** 서재, 작업실; 굴
Your den is a quiet room in your house where you can go to study, work, or carry on a hobby without being disturbed.

★ **display** [displéi] v. 전시하다; 내보이다; (정보를) 보여주다; n. 전시, 진열; 표현; 디스플레이
If you display something that you want people to see, you put it in a particular place, so that people can see it easily.

memento [məméntou] n. 기념품
A memento is an object which you keep because it reminds you of a person or a special occasion.

front-page [frʌnt-péidʒ] a. 신문 제1면의
A front-page article or picture appears on the front page of a newspaper because it is very important or interesting.

복습 **headline** [hédlain] n. (신문 기사의) 표제; v. (기사에) 표제를 달다
A headline is the title of a newspaper story, printed in large letters at the top of the story, especially on the front page.

★ **countless** [káuntlis] a. 셀 수 없는, 무수한
Countless means very many.

★ **triumph** [tráiəmf] n. 업적, 승리; 승리감, 환희; v. 승리를 거두다, 이기다
A triumph is a great success or achievement, often one that has been gained with a lot of skill or effort.

centerpiece [séntərpi:s] n. 중심 항목; (식탁 중앙에 놓는) 장식물
The centerpiece of something is the best or most interesting part of it.

★ **mount** [maunt] v. 끼우다, 고정시키다; (자전거·말 등에) 올라타다; n. (전시품을 세우는) 판; 산
If you mount an object on something, you fix it there firmly.

복습 **sheet** [ʃi:t] n. (종이) 한 장; (물·얼음·불 등의) 넓은 층; 얇은 천
A sheet of glass, metal, or wood is a large, flat, thin piece of it.

복습 **suit** [su:t] n. (특정한 활동 때 입는) 옷; 정장; 소송; v. ~에게 편리하다; 어울리다
A particular type of suit is a piece of clothing that you wear for a particular activity.

briefcase [brí:fkeis] n. 서류 가방
A briefcase is a case used for carrying documents in.

★★★ **employ** [implɔ́i] v. 고용하다 (employee n. 직원)
An employee is a person who is paid to work for an organization or for another person.

★ **manual** [mǽnjuəl] **n.** 설명서; **a.** 손으로 하는, 육체노동의; 수동의
A manual is a book which tells you how to do something or how a piece of machinery works.

★ **toss** [tɔːs] **v.** (가볍게) 던지다; (고개를) 홱 쳐들다; **n.** 던지기
If you toss something somewhere, you throw it there lightly, often in a rather careless way.

★ **trash** [træʃ] **n.** 쓰레기; **v.** 부수다; (필요 없는 것을) 버리다
Trash consists of unwanted things or waste material such as used paper, empty containers and bottles, and waste food.

clunk [klʌŋk] **n.** 탁 하는 소리
A clunk is a sound made by a heavy object hitting something hard.

★ **envelope** [énvəlòup] **n.** 봉투
An envelope is the rectangular paper cover in which you send a letter to someone through the post.

복습 **flat** [flæt] **a.** 납작한; 평평한, 편평한; 단호한; **ad.** 평평하게, 반듯이
A flat object is not very tall or deep in relation to its length and width.

★ **panel** [pænl] **n.** 판; (자동차 등의) 계기판; 패널, 자문단
A panel is a flat rectangular piece of wood or other material that forms part of a larger object such as a door.

squint [skwint] **v.** 눈을 가늘게 뜨고 보다; 사시이다; **n.** 사시; 잠깐 봄
If you squint at something, you look at it with your eyes partly closed.

★★ **project** [prádʒekt] **v.** (빛·영상 등을) 비추다; 발사하다, 내뿜다; 계획하다; **n.** 계획, 프로젝트
If you project a film or picture onto a screen or wall, you make it appear there.

grid [grid] **n.** 격자무늬; (지도의) 격자 눈금; (자동차 경주에서) 출발점
A grid is something which is in a pattern of straight lines that cross over each other, forming squares.

robotic [roubátik] **a.** 로봇 같은; 로봇식의
Robotic equipment can perform certain tasks automatically.

★★ **match** [mætʃ] **v.** 일치하다; 어울리다; 맞먹다; **n.** 똑같은 것; 경쟁 상대; 성냥
If something such as an amount or a quality matches with another amount or quality, they are both the same or equal.

★ **rod** [rad] **n.** (목재 · 금속 · 유리 소재의) 막대, 장대; 가는 봉
A rod is a long, thin metal or wooden bar.

복습 **scan** [skæn] **v.** (빛 · 레이더 등이) 훑다; (유심히) 살피다; 정밀 촬영하다; **n.** 정밀 검사
If a radar or sonar machine scans an area, it examines or searches it by sending radar or sonar beams over it.

★ **secure** [sikjúər] **a.** 안전한; 안심하는; **v.** 얻어 내다; (단단히) 고정시키다
A secure place is tightly locked or well protected, so that people cannot enter it or leave it.

★ **commence** [kəméns] **v.** 시작하다
When something commences or you commence it, it begins.

turn into **idiom** ~이 되다, ~으로 변하다
To turn or be turned into something means to change, or to make a thing change, into something different.

rest assured **idiom** (자신이 하는 말을 강조하여) 믿어도 된다
If you say that someone can rest assured that something is the case, you mean that it is definitely the case, so they do not need to worry about it.

according to **prep.** ~에 따르면, ~에 따라
If someone says that something is true according to a particular person, book, or other source of information, they are indicating where they got their information.

mesmerize [mézməràiz] **v.** 마음을 사로잡다, 완전 넋을 빼놓다
If you are mesmerized by something, you are so interested in it or so attracted to it that you cannot think about anything else.

★★ **represent** [rèprizént] **v.** 대표하다; 보여주다, 제시하다; 상징하다
If you represent a person or group at an official event, you go there on their behalf.

★ **division** [divíʒən] **n.** (조직의) 부; 분할; 분열
In a large organization, a division is a group of departments whose work is done in the same place or is connected with similar tasks.

★★ **design** [dizáin] **v.** 설계하다; 고안하다; **n.** 설계; 계획, 의도
When someone designs a garment, building, machine, or other object, they plan it and make a detailed drawing of it from which it can be built or made.

★ **experimental** [ikspèrəméntl] **a.** 실험적인
Something that is experimental is new or uses new ideas or methods, and might be modified later if it is unsuccessful.

★★ **technology** [teknálədʒi] **n.** (과학) 기술; 기계, 장비
Technology refers to methods, systems, and devices which are the result of scientific knowledge being used for practical purposes.

★★ **pause** [pɔːz] **v.** (말 · 일을) 잠시 멈추다; (테이프 · 시디 등을) 정지시키다; **n.** (말 · 행동 등의) 멈춤
If you pause while you are doing something, you stop for a short period and then continue.

★ **unique** [juːníːk] **a.** 특별한; 유일무이한, 독특한
You can use unique to describe things that you admire because they are very unusual and special.

★ **remote** [rimóut] **a.** 외진, 외딴; 원격의; 먼; **n.** (= remote control) 리모콘; 원격 조종
Remote areas are far away from cities and places where most people live, and are therefore difficult to get to.

★ **facility** [fəsíləti] **n.** 시설; 기관; 기능, 특징
Facilities are buildings, pieces of equipment, or services that are provided for a particular purpose.

prototype [próutoutaip] **n.** 원형, 시제품
A prototype is a new type of machine or device which is not yet ready to be made in large numbers and sold.

복습 **control** [kəntróul] **n.** 통제, 제어; (기계 · 차량의) 제어 장치; **v.** 지배하다; 조정하다
If you have control of something or someone, you are able to make them do what you want them to do.

복습 **threaten** [θretn] **v.** 위협하다; 협박하다; (나쁜 일이 있을) 조짐을 보이다
If a person threatens to do something unpleasant to you, or if they threaten you, they say or imply that they will do something unpleasant to you, especially if you do not do what they want.

incalculable [inkǽlkjuləbl] **a.** 헤아릴 수 없이 많은, 막대한
Something that is incalculable cannot be calculated or estimated because it is so great.

★★ **damage** [dǽmidʒ] **n.** 손상, 피해; 훼손; **v.** 손상을 주다, 피해를 입히다, 훼손하다
Damage is physical harm that is caused to an object.

복습 **grab** [græb] **v.** (와락 · 단단히) 붙잡다; 급히 ~하다; **n.** 와락 잡아채려고 함
If you grab something, you take it or pick it up suddenly and roughly.

★★ **sensitive** [sénsətiv] **a.** 민감한; 세심한; 감성 있는
A sensitive subject or issue needs to be dealt with carefully because it is likely to cause disagreement or make people angry or upset.

★★★ **nature** [néiʧər] **n.** 본질; 천성, 본성; 자연
The nature of something is its basic quality or character.

★ **mission** [míʃən] **n.** 임무; 사명; **v.** 길고 험난한 여정에 나서다
A mission is an important task that people are given to do, especially one that involves traveling to another country.

복습 **payment** [péimənt] **n.** 지불, 납입
A payment is an amount of money that is paid to someone, or the act of paying this money.

triple [tripl] **a.** 3배의; **v.** 3배가 되다
If something is triple the amount or size of another thing, it is three times as large.

★★ **current** [kə́:rənt] **a.** 현재의, 지금의; **n.** (물 · 공기의) 흐름, 해류; 전류
Current means happening, being used, or being done at the present time.

★★ **annual** [ǽnjuəl] **a.** 연간의, 한 해의; 매년의, 연례의
Annual quantities or rates relate to a period of one year.

★ **salary** [sǽləri] **n.** 급여, 월급
A salary is the money that someone is paid each month by their employer, especially when they are in a profession such as teaching, law, or medicine.

★★ **jaw** [dʒɔ:] **n.** 턱
Your jaw is the lower part of your face below your mouth.

★ **blank** [blæŋk] **a.** 멍한, 무표정한; 빈; **n.** 빈칸, 여백; **v.** (갑자기) 멍해지다 (blankly **ad.** 멍하니)
If you look blank, your face shows no feeling, understanding, or interest.

scribble [skribl] **v.** 갈겨쓰다, 휘갈기다; 낙서하다; **n.** 낙서
If you scribble something, you write it quickly and roughly.

★ **pad** [pæd] **n.** (메모지 등의) 묶음; (우주선) 발사대; 패드; **v.** 소리 안 나게 걷다; 완충재를 대다
A pad of paper is a number of pieces of paper which are fixed together along the top or the side, so that each piece can be torn off when it has been used.

★ **instruct** [instrʌ́kt] **v.** 지시하다; 가르치다; (정보를) 알려 주다
If you instruct someone to do something, you formally tell them to do it.

business card [bíznis ka:rd] n. 명함
A person's business card is a small card which they give to other people, and which has their name and details of their job and company printed on it.

복습 **spit** [spit] v. (spit/spat-spit/spat) ~에서 나오다; (~을) 뱉다; n. 침; (침 등을) 뱉기
To spit out of somewhere means to send out forcefully from there.

⋆ **ensure** [inʃúər] v. 반드시 ~하게 하다, 보장하다
To ensure something, or to ensure that something happens, means to make certain that it happens.

⋆ **security** [sikjúərəti] n. 보안, 경비; 경비 담당 부서; 안도감, 안심
Security refers to all the measures that are taken to protect a place, or to ensure that only people with permission enter it or leave it.

⋆⋆ **smooth** [smu:ð] a. (소리가) 감미로운; 부드러운; 매끈한; v. 매끈하게 하다
(smoothly ad. 차분하게)
A voice or music that is smooth is soft and pleasant to listen to.

reel [ri:l] v. (마음이) 어지럽다; 비틀거리다; n. 릴, 물레
If you are reeling from a shock, you are feeling extremely surprised or upset because of it.

self-destruct [self-distrʌ́kt] v. 저절로 폭파되다, 못 쓰게 되다
If something self-destructs, it destroys itself, especially by exploding.

muffle [mʌfl] v. (소리를) 죽이다; (따뜻하게) 감싸다
If something muffles a sound, it makes it quieter and more difficult to hear.

복습 **boom** [bu:m] n. 쾅 (하는 소리); v. 쾅 하는 소리를 내다; 굵은 목소리로 말하다
A boom is a deep loud sound that continues for some time, for example the noise of thunder or an explosion.

복습 **go off** idiom (경보기 등이) 울리다; 폭발하다; 발사되다
If something like an alarm goes off, it starts making a noise as a signal or warning.

복습 **distract** [distrǽkt] v. (주의를) 딴 데로 돌리다, 집중이 안 되게 하다
(distracted a. (정신이) 산만해진)
If you are distracted, you are not concentrating on something because you are worried or are thinking about something else.

복습 **frustrate** [frʌ́streit] v. 좌절감을 주다, 불만스럽게 하다; 방해하다
(frustrating a. 불만스러운, 좌절감을 주는)
Something that is frustrating annoys you or makes you angry because you cannot do anything about the problems it causes.

stay at it idiom 견뎌 내다
If you stay at it, you continue doing something even if you want to stop.

* **stammer** [stǽmər] v. 말을 더듬다; n. 말 더듬기
If you stammer, you speak with difficulty, hesitating and repeating words or sounds.

gulp [gʌlp] v. 침을 꿀떡 삼키다; (숨을) 깊이 들이마시다; n. 꿀꺽 마시기
If you gulp, you swallow air, often making a noise in your throat as you do so, because you are nervous or excited.

* **conference** [kánfərəns] n. 회의, 학회; 회견
A conference is a meeting, often lasting a few days, which is organized on a particular subject or to bring together people who have a common interest.

** **hopeful** [hóupfəl] a. 희망에 찬, 기대하는; 희망적인 (hopefully ad. 희망을 갖고)
If you do something hopefully, you do it in a way that expresses desire with an expectation of fulfillment.

복습 **recognize** [rékəgnàiz] v. 알아보다; 인식하다; 공인하다
If someone says that they recognize something, they acknowledge that it exists or that it is true.

복습 **talent** [tǽlənt] n. 재주, (타고난) 재능; 재능 있는 사람
Talent is the natural ability to do something well.

** **hug** [hʌg] n. 포옹; v. 껴안다, 포옹하다
A hug is the act of holding someone or something close to your body with your arms.

* **dial** [dáiəl] v. 다이얼을 돌리다, 전화를 걸다; n. (시계 · 계기 등의) 문자반
If you dial or if you dial a number, you turn the dial or press the buttons on a telephone in order to phone someone.

hang up idiom 전화를 끊다; ~을 중지하다
To hang up means to end a telephone conversation, often very suddenly.

복습 **glance** [glæns] v. 흘깃 보다; 대충 훑어보다; n. 흘낏 봄
If you glance at something or someone, you look at them very quickly and then look away again immediately.

Check Your Reading Speed

1분에 몇 단어를 읽는지 리딩 속도를 측정해보세요.

$$\frac{\text{812 words}}{\text{reading time (} \quad \text{) sec}} \times 60 = (\quad) \text{ WPM}$$

Build Your Vocabulary

복습 **sleek** [sli:k] a. (모양이) 매끈한; 윤이 나는
Sleek vehicles, furniture, or other objects look smooth, shiny, and expensive.

⋆ **luxurious** [lʌgʒúəriəs] a. 호화로운, 아주 편안한
If you describe something as luxurious, you mean that it is very comfortable and expensive.

⋆ **jet** [dʒet] n. 제트기; 분출; v. 급속히 움직이다; 분출하다
A jet is an aircraft that is powered by jet engines.

⋆ **slice** [slais] v. (하늘 · 물 등을) 가르듯이 달리다; 베다; n. (얇게 썬) 조각; 부분, 몫
To slice through something means to pass through it very easily.

복습 **remote** [rimóut] a. 외진, 외딴; 원격의; 먼; n. (= remote control) 리모콘; 원격 조종
Remote areas are far away from cities and places where most people live, and are therefore difficult to get to.

⋆ **location** [loukéiʃən] n. 장소, 위치
A location is the place where something happens or is situated.

clad [klæd] a. ~을 입은; ~이 덮인
If you are clad in particular clothes, you are wearing them.

⋆ **brief** [bri:f] v. ~에게 알려주다; a. (시간이) 짧은; 간단한
If someone briefs you, especially about a piece of work or a serious matter, they give you information that you need before you do it or consider it.

upcoming [ʌpkʌ́miŋ] a. 다가오는, 곧 있을
Upcoming events will happen in the near future.

복습 **mission** [míʃən] n. 임무; 사명; v. 길고 험난한 여정에 나서다
A mission is an important task that people are given to do, especially one that involves traveling to another country.

복습 **prototype** [próutoutaip] n. 원형, 시제품
A prototype is a new type of machine or device which is not yet ready to be made in large numbers and sold.

복습 **battle** [bætl] n. 전투; 싸움; v. 싸우다, 투쟁하다
A battle is a violent fight between groups of people, especially one between military forces during a war.

★ **artificial** [àːrtəfíʃəl] a. 인공의; 인위적인; 거짓된, 꾸민
Artificial objects, materials, or processes do not occur naturally and are created by human beings, for example using science or technology.

★★ **intelligence** [intélədʒəns] n. 지능; 기밀, 정보
Intelligence is the ability to think, reason, and understand instead of doing things automatically or by instinct.

★★ **enable** [inéibl] v. ~을 할 수 있게 하다; 가능하게 하다
If someone or something enables you to do a particular thing, they give you the opportunity to do it.

★★ **unfortunately** [ʌnfɔ́ːrʧənətli] ad. 불행하게도, 유감스럽게도
You can use unfortunately to introduce or refer to a statement when you consider that it is sad or disappointing, or when you want to express regret.

복습 **loose** [luːs] a. 마음대로 돌아다니는; 흩어진; 꽉 죄지 않는
If people or animals break loose or are set loose, they are no longer held, tied, or kept somewhere and can move around freely.

★ **jungle** [dʒʌŋgl] n. 밀림 (지대), 정글
A jungle is a forest in a tropical country where large numbers of tall trees and plants grow very close together.

★ **tone** [toun] n. 어조, 말투; (글 등의) 분위기; 음색
Someone's tone is a quality in their voice which shows what they are feeling or thinking.

airdrop [ɛ́ərdrap] n. (항공기에서 낙하산으로 하는 공중) 투하
An airdrop is a delivery of supplies by aircraft to an area that is hard to get to. The supplies are dropped from the aircraft on parachutes.

★★ **obvious** [ábviəs] a. 분명한, 확실한; 명백한 (obviously ad. 분명히)
You use obviously when you are stating something that you expect the person who is listening to know already.

복습 **represent** [rèprizént] v. 보여주다, 제시하다; 대표하다; 상징하다
If you say that something represents a change, achievement, or victory, you mean that it is a change, achievement, or victory.

⋆ **significant** [signífikənt] a. 중요한, 의미 있는
A significant amount or effect is large enough to be important or affect a situation to a noticeable degree.

⋆ **invest** [invést] v. 투자하다; (권력 · 권한 등을) 부여하다 (investment n. 투자)
If you invest in something, or if you invest a sum of money, you use your money in a way that you hope will increase its value, for example by paying it into a bank, or buying shares or property.

shut down idiom (기계가) 멈추다; 문을 닫다
If a machine shuts down, or someone shuts it down, it stops working.

pod [pad] n. (우주선 · 선박의 본체에서) 분리 가능한 부분; (콩이 들어 있는) 꼬투리
A pod is a detachable or self-contained unit on an aircraft, spacecraft, vehicle, or vessel, having a particular function.

bay [bei] n. 구역, 구간; 만(灣)
A bay is a partly enclosed area, inside or outside a building, that is used for a particular purpose.

⋆⋆ **prove** [pru:v] v. (~임이) 드러나다; 입증하다, 증명하다
If something proves to be true or to have a particular quality, it becomes clear after a period of time that it is true or has that quality.

feat [fi:t] n. 공적, 위업; 묘기, 재주
If you refer to an action, or the result of an action, as a feat, you admire it because it is an impressive and difficult achievement.

⋆⋆ **successful** [səksésfəl] a. 성공한, 성공적인 (unsuccessful a. 성공하지 못한)
Something that is unsuccessful does not achieve what it was intended to achieve.

⋆ **squeeze** [skwi:z] v. (좁은 곳에) 비집고 들어가다; (꼭) 쥐다; n. (손으로 꼭) 쥐기
If you squeeze a person or thing somewhere or if they squeeze there, they manage to get through or into a small space.

cram [kræm] v. (억지로) 밀어 넣다
If you cram things or people into a container or place, you put them into it, although there is hardly enough room for them.

admittedly [ædmítidli] ad. 인정하건대
You use admittedly when you are saying something which weakens the importance or force of your statement.

* **press** [pres] v. 누르다; (무엇에) 바싹 대다; 꾹 밀어 넣다; n. 언론
If you press a button or switch, you push it with your finger in order to make a machine or device work.

복습 **switch** [switʃ] n. 스위치; 전환; v. 전환하다, 바꾸다
A switch is a small control for an electrical device which you use to turn the device on or off.

* **beat** [bi:t] v. (게임 · 시합에서) 이기다; 때리다; (심장이) 고동치다; n. 리듬; 고동, 맥박
If you beat someone in a competition or election, you defeat them.

복습 **instruct** [instrʌ́kt] v. 지시하다; 가르치다; (정보를) 알려 주다 (instruction n. 지시)
An instruction is something that someone tells you to do.

복습 **blast** [blæst] v. 빠르게 가다; 확 뿌리다; 폭발시키다; n. 폭발; (한 줄기의) 강한 바람
If someone or something blasts in a particular direction, they move very quickly and loudly in that direction.

복습 **tear** [tɛər] ① v. 뜯어 내다; 찢다, 뜯다; 부리나케 가다; n. 찢어진 곳, 구멍 ② n. 눈물
To tear something from somewhere means to remove it roughly and violently.

*** **free** [fri:] v. (freed-freed) (갇히거나 걸린 데서) 풀어 주다; a. 자유로운; 무료의
If you free someone or something, you remove them from the place in which they have been trapped or become fixed.

복습 **track** [træk] v. 추적하다, 뒤쫓다; n. (기차) 선로; 경주로, 트랙; 자국
To track someone or something means to follow their movements by means of a special device, such as a satellite or radar.

out of shape idiom 몸매가 엉망인; (정상적인) 제 모양이 아닌
If you are out of shape, you are not in good physical condition.

복습 **sign** [sain] n. 기색, 흔적; 표지판; 몸짓; v. 서명하다; 신호를 보내다
If there is a sign of something, there is something which shows that it exists or is happening.

복습 **overweight** [òuvərwéit] a. 과체중의, 비만의; 중량 초과의
Someone who is overweight weighs more than is considered healthy or attractive.

⋆ **rusty** [rʌ́sti] **a.** 예전 같지 않은; 녹슨, 녹투성이의
If a skill that you have or your knowledge of something is rusty, it is not as good as it used to be, because you have not used it for a long time.

⋆⋆ **struggle** [strʌgl] **v.** 애쓰다; 몸부림치다, 허우적거리다; 힘겹게 나아가다; **n.** 투쟁, 분투; 몸부림
If you struggle to do something, you try hard to do it, even though other people or things may be making it difficult for you to succeed.

복습 **nearby** [nìərbái] **a.** 인근의, 가까운 곳의; **ad.** 가까운 곳에
If something is nearby, it is only a short distance away.

⋆ **lava** [lá:və] **n.** 용암
Lava is the very hot liquid rock that comes out of a volcano.

⋆⋆ **pool** [pu:l] **n.** (웅덩이처럼) 고여 있는 곳; 웅덩이; **v.** (자금 · 정보 등을) 모으다; 고이다
A pool of liquid or light is a small area of it on the ground or on a surface.

⋆⋆ **process** [práses] **n.** 과정, 절차; 공정; **v.** (공식적으로) 처리하다; 가공하다
If you are doing something and you do something else in the process, you do the second thing as part of doing the first thing.

⋆ **emerge** [imə́:rdʒ] **v.** 나오다, 모습을 드러내다; (어려움 등을) 헤쳐 나오다
To emerge means to come out from an enclosed or dark space such as a room or a vehicle, or from a position where you could not be seen.

⋆ **claw** [klɔ:] **n.** 갈고리 모양의 기계; (동물 · 새의) 발톱; **v.** (손톱 · 발톱으로) 할퀴다
A claw is a curved end on a tool or machine, used for pulling or picking things up.

복습 **crack** [kræk] **v.** 날카로운 소리가 나다; 깨지다, 부서지다; **n.** 날카로운 소리; 금; (좁은) 틈
If something cracks, or if you crack it, it makes a sharp sound like the sound of a piece of wood breaking.

복습 **slip** [slip] **v.** 슬며시 가다; 미끄러지다; (옷 등을) 재빨리 벗다; **n.** (작은) 실수; 미끄러짐
If you slip somewhere, you go there quickly and quietly.

복습 **eventually** [ivéntʃuəli] **ad.** 결국, 마침내
Eventually means at the end of a situation or process or as the final result of it.

복습 **headquarter** [hédkwɔ:rtər] **n.** (pl.) 본사, 본부; **v.** ~에 본부를 두다
The headquarters of an organization are its main offices.

복습 **mysterious** [mistíəriəs] **a.** 신비한; 비밀스러운; 기이한
Someone or something that is mysterious is strange and is not known about or understood.

복습 **employ** [implɔ́i] v. 고용하다 (employer n. 고용주)
Your employer is the person or organization that you work for.

복습 **display** [displéi] n. 디스플레이; 전시, 진열; 표현; v. (정보를) 보여주다; 전시하다; 내보이다
The display on a computer screen is the information that is shown there.

⁑ **mystery** [místəri] n. 신비스러운 사람, 것; 수수께끼, 미스터리
A mystery person or thing is one whose identity or nature is not known.

⁑ **comment** [káment] v. 논평하다, 견해를 밝히다; n. 논평, 언급
If you comment on something, you give your opinion about it or you give an explanation for it.

복습 **handsome** [hǽnsəm] a. 보기 좋은, 멋진; 멋진, 잘생긴 (handsomely ad. 훌륭하게, 멋지게)
Handsomely means in a smart and attractive manner or style.

복습 **enormous** [inɔ́:rməs] a. 막대한, 거대한
Something that is enormous is extremely large in size or amount.

* **terrace** [térəs] n. 테라스, 작은 발코니
A terrace is a flat area of stone or grass next to a building where people can sit.

* **overlook** [ouvərlúk] v. 바라보다, 내려다보다; 눈감아주다; n. 전망이 좋은 곳, 높은 곳
If a building or window overlooks a place, you can see the place clearly from the building or window.

lush [lʌʃ] a. (식물 · 정원 등이) 무성한, 우거진; 멋진
Lush fields or gardens have a lot of very healthy grass or plants.

* **tropical** [trápikəl] a. 열대의, 열대지방의
Tropical means belonging to or typical of the tropics.

lavish [lǽviʃ] a. 풍성한; 호화로운; 아주 후한 (lavishly ad. 풍성하게)
If you describe something as lavish, you mean that it is very elaborate and impressive and a lot of money has been spent on it.

* **impressive** [imprésiv] a. 인상적인, 감명 깊은
Something that is impressive impresses you, for example because it is great in size or degree, or is done with a great deal of skill.

* **waterfall** [wɔ́:tərfɔ:l] n. 폭포
A waterfall is a place where water flows over the edge of a steep, high cliff in hills or mountains, and falls into a pool below.

★★ **melt** [melt] v. 녹다; (감정 등이) 누그러지다; n. 용해 (molten a. 녹은)
Molten rock, metal, or glass has been heated to a very high temperature and has become a hot thick liquid.

rumble [rʌmbl] n. 우르렁거리는 소리; v. 웅웅거리는 소리를 내다; 덜커덩거리며 나아가다
A rumble is a low continuous noise.

★★★ **part** [pa:rt] v. (두 사물 · 부분이) 갈라지다; (~와) 헤어지다; n. 일부, 약간; 부분
If things that are next to each other part or if you part them, they move in opposite directions, so that there is a space between them.

복습 **reveal** [riví:l] v. (보이지 않던 것을) 드러내 보이다; (비밀 등을) 밝히다
If you reveal something that has been out of sight, you uncover it so that people can see it.

passageway [pǽsidʒwèi] n. 복도, 통로
A passageway is a long narrow space with walls or fences on both sides, which connects one place or room with another.

복습 **peek** [pi:k] v. (재빨리) 훔쳐보다; 살짝 보이다; n. 엿보기
If you peek at something or someone, you have a quick look at them, often secretly.

★★★ **figure** [fígjər] n. (멀리서 흐릿하게 보이는) 사람; 수치; (중요한) 인물; v. 생각하다; 중요하다
You refer to someone that you can see as a figure when you cannot see them clearly or when you are describing them.

★ **obscure** [əbskjúər] v. 보기 어렵게 하다; a. 잘 알려져 있지 않은; 모호한
If one thing obscures another, it prevents it from being seen or heard properly.

복습 **glow** [glou] n. (은은한) 불빛; 홍조; v. 빛나다, 타다; (얼굴이) 상기되다
A glow is a dull, steady light, for example the light produced by a fire when there are no flames.

seeming [sí:miŋ] a. 외견상의, 겉보기의 (seemingly ad. 외견상으로, 겉보기에는)
If something is seemingly the case, you mean that it appears to be the case, even though it may not really be so.

overdressed [òuvərdrést] a. 옷을 지나치게 차려입은
If you say that someone is overdressed, you are criticizing them for wearing clothes that are not appropriate for the occasion because they are too formal or too smart.

approving [əprúːviŋ] a. 찬성하는, 좋다고 여기는 (approvingly ad. 만족스러운 듯이)
An approving reaction or remark shows support for something, or satisfaction with it.

dashing [dǽʃiŋ] a. 늠름한; 멋진, 근사한
A dashing person or thing is very stylish and attractive.

⋆ **host** [houst] n. (초대한) 주인; (TV · 라디오 프로의) 진행자; v. 주최하다; 진행하다
The host at a party is the person who has invited the guests and provides the food, drink, or entertainment.

복습 **wave** [weiv] n. (손 · 팔을) 흔들기; 물결; (열 · 소리·빛 등의) -파; v. (손 · 팔을) 흔들다; 손짓하다
A wave is a movement of your hand used for saying hello or goodbye to someone or for giving a signal.

⋆⋆ **casual** [kǽʒuəl] a. 태평스러운 (듯한), 무심한; 격식을 차리지 않는
(casually ad. 무심하게; 우연히)
If you are casual, you are, or you pretend to be, relaxed and not very concerned about what is happening or what you are doing.

make it a point to idiom 반드시 ~하다
If you make it a point to do something, you do it in a very deliberate or obvious way.

복습 **anonymous** [ənánəməs] a. 익명인; 익명으로 된 (anonymity n. 익명)
If you remain anonymous when you do something, you do not let people know that you were the person who did it.

⋆ **surrounding** [səráundiŋ] n. (pl.) 환경, 주위의 상황; a. 인근의, 주위의
When you are describing the place where you are at the moment, or the place where you live, you can refer to it as your surroundings.

복습 **settle** [setl] v. 자리를 잡다; (서서히) 가라앉다; 결정하다 (settle down idiom 정착하다)
When someone settles down, they start living in a place where they intend to stay for a long time.

⋆ **volcano** [valkéinou] n. 화산
A volcano is a mountain from which hot melted rock, gas, steam, and ash from inside the earth sometimes burst.

⋆⋆ **lean** [liːn] v. 기울이다, (몸을) 숙이다; ~에 기대다; a. 군살이 없는, 호리호리한
When you lean in a particular direction, you bend your body in that direction.

* **stable** [steibl] **a.** 안정된, 안정적인; 차분한; **n.** 마구간 (unstable **a.** 불안정한)
If people are unstable, their emotions and behavior keep changing because their minds are disturbed or upset.

misunderstand [mìsʌndərstǽnd] **v.** 오해하다 (misunderstood **a.** 오해를 받는)
If you describe someone or something as misunderstood, you mean that people do not understand them and have a wrong impression or idea of them.

Check Your Reading Speed

1분에 몇 단어를 읽는지 리딩 속도를 측정해보세요.

$$\frac{\text{813 words}}{\text{reading time (\quad) sec}} \times 60 = (\quad) \text{ WPM}$$

Build Your Vocabulary

work out **idiom** (건강 · 몸매 관리 등을 위해) 운동하다; (일이) 잘 풀리다
If you work out, you do physical exercises in order to make your body fit and strong.

get in shape **idiom** 좋은 몸매를 유지하다
If you get in shape, you become strong or fit.

brand-new [brænd-njú:] **a.** 아주 새로운, 신상품의
A brand-new object is completely new.

복습 **incredible** [inkrédəbl] **a.** 믿을 수 없는, 믿기 힘든
If you describe something or someone as incredible, you like them very much or are impressed by them, because they are extremely or unusually good.

⋆ **tailor** [téilər] **v.** 양복을 짓다; 맞추다, 조정하다; **n.** 재단사 (tailored **a.** (옷이) 잘 맞도록 만든)
Tailored clothes are designed to fit close to the body, rather than being loose.

복습 **notice** [nóutis] **v.** 알아채다, 인지하다; 주의하다; **n.** 신경 씀, 알아챔; 통지, 예고
If you notice something or someone, you become aware of them.

⋆ **stuff** [stʌf] **v.** 쑤셔 넣다; 채워 넣다; **n.** 것, 물건
If you stuff something somewhere, you push it there quickly and roughly.

복습 **briefcase** [brí:fkeis] **n.** 서류 가방
A briefcase is a case used for carrying documents in.

복습 **snap** [snæp] **v.** 탁 하고 움직이다; 급히 움직이다; 날카롭게 말하다; 툭 부러지다; **n.** 탁 하는 소리
If you snap something into a particular position, or if it snaps into that position, it moves quickly into that position, with a sharp sound.

복습 **hug** [hʌg] **v.** 껴안다, 포옹하다; **n.** 포옹
When you hug someone, you put your arms around them and hold them tightly.

⋆ **doorstep** [dɔ́:rstep] **n.** 문간(의 계단)
A doorstep is a step in front of a door on the outside of a building.

복습 **customer** [kʌ́stəmər] **n.** 손님, 고객
A customer is someone who buys goods or services, especially from a shop.

⋆ **ladder** [lǽdər] **n.** (조직 · 활동 분야 등에서) 단계; 사다리
You can use the ladder to refer to something such as a society, organization, or system which has different levels that people can progress up or drop down.

⋆ **brighten** [braitn] **v.** (기쁨 · 희망으로) 밝아지다; (얼굴 등이) 환해지다; 반짝이다
If someone brightens or their face brightens, they suddenly look happier.

⋆⋆ **attitude** [ǽtitjù:d] **n.** (정신적인) 태도, 사고방식; 반항적인 태도
Your attitude to something is the way that you think and feel about it, especially when this shows in the way you behave.

rev [rev] **v.** (엔진의) 회전 속도를 올리다; **n.** (엔진의) 회전 속도
When the engine of a vehicle revs, or when you rev it, the engine speed is increased as the accelerator is pressed.

복습 **driveway** [dráivwèi] **n.** (주택의) 진입로
A driveway is a piece of hard ground that leads from the road to the front of a house or other building.

pull up **idiom** (차량 · 운전자가) 멈추다, 서다
If a vehicle or driver pulls up, they stop.

⋆ **web** [web] **v.** 거미줄 모양이 되다; ~에 거미줄을 치다; **n.** 거미줄; ~망 (webbed **a.** 거미집 모양의)
If something is webbed, it is made like a web, as if by weaving.

⋆ **beam** [bi:m] **n.** 빛줄기; 기둥; **v.** 활짝 웃다; 비추다
A beam is a line of energy, radiation, or particles sent in a particular direction.

복습 **lean** [li:n] **v.** 기울이다, (몸을) 숙이다; ~에 기대다; **a.** 군살이 없는, 호리호리한
When you lean in a particular direction, you bend your body in that direction.

복습 **security** [sikjúərəti] **n.** 보안, 경비; 경비 담당 부서; 안도감, 안심
Security refers to all the measures that are taken to protect a place, or to ensure that only people with permission enter it or leave it.

복습 **appointment** [əpɔ́intmənt] **n.** 약속; 임명, 지명
If you have an appointment with someone, you have arranged to see them at a particular time, usually in connection with their work or for a serious purpose.

* **guard** [gaːrd] **n.** 경비 요원; 경비, 감시; 보호물; **v.** 지키다, 보호하다
A guard is a specially organized group of people, such as soldiers or policemen, who protect or watch someone or something.

* **stiff** [stif] **a.** 딱딱한, 경직된; 뻣뻣한; 심한; **ad.** 몹시, 극심하게 (stiffly **ad.** 딱딱하게)
Stiff behavior is rather formal and not very friendly or relaxed.

husky [hʌ́ski] **a.** (목소리가) 약간 쉰 듯한; 건장한, 튼튼한
If someone's voice is husky, it is low and rather rough, often in an attractive way.

* **bark** [baːrk] **v.** (명령 · 질문 등을) 빽 내지르다; (개가) 짖다; **n.** 나무껍질; (개 등이) 짖는 소리
If you bark at someone, you shout at them aggressively in a loud, rough voice.

* **electric** [iléktrik] **a.** 전기의; 전기를 이용하는
An electric device or machine works by means of electricity, rather than using some other source of power.

* **fence** [fens] **n.** 울타리; 장애물; **v.** 울타리를 치다
A fence is a barrier between two areas of land, made of wood or wire supported by posts.

* **rim** [rim] **v.** 테를 이루다; **n.** (둥근 물건의) 가장자리, 테두리 (rimmed **a.** 테를 두른)
If something is rimmed with a substance or color, it has that substance or color around its border.

* **international** [ìntərnǽʃənəl] **a.** 국제적인 (internationally **ad.** 국제적으로)
International means between or involving different countries.

복습 **design** [dizáin] **v.** 설계하다; 고안하다; **n.** 설계; 계획, 의도 (designer **n.** 디자이너)
A designer is a person whose job is to design things by making drawings of them.

brusque [brʌsk] **a.** 무뚝뚝한, 퉁명스러운
If you describe a person or their behavior as brusque, you mean that they deal with things, or say things, quickly and shortly, so that they seem to be rude.

* **fabulous** [fǽbjuləs] **a.** 기막히게 좋은; 엄청난, 굉장한
If you describe something as fabulous, you are emphasizing that you like it a lot or think that it is very good.

* **accent** [ǽksent] **n.** 말씨, 악센트; 강조; 억양; **v.** (어떤 부분을) 강조하다
Someone who speaks with a particular accent pronounces the words of a language in a distinctive way that shows which country, region, or social class they come from.

★★ **grin** [grin] **v.** 활짝 웃다; **n.** 활짝 웃음
When you grin, you smile broadly.

복습 **stun** [stʌn] **v.** 어리벙벙하게 하다; 깜짝 놀라게 하다; 기절시키다
If you are stunned by something, you are extremely shocked or surprised by it and are therefore unable to speak or do anything.

복습 **shut down** **idiom** (기계가) 멈추다; 문을 닫다
If a machine shuts down, or someone shuts it down, it stops working.

★★ **greet** [gri:t] **v.** 인사하다; 환영하다; 반응을 보이다
When you greet someone, you say 'Hello' or shake hands with them.

★ **gigantic** [dʒaigǽntik] **a.** 거대한
If you describe something as gigantic, you are emphasizing that it is extremely large in size, amount, or degree.

복습 **sigh** [sai] **v.** 한숨을 쉬다, 한숨짓다; 탄식하듯 말하다; **n.** 한숨
When you sigh, you let out a deep breath, as a way of expressing feelings such as disappointment, tiredness, or pleasure.

★ **darling** [dá:rliŋ] **n.** 자기, 얘야; **a.** (대단히) 사랑하는; 굉장히 멋진
You call someone darling if you love them or like them very much.

복습 **hopeful** [hóupfəl] **a.** 희망에 찬, 기대하는; 희망적인 (hopefully **ad.** 희망을 갖고)
If you do something hopefully, you do it in a way that expresses desire with an expectation of fulfillment.

★★ **challenge** [ʧǽlindʒ] **n.** 도전; 저항; **v.** 도전하다; 도전 의식을 북돋우다
A challenge is something new and difficult which requires great effort and determination.

★ **patch** [pæʧ] **n.** 조각; 부분; **v.** 덧대다, 때우다
A patch is a piece of material which you use to cover a hole in something.

mega [mégə] **a.** 엄청나게 큰, 인상적인
Mega- combines with nouns and adjectives in order to emphasize the size, quality, or importance of something.

복습 **mesh** [meʃ] **n.** 망사; 그물망, 철망; **v.** 꼭 들어맞게 하다; 맞물리다
Mesh is material like a net made from wire, thread, or plastic.

★ **impatient** [impéiʃənt] **a.** 짜증난, 안달하는; 어서 ~하고 싶어 하는 (impatiently **ad.** 성급하게)
If you are impatient, you are annoyed because you have to wait too long for something.

outmode [àutmóud] v. 시대에 뒤떨어지다 (outmoded a. 유행에 뒤떨어진)
If you describe something as outmoded, you mean that you think it is old-fashioned and no longer useful or relevant to modern life.

⋆ **sturdy** [stə́:rdi] a. 튼튼한, 견고한; 건장한; 확고한
Someone or something that is sturdy looks strong and is unlikely to be easily injured or damaged.

⋆ **moonlight** [mú:nlait] v. (은밀히) 부업을 하다; n. 달빛
If someone moonlights, they have a second job in addition to their main job, often without informing their main employers or the tax office.

복습 **casual** [kǽʒuəl] a. 태평스러운 (듯한), 무심한; 격식을 차리지 않는
If you are casual, you are, or you pretend to be, relaxed and not very concerned about what is happening or what you are doing.

복습 **knowingly** [nóuiŋli] ad. 다 알고 있다는 듯이; 고의로
If you do something knowingly, you do it in a way that suggests one has secret knowledge or awareness.

hobo [hóubou] n. 떠돌이, 부랑자
A hobo is a person who has no home, especially one who travels from place to place and gets money by begging.

복습 **announce** [ənáuns] v. 선언하다; 발표하다, 알리다
If you announce something, you tell people about it publicly or officially.

복습 **firm** [fə:rm] a. 단호한, 확고한; 단단한 (firmly ad. 단호히)
If you describe someone as firm, you mean they behave in a way that shows that they are not going to change their mind, or that they are the person who is in control.

복습 **trash** [træʃ] n. 쓰레기; v. 부수다; (필요 없는 것을) 버리다
Trash consists of unwanted things or waste material such as used paper, empty containers and bottles, and waste food.

⋆⋆ **rush** [rʌʃ] v. 급히 움직이다; 서두르다; n. (감정이 갑자기) 치밀어 오름; 혼잡; 기쁨, 흥분
If you rush somewhere, you go there quickly.

retrieve [ritrí:v] v. 되찾아오다, 회수하다; 수습하다
If you retrieve something, you get it back from the place where you left it.

look back idiom (과거를) 되돌아보다
If you look back, you think about a time or event in the past.

복습 **distract** [distrǽkt] v. (주의를) 딴 데로 돌리다, 집중이 안 되게 하다
If something distracts you or your attention from something, it takes your attention away from it.

★ **sane** [sein] a. 제정신의, 정신이 온전한; 분별 있는
Someone who is sane is able to think and behave normally and reasonably, and is not mentally ill.

★ **hint** [hint] n. 힌트, 암시; (약간의) 기미; v. 넌지시 알려주다, 힌트를 주다
A hint is a suggestion about something that is made in an indirect way.

복습 **confuse** [kənfjú:z] v. (사람을) 혼란시키다; 혼동하다 (confused a. 혼란스러워하는)
If you are confused, you do not know exactly what is happening or what to do.

★★ **gesture** [dʒésʧər] v. (손 · 머리 등으로) 가리키다; 몸짓을 하다; n. 몸짓; (감정 · 의도의) 표시
If you gesture, you use movements of your hands or head in order to tell someone something or draw their attention to something.

★ **bold** [bould] a. 선명한, 굵은; 용감한, 대담한
A bold color or pattern is very bright and noticeable.

★ **dramatic** [drəmǽtik] a. 감격적인, 인상적인; 극적인; 과장된
A dramatic change or event happens suddenly and is very noticeable and surprising.

★ **heroic** [hiróuik] a. 영웅적인, 용감무쌍한; 영웅의; n. (pl.) 영웅적 행동
If you describe a person or their actions as heroic, you admire them because they show extreme bravery.

복습 **enthusiastic** [inθù:ziǽstik] a. 열렬한, 열광적인 (enthusiastically ad. 열광적으로)
If you are enthusiastic about something, you show how much you like or enjoy it by the way that you behave and talk.

★★ **classic** [klǽsik] a. 고전적인; 일류의, 최고 수준의; n. 고전; 모범
Classic style is simple and traditional and is not affected by changes in fashion.

복습 **cape** [keip] n. 망토
A cape is a short cloak.

복습 **boot** [bu:t] n. 목이 긴 신발, 부츠; v. 세게 차다; (컴퓨터를) 부팅하다
Boots are shoes that cover your whole foot and the lower part of your leg.

cut off idiom (말을) 중단시키다; 단절시키다
To cut off means to prevent someone from continuing what they are saying.

★ **stiffen** [stífən] v. (화 · 공포로 몸이) 경직되다; 뻣뻣해지다; (태도 · 생각을) 강화시키다
If you stiffen, you stop moving and stand or sit with muscles that are suddenly tense, for example because you feel afraid or angry.

복습 **remind** [rimáind] v. 상기시키다, 다시 한 번 알려 주다
If someone reminds you of a fact or event that you already know about, they say something which makes you think about it.

cringe [krindʒ] v. (겁이 나서) 움츠리다, 움찔하다; 민망하다
If you cringe at something, you feel embarrassed or disgusted, and perhaps show this feeling in your expression or by making a slight movement.

복습 **storm** [stɔːrm] n. 폭풍, 폭풍우; v. 쿵쾅대며 가다, 뛰쳐나가다; 기습하다
A storm is very bad weather, with heavy rain, strong winds, and often thunder and lightning.

snag [snæg] v. (날카롭거나 튀어나온 것에) 걸리다; 잡아채다, 낚아채다; n. 문제; 날카로운 것
If you snag part of your clothing on a sharp or rough object or if it snags, it gets caught on the object and tears.

★ **missile** [mísəl] n. 미사일
A missile is a tube-shaped weapon that travels long distances through the air and explodes when it reaches its target.

fin [fin] n. (기계의) 지느러미 비슷한 부분; (물고기의) 지느러미
A fin on something such as an airplane, rocket, or bomb is a flat part which sticks out and which is intended to help control its movement.

복습 **bulb** [bʌlb] n. 전구
A bulb is the glass part of an electric lamp, which gives out light when electricity passes through it.

복습 **eyebrow** [áibràu] n. 눈썹
Your eyebrows are the lines of hair which grow above your eyes.

doom [duːm] v. 불행한 운명을 맞게 하다; n. 죽음, 파멸, 비운 (doomed a. 불운한)
Someone or something that is doomed is certain to fail or be destroyed.

복습 **jet** [dʒet] n. 제트기; 분출; v. 급속히 움직이다; 분출하다
A jet is an aircraft that is powered by jet engines.

복습 **takeoff** [téikɔ̀ːf] n. 이륙, 도약; 제거, 분리
Takeoff is the beginning of a flight, when an aircraft leaves the ground.

복습 **glare** [glɛər] **v.** 노려보다; 환하다, 눈부시다; **n.** 노려봄; 환한 빛, 눈부심
If you glare at someone, you look at them with an angry expression on your face.

finality [fainǽləti] **n.** 최후의 언행; 종국, 결말
If you say something with finality, you say it in a way that shows that you have made up your mind about something and do not want to discuss it further.

복습 **be about to** **idiom** 막 ~하려는 참이다
If you are about to do something, you are going to do it immediately.

복습 **go on** **idiom** 자자, 어서; 말을 계속하다; (어떤 상황이) 계속되다
You can say 'go on' to someone to encourage them to do something.

⋆ **assign** [əsáin] **v.** (일 · 책임 등을) 맡기다; (사람을) 배치하다; ~의 탓으로 하다
(assignment **n.** 임무)
An assignment is a task or piece of work that you are given to do, especially as part of your job or studies.

⋆ **sentimental** [sèntəméntl] **a.** 감상적인; 정서적인
Sentimental means relating to or involving feelings such as pity or love, especially for things in the past.

복습 **fix** [fiks] **v.** 수리하다; 준비하다; 고정시키다; **n.** 해결책; 곤경
If you fix something which is damaged or which does not work properly, you repair it.

Chapters 13~15

1. What first made Helen suspicious of Bob?

A. Hearing Bob make several phone calls

B. Finding a blond hair on Bob's jacket

C. Seeing Bob leave home on a jet

D. Catching Bob in a meeting with Mirage

2. Why did Helen call Edna?

A. She wanted to beg Edna for a new suit.

B. She wanted to find out how Edna was doing.

C. She wanted to know why Edna had fixed Bob's suit.

D. She wanted to ask Edna for advice about Super work.

3. What was true about Syndrome?

A. He had always hated Mr. Incredible.

B. He still respected Mr. Incredible.

C. He was the leader of multiple countries.

D. He made money by creating weapons.

4. What did Mr. Incredible notice about Gazerbeam?

A. He had left a message on a wall before he died.

B. He had lost his glasses before he died.

C. He died because he was hit with a laser.

D. He died because he lost his laser power.

5. Why did Mr. Incredible crawl under Gazerbeam's skeleton?

A. To hide from an explosion

B. To look for a clue

C. So that he would not drown

D. So that a probe would not detect him

Check Your Reading Speed

1분에 몇 단어를 읽는지 리딩 속도를 측정해보세요.

$$\frac{\text{361 words}}{\text{reading time (}\quad\text{) sec}} \times 60 = (\quad\quad) \text{ WPM}$$

Build Your Vocabulary

glint [glint] **n.** 반짝임; (눈이 강하게) 번득임; **v.** 반짝거리다; (눈이 강하게) 번득이다
A glint is a quick flash of light.

복습 **blond** [bland] **a.** (= blonde) (남자가) 금발인
A woman who has blonde hair has pale-colored hair. Blonde hair can be very light brown or light yellow. The form blond is used when describing men.

복습 **yell** [jel] **v.** 고함치다, 소리 지르다; **n.** 고함, 외침
If you yell, you shout loudly, usually because you are excited, angry, or in pain.

복습 **den** [den] **n.** 서재, 작업실; 굴
Your den is a quiet room in your house where you can go to study, work, or carry on a hobby without being disturbed.

★ **sly** [slai] **a.** 은밀한; 교활한, 음흉한; 다 알고 있다는 듯한 (slyly **ad.** 몰래, 은밀히)
A sly look, expression, or remark shows that you know something that other people do not know or that was meant to be a secret.

복습 **hang up** **idiom** 전화를 끊다; ~을 중지하다
To hang up means to end a telephone conversation, often very suddenly.

복습 **shrug** [ʃrʌg] **v.** (어깨를) 으쓱하다; **n.** 어깨를 으쓱하기
If you shrug, you raise your shoulders to show that you are not interested in something or that you do not know or care about something.

복습 **conference** [kánfərəns] **n.** 회의, 학회; 회견
A conference is a meeting, often lasting a few days, which is organized on a particular subject or to bring together people who have a common interest.

★★ **duty** [djú:ti] **n.** 직무, 임무; (도덕적 · 법률적) 의무
Duty is work that you have to do for your job.

복습 **suspicious** [səspíʃəs] **a.** 의혹을 갖는; 의심스러운; 의심스러워하는
If you are suspicious of someone or something, you believe that they are probably involved in a crime or some dishonest activity.

복습 **luxurious** [lʌgʒúəriəs] **a.** 호화로운, 아주 편안한
If you describe something as luxurious, you mean that it is very comfortable and expensive.

복습 **surrounding** [səráundiŋ] **n.** (pl.) 환경, 주위의 상황; **a.** 인근의, 주위의
When you are describing the place where you are at the moment, or the place where you live, you can refer to it as your surroundings.

복습 **sleek** [sli:k] **a.** (모양이) 매끈한; 윤이 나는
Sleek vehicles, furniture, or other objects look smooth, shiny, and expensive.

복습 **dramatic** [drəmǽtik] **a.** 감격적인, 인상적인; 극적인; 과장된
A dramatic change or event happens suddenly and is very noticeable and surprising.

복습 **heroic** [hiróuik] **a.** 영웅적인, 용감무쌍한; 영웅의; **n.** (pl.) 영웅적 행동
If you describe a person or their actions as heroic, you admire them because they show extreme bravery.

★ **sip** [sip] **v.** (음료를) 홀짝거리다, 조금씩 마시다; **n.** 한 모금
If you sip a drink or sip at it, you drink by taking just a small amount at a time.

autopilot [ɔ́:toupàilət] **n.** (항공기 · 배의) 자동 조종 장치
An automatic pilot or an autopilot is a device in an aircraft that automatically keeps it on a particular course.

automate [ɔ́:təmèit] **v.** 자동화하다 (automated **a.** 자동화된, 자동의)
An automated factory, office, or industrial process uses machines to do the work instead of people.

★★ **captain** [kǽptən] **n.** (항공기의) 기장; 선장; (스포츠 팀의) 주장; **v.** (운동 팀의) 주장이 되다
The captain of an airplane is the pilot in charge of it.

복습 **current** [kə́:rənt] **a.** 현재의, 지금의; **n.** (물 · 공기의) 흐름, 해류; 전류 (currently **ad.** 현재, 지금)
Current means happening, being used, or being done at the present time.

★ **fasten** [fæsn] **v.** 매다, 채우다; (단단히) 잠그다; 고정시키다
When you fasten something, you close it by means of buttons or a strap, or some other device.

★ **descend** [disénd] **v.** 내려오다, 내려가다; (아래로) 경사지다 (descent **n.** 하강, 강하)
A descent is a movement from a higher to a lower level or position.

복습 **lush** [lʌʃ] **a.** (식물 · 정원 등이) 무성한, 우거진; 멋진
Lush fields or gardens have a lot of very healthy grass or plants.

복습 **volcano** [valkéinou] **n.** 화산 (volcanic **a.** 화산의)
Volcanic means coming from or created by volcanoes.

terrain [təréin] **n.** 지형, 지역
Terrain is used to refer to an area of land or a type of land when you are considering its physical features.

★ **plunge** [plʌndʒ] **v.** (갑자기) 거꾸러지다; 급락하다; **n.** (갑자기) 떨어져 내림; 급락
If something or someone plunges in a particular direction, especially into water, they fall, rush, or throw themselves in that direction.

★★★ **nose** [nouz] **n.** (항공기 · 우주선 등의) 앞부분; 코; **v.** 천천히 조심스럽게 나아가다
The nose of a vehicle such as a car or airplane is the front part of it.

★★ **surface** [sə́:rfis] **n.** 수면, 표면, 지면; 외관; **v.** 수면으로 올라오다; (갑자기) 나타나다
The surface of something is the flat top part of it or the outside of it.

복습 **convert** [kənvə́:rt] **v.** 전환시키다, 개조하다; (의견 · 습관 등을) 바꾸다
If one thing is converted or converts into another, it is changed into a different form.

submersible [səbmə́:rsəbl] **n.** 잠수정; **a.** 물속에서 쓸 수 있는
A submersible is a type of ship that can travel underwater, especially one that operates without people being in it.

복습 **maneuver** [mənú:vər] **v.** (조심조심) 움직이다; 계책을 부리다; **n.** (기술적인) 동작; 묘책
If you maneuver something into or out of an awkward position, you skillfully move it there.

★ **formation** [fɔ:rméiʃən] **n.** 형성물; (특정한) 대형, 편대
A rock or cloud formation is rock or cloud of a particular shape or structure.

★ **spectacular** [spektǽkjulər] **a.** 장관을 이루는; 극적인; **n.** 화려한 쇼
Something that is spectacular is very impressive or dramatic.

★ **underwater** [ʌndərwɔ́:tər] **a.** 물속의, 수중의; **ad.** 수면 아래로, 물속에서
Something that exists or happens underwater exists or happens below the surface of the sea, a river, or a lake.

⋆ **scenery** [sí:nəri] n. 경치, 풍경; 배경, 무대 장치
The scenery in a country area is the land, water, or plants that you can see around you.

⋆ **dock** [dak] v. (배를) 부두에 대다; n. 부두, 선창
When a ship docks or is docked, it is brought into a dock.

복습 **bay** [bei] n. 구역, 구간; 만(灣)
A bay is a partly enclosed area, inside or outside a building, that is used for a particular purpose.

⋆ **bubble** [bʌbl] n. 거품; (감정의) 약간; v. (감정이) 차오르다; 거품이 일다
Bubbles are small balls of air or gas in a liquid.

복습 **lava** [lá:və] n. 용암
Lava is the very hot liquid rock that comes out of a volcano.

복습 **land** [lænd] v. (땅 · 표면에) 내려앉다, 착륙하다; 놓다, 두다; n. 육지, 땅; 지역 (landing n. 착륙)
A landing is an act of bringing an aircraft or spacecraft down to the ground.

⋆ **drain** [drein] v. (액체를) 따라 내다; (힘 · 돈 등을) 빼내 가다; n. 배수관
If you drain a liquid from a place or object, you remove the liquid by causing it to flow somewhere else.

복습 **clunk** [klʌŋk] n. 탁 하는 소리
A clunk is a sound made by a heavy object hitting something hard.

⋆⋆ **tube** [tju:b] n. 관; 튜브; 통
A tube is a long hollow object that is usually round, like a pipe.

⋆ **attach** [ətǽʧ] v. 붙이다, 첨부하다; 연관되다
If you attach something to an object, you join it or fasten it to the object.

복습 **pod** [pad] n. (우주선 · 선박의 본체에서) 분리 가능한 부분; (콩이 들어 있는) 꼬투리
A pod is a detachable or self-contained unit on an aircraft, spacecraft, vehicle, or vessel, having a particular function.

복습 **zoom** [zu:m] v. 쌩 하고 가다; 급등하다; n. (빠르게) 쌩 하고 지나가는 소리
If you zoom somewhere, you go there very quickly.

lagoon [ləgú:n] n. 석호(潟湖)
A lagoon is an area of calm sea water that is separated from the ocean by a line of rock or sand.

복습 **jungle** [dʒʌŋgl] **n.** 밀림 (지대), 정글
A jungle is a forest in a tropical country where large numbers of tall trees and plants grow very close together.

복습 **headquarter** [hédkwɔ:rtər] **n.** (pl.) 본사, 본부; **v.** ~에 본부를 두다
The headquarters of an organization are its main offices.

★ **escort** [éskɔ:rt] **v.** 호송하다, 호위하다; **n.** 호위대
If you escort someone somewhere, you accompany them there, usually in order to make sure that they leave a place or get to their destination.

★★ **quarter** [kwɔ́:rtər] **n.** (pl.) 숙소, 막사; 4분의 1; 구역; **v.** 4등분하다; 숙소를 제공하다
The rooms provided for soldiers, sailors, or servants to live in are called their quarters.

복습 **brief** [bri:f] **v.** ~에게 알려주다; **a.** (시간이) 짧은; 간단한
If someone briefs you, especially about a piece of work or a serious matter, they give you information that you need before you do it or consider it.

Check Your Reading Speed

1분에 몇 단어를 읽는지 리딩 속도를 측정해보세요.

$$\frac{\text{257 words}}{\text{reading time (} \qquad \text{) sec}} \times 60 = (\qquad) \text{ WPM}$$

Build Your Vocabulary

복습 **tidy** [táidi] v. 치우다, 정돈하다; a. 단정한, 말쑥한, 깔끔한
When you tidy a place such as a room or cupboard, you make it neat by putting things in their proper places.

복습 **den** [den] n. 서재, 작업실; 굴
Your den is a quiet room in your house where you can go to study, work, or carry on a hobby without being disturbed.

★ **dust** [dʌst] v. 먼지를 털다; (고운 가루를) 뿌리다; n. (흙)먼지
When you dust something such as furniture, you remove dust from it, usually using a cloth.

★ **microscope** [máikrəskòup] n. 현미경 (microscopic a. 미세한, 현미경으로 봐야만 보이는)
Microscopic objects are extremely small, and usually can be seen only through a microscope.

★ **stitch** [stitʃ] n. 바늘땀; 한 바늘, 한 땀; v. 꿰매다, 바느질하다
Stitches are the short pieces of thread that have been sewn in a piece of cloth.

복습 **suit** [suːt] n. (특정한 활동 때 입는) 옷; 정장; 소송; v. ~에게 편리하다; 어울리다
A particular type of suit is a piece of clothing that you wear for a particular activity.

★★ **repair** [ripέər] v. 수리하다; (상황을) 바로잡다; n. 수리, 보수, 수선
If you repair something that has been damaged or is not working properly, you mend it.

craftsmanship [krǽftsmənʃìp] n. 솜씨; 손재주
Craftsmanship is the quality that something has when it is beautiful and has been very carefully made.

on the side idiom 부업으로; 비밀스럽게
If you do something on the side, you do work in addition to your regular job.

복습 **dial** [dáiəl] v. 다이얼을 돌리다, 전화를 걸다; n. (시계·계기 등의) 문자반
If you dial or if you dial a number, you turn the dial or press the buttons on a telephone in order to phone someone.

복습 **husky** [hʌ́ski] a. (목소리가) 약간 쉰 듯한; 건장한, 튼튼한
If someone's voice is husky, it is low and rather rough, often in an attractive way.

⋆ **thrill** [θril] v. 열광시키다, 정말 신나게 하다; n. 흥분, 설렘; 전율 (thrilled a. 아주 흥분한, 신이 난)
If someone is thrilled, they are extremely pleased about something.

복습 **darling** [dá:rliŋ] n. 자기, 얘야; a. (대단히) 사랑하는; 굉장히 멋진
You call someone darling if you love them or like them very much.

복습 **hesitate** [hézətèit] v. 망설이다, 주저하다; 거리끼다
If you hesitate, you do not speak or act for a short time, usually because you are uncertain, embarrassed, or worried about what you are going to say or do.

복습 **patch** [pæʧ] v. 덧대다, 때우다; n. 부분; 조각
If you patch something that has a hole in it, you mend it by fastening a patch over the hole.

⋆ **marvelous** [má:rvələs] a. 기막히게 좋은, 경탄할 만한
If you describe someone or something as marvelous, you are emphasizing that they are very good.

⋆ **pajamas** [pədʒá:məz] n. (바지와 상의로 된) 잠옷
A pair of pajamas consists of loose trousers and a loose jacket that people, especially men, wear in bed.

⋆ **beg** [beg] v. 간청하다, 애원하다; 구걸하다
If you beg someone to do something, you ask them very anxiously or eagerly to do it.

복습 **insist** [insíst] v. 고집하다, 주장하다, 우기다
If you insist that something should be done, you say so very firmly and refuse to give in about it.

Check Your Reading Speed

1분에 몇 단어를 읽는지 리딩 속도를 측정해보세요.

$$\frac{\text{711 words}}{\text{reading time (\qquad) sec}} \times 60 = (\qquad) \text{ WPM}$$

Build Your Vocabulary

복습 **enormous** [inɔ́:rməs] a. 막대한, 거대한
Something that is enormous is extremely large in size or amount.

복습 **conference** [kánfərəns] n. 회의, 학회; 회견
A conference is a meeting at which formal discussions take place.

복습 **brief** [bri:f] v. ~에게 알려주다; a. (시간이) 짧은; 간단한
If someone briefs you, especially about a piece of work or a serious matter, they give you information that you need before you do it or consider it.

복습 **mission** [míʃən] n. 임무; 사명; v. 길고 험난한 여정에 나서다
A mission is an important task that people are given to do, especially one that involves traveling to another country.

복습 **slam** [slæm] v. 세게 치다, 놓다; 쾅 닫다; n. 쾅 하고 닫기; 탕 하는 소리
If you slam a door or window or if it slams, it shuts noisily and with great force.

hangar [hǽŋər] n. 격납고
A hangar is a large building in which aircraft are kept.

복습 **doorway** [dɔ́:rwèi] n. 출입구
A doorway is a space in a wall where a door opens and closes.

⋆ **echo** [ékou] v. (소리가) 울리다; 그대로 따라 하다; n. (소리의) 울림, 메아리; 반복
If a sound echoes, it is reflected off a surface and can be heard again after the original sound has stopped.

loudspeaker [láudspì:kər] n. 확성기
A loudspeaker is a piece of equipment that converts electric signals to audible sound.

복습 **maneuver** [mənúːvər] **v.** (조심조심) 움직이다; 계책을 부리다; **n.** (기술적인) 동작; 묘책
If you maneuver something into or out of an awkward position, you skillfully move it there.

★ **anticipate** [æntísəpèit] **v.** 예상하다; 기대하다, 고대하다
If you anticipate something, you do it, think it, or say it before someone else does.

복습 **boom** [buːm] **v.** 굵은 목소리로 말하다; 쾅 하는 소리를 내다; **n.** 쾅 (하는 소리)
When something such as someone's voice, a cannon, or a big drum booms, it makes a loud, deep sound that lasts for several seconds.

복습 **grab** [græb] **v.** (와락 · 단단히) 붙잡다; 급히 ~하다; **n.** 와락 잡아채려고 함
If you grab something, you take it or pick it up suddenly and roughly.

복습 **claw** [klɔː] **n.** 갈고리 모양의 기계; (동물 · 새의) 발톱; **v.** (손톱 · 발톱으로) 할퀴다
A claw is a curved end on a tool or machine, used for pulling or picking things up.

★★ **fling** [fliŋ] **v.** (flung-flung) (힘껏) 던지다; (머리 · 팔 등을) 휘두르다; **n.** (한바탕) 실컷 즐기기
If you fling something somewhere, you throw it there using a lot of force.

★ **clearing** [klíəriŋ] **n.** (숲 속의) 빈터
A clearing is a small area in a forest where there are no trees or bushes.

★ **seize** [siːz] **v.** 와락 붙잡다; (기회 · 주도권 등을) 잡다; 장악하다
If you seize something, you take hold of it quickly, firmly, and forcefully.

★★ **spin** [spin] **v.** (빙빙) 돌다; 돌아서다; **n.** 회전
If something spins or if you spin it, it turns quickly around a central point.

close in idiom (~에) 접근하다
To close in someone or close in on someone means to move nearer to them, especially in order to surround them and stop them from escaping.

복습 **chunk** [ʧʌŋk] **n.** 덩어리; 상당히 많은 양; **v.** 덩어리로 나누다 (chunky **a.** 땅딸막한)
A chunky person is broad and heavy.

복습 **figure** [fígjər] **n.** (멀리서 흐릿하게 보이는) 사람; 수치; (중요한) 인물; **v.** 생각하다; 중요하다
You refer to someone that you can see as a figure when you cannot see them clearly or when you are describing them.

복습 **trash** [træʃ] **v.** 부수다; (필요 없는 것을) 버리다; **n.** 쓰레기
If someone trashes a place or vehicle, they deliberately destroy it or make it very dirty.

★ **modify** [mádəfài] v. 수정하다, 변경하다; 조정하다 (modification n. 수정, 변경)
If you modify something, you change it slightly, usually in order to improve it.

after all idiom 어쨌든; 결국에는
You can use after all when giving a reason to explain what you have just said.

복습 **realize** [ríːəlàiz] v. 깨닫다, 알아차리다; 실현하다, 달성하다 (realization n. 깨달음, 자각)
If you realize that something is true, you become aware of that fact or understand it.

복습 **press** [pres] v. 누르다; (무엇에) 바짝 대다; 꾹 밀어 넣다; n. 언론
If you press a button or switch, you push it with your finger in order to make a machine or device work.

★ **wrist** [rist] n. 손목
Your wrist is the part of your body between your hand and your arm which bends when you move your hand.

복습 **sail** [seil] v. 항해하다; 미끄러지듯 나아가다; n. 돛 (that ship has sailed idiom 기회를 놓치다)
You can say 'that ship has sailed' in order to tell someone that an opportunity has passed or a situation can no longer be changed.

★★★ **treat** [triːt] v. (특정한 태도로) 대하다; 여기다, 치부하다; n. (대접하여 하는) 특별한 것, 대접
If you treat someone or something in a particular way, you behave toward them or deal with them in that way.

★★ **respect** [rispékt] v. 존경하다; 존중하다; n. 존경(심), 경의; 존중, 정중
If you respect someone, you have a good opinion of their character or ideas.

★★ **threat** [θret] n. 위협적인 존재; 위험; 협박
A threat to a person or thing is a danger that something unpleasant might happen to them.

turn out idiom ~인 것으로 드러나다; 되어 가다; 나타나다
If things turn out, they are discovered or they prove to be the case finally and surprisingly.

pay through the nose idiom (~에 대해) 터무니없이 많은 돈을 주다
If you say that you paid through the nose for something, you are emphasizing that you had to pay what you consider too high a price for it.

복습 **invent** [invént] v. 발명하다; (사실이 아닌 것을) 지어내다
If you invent something such as a machine or process, you are the first person to think of it or make it.

⁑ **weapon** [wépən] n. 무기, 흉기
A weapon is an object such as a gun, a knife, or a missile, which is used to kill or hurt people in a fight or a war.

복습 **defeat** [difí:t] v. 물리치다; 좌절시키다; 이해가 안 되다; n. 패배
If you defeat someone, you win a victory over them in a battle, game, or contest.

leash [li:ʃ] v. 속박하다, 억제하다; 가죽끈으로 매다; n. 가죽 끈; 통제
(unleash v. 풀어놓다; 해방하다)
If you say that someone or something unleashes a powerful force, feeling, activity, or group, you mean that they suddenly start it or send it somewhere.

⋆ **log** [lɔ:g] n. 통나무
A log is a piece of a thick branch or of the trunk of a tree that has been cut so that it can be used for fuel or for making things.

⋆ **hurl** [hə:rl] v. (거칠게) 던지다; (욕 · 비난 · 모욕 등을) 퍼붓다
If you hurl something, you throw it violently and with a lot of force.

duck [dʌk] v. (머리나 몸을) 휙 수그리다; 급히 움직이다; n. [동물] 오리
If you duck, you move your head or the top half of your body quickly downward to avoid something that might hit you, or to avoid being seen.

복습 **beam** [bi:m] n. 빛줄기; 기둥; v. 활짝 웃다; 비추다
A beam is a line of energy, radiation, or particles sent in a particular direction.

⋆ **index finger** [índeks fiŋgər] n. 집게손가락
Your index finger is the finger that is next to your thumb.

복습 **freeze** [fri:z] v. (froze-frozen) (두려움 등으로 몸이) 얼어붙다; 얼다; n. 동결; 한파
If someone who is moving freezes, they suddenly stop and become completely still and quiet.

복습 **midair** [midέər] n. 공중, 상공
If something happens in midair, it happens in the air, rather than on the ground.

복습 **sly** [slai] a. 교활한, 음흉한; 은밀한; 다 알고 있다는 듯한
If you describe someone as sly, you disapprove of them because they keep their feelings or intentions hidden and are clever at deceiving people.

복습 **monologue** [mánəlɔ̀:g] v. 독백하다; n. 독백
If you monologue, you deliver a monologue or long speech.

⋆ **chuckle** [ʧʌkl] v. 킬킬 웃다; 빙그레 웃다; n. 킬킬거림; 속으로 웃기
When you chuckle, you laugh quietly.

복습 **admire** [ædmáiər] v. 감탄하며 바라보다; 존경하다, 칭찬하다 (admiration n. 감탄, 존경)
Admiration is a feeling of great liking and respect for a person or thing.

⋆ **jerk** [dʒəːrk] v. 홱 움직이다; n. 얼간이; 홱 움직임
If you jerk something or someone in a particular direction, or they jerk in a particular direction, they move a short distance very suddenly and quickly.

effortless [éfərtlis] a. 힘이 들지 않는; 수월해 보이는 (effortlessly ad. 쉽게)
Something that is effortless is done easily and well.

복습 **toss** [tɔːs] v. (가볍게) 던지다; (고개를) 홱 쳐들다; n. 던지기
If you toss something somewhere, you throw it there lightly, often in a rather careless way.

복습 **tremendous** [triméndəs] a. 엄청난; 굉장한, 대단한
You use tremendous to emphasize how strong a feeling or quality is, or how large an amount is.

복습 **force** [fɔːrs] n. 힘; 작용력; 영향력; v. 억지로 ~하다; ~를 강요하다
If someone uses force to do something, or if it is done by force, strong and violent physical action is taken in order to achieve it.

⋆⋆ **slight** [slait] a. 약간의, 조금의; 작고 여윈
Something that is slight is very small in degree or quantity.

복습 **ray** [rei] n. 광선; 약간, 소량
Rays of light are narrow beams of light.

taunt [tɔːnt] v. 놀리다, 비웃다, 조롱하다; n. 놀림, 비웃음, 조롱
If someone taunts you, they say unkind or insulting things to you, especially about your weaknesses or failures.

nemesis [néməsis] n. 강적; 응당 받아야 할 천벌
A nemesis is someone or something that continues to oppose you and cannot easily be defeated.

catch oneself idiom 하던 말을 멈추다
If you catch yourself doing something, especially something surprising, you suddenly become aware that you are doing it.

canopy [kǽnəpi] n. 숲의 우거진 윗부분; (늘어뜨린) 덮개
A canopy is a layer of something that spreads out and covers an area, for example the branches and leaves that spread out at the top of trees in a forest.

복습 **dive** [daiv] v. (물속으로) 뛰어들다; 급히 움직이다; 급강하하다; n. 급강하; (물속으로) 뛰어들기
If you dive into some water, you jump in head-first with your arms held straight above your head.

★ **massive** [mǽsiv] a. (육중하면서) 거대한; 엄청나게 심각한
Something that is massive is very large in size, quantity, or extent.

복습 **waterfall** [wɔ́:tərfɔ:l] n. 폭포
A waterfall is a place where water flows over the edge of a steep, high cliff in hills or mountains, and falls into a pool below.

복습 **ledge** [ledʒ] n. 절벽에서 튀어나온 바위; (벽에서 튀어나온) 선반
A ledge is a piece of rock on the side of a cliff or mountain, which is in the shape of a narrow shelf.

복습 **crash** [kræʃ] v. 부딪치다; 충돌하다; 굉음을 내다; n. (자동차 · 항공기) 사고; 요란한 소리
If something crashes somewhere, it moves and hits something else violently, making a loud noise.

★ **furious** [fjúəriəs] a. 몹시 화가 난; 맹렬한
Someone who is furious is extremely angry.

복습 **engage** [ingéidʒ] v. 기계 부품이 맞물리다; 약속하다; 교전을 시작하다; 관여하다
When a part of a machine or other mechanism engages or when you engage it, it moves into a position where it fits into something else.

lollipop [lálipàp] n. 막대 사탕
A lollipop is a sweet consisting of a hard disc or ball of a sugary substance on the end of a stick.

★ **device** [diváis] n. 장치, 기구; 폭발물; 방법
A device is an object that has been invented for a particular purpose, for example for recording or measuring something.

복습 **powerful** [páuərfəl] a. 강력한; 영향력 있는, 유력한
A powerful machine or substance is effective because it is very strong.

복습 **explode** [iksplóud] v. 폭발하다; (갑자기 강한 감정을) 터뜨리다 (explosive n. 폭발물)
An explosive is a substance or device that can cause an explosion.

복습 **wave** [weiv] n. (열 · 소리 · 빛 등의) -파; (손 · 팔을) 흔들기; 물결; v. (손 · 팔을) 흔들다; 손짓하다
A wave is a sudden increase in heat or energy that spreads out from an earthquake or explosion.

복습 **blow** [blou] v. (blew-blown) (바람 · 입김에) 날리다; (비밀을) 누설하다다; (타이어가) 터지다; n. 강타
If the wind blows something somewhere or if it blows there, the wind moves it there.

⋆ **cave** [keiv] n. 동굴
A cave is a large hole in the side of a cliff or hill, or one that is under the ground.

grotto [grátou] n. 작은 동굴
A grotto is a small cave with interesting or attractively shaped rocks.

⋆ **exhaust** [igzɔ́:st] v. 기진맥진하게 하다; 다 써 버리다; n. (자동차 등의) 배기가스
(exhausted a. 기진맥진한)
If something exhausts you, it makes you so tired, either physically or mentally, that you have no energy left.

⋆ **skeleton** [skélətn] n. 해골; 골격; (건물 등의) 뼈대
Your skeleton is the framework of bones in your body.

복습 **recognize** [rékəgnàiz] v. 알아보다; 인식하다; 공인하다
If you recognize someone or something, you know who that person is or what that thing is.

⋆ **skull** [skʌl] n. 두개골, 해골
Your skull is the bony part of your head which encloses your brain.

have to hand it to idiom ~는 인정해 줘야 한다
If you have to hand it to someone, you admire them for something that they have done.

복습 **burn** [bə:rn] v. 태우다; 불에 타다; 상기되다; n. 화상
If you burn something, you destroy or damage it with fire.

⋆ **click** [klik] n. 딸깍 (하는 소리); v. 딸깍 하는 소리를 내다; 분명해지다
A click is a short, sharp sound as of a switch being operated or of two hard objects coming smartly into contact.

복습 **electronic** [ilektránik] a. 전자의, 전자 장비와 관련된
An electronic device has transistors or silicon chips which control and change the electric current passing through the device.

⋆ **probe** [proub] n. 탐침, 탐색침; (철저한) 조사; v. 조사하다; (길고 가느다란 기구로) 살피다
A probe is a long thin instrument that doctors and dentists use to examine parts of the body.

crawl [krɔ:l] v. 기어가다; 우글거리다; n. 기어가기
When you crawl, you move forward on your hands and knees.

복습 **scan** [skæn] v. (빛 · 레이더 등이) 훑다; (유심히) 살피다; 정밀 촬영하다; n. 정밀 검사
If a radar or sonar machine scans an area, it examines or searches it by sending radar or sonar beams over it.

복습 **fix** [fiks] v. 고정시키다; 수리하다; 준비하다; n. 해결책; 곤경
If you fix your eyes on someone or something or if your eyes fix on them, you look at them with complete attention.

복습 **hold one's breath** idiom (흥분 · 공포 등으로) 숨을 죽이다
If you say that someone is holding their breath, you mean that they are waiting anxiously or excitedly for something to happen.

chirp [ʧə:rp] v. 찍찍거리다; 재잘거리다
When a bird or an insect such as a cricket or grasshopper chirps, it makes short high-pitched sounds.

reading [rí:diŋ] n. 수치, 측정값; 읽기; 이해, 해석
The reading on a measuring device is the figure or measurement that it shows.

negative [négətiv] a. (테스트 결과가) 음성의; 부정적인, 나쁜; n. 부정, 거부; 음성 (결과)
If a medical test or scientific test is negative, it shows no evidence of the medical condition or substance that you are looking for.

terminate [tə́:rmənèit] v. 살해하다; 끝내다, 종료하다; 종점에 닿다
If you terminate someone, you murder them.

복습 **bow** [bau] ① v. (고개를) 숙이다; 절하다; n. (고개 숙여 하는) 인사 ② n. 나비 모양 (매듭 · 리본)
If you bow your head, you bend it downward so that you are looking toward the ground, for example because you want to show respect or because you are thinking deeply about something.

복습 **former** [fɔ́:rmər] a. (시간적으로) 이전의, 먼저의; n. 전자
Former is used to describe someone who used to have a particular job, position, or role, but no longer has it.

idol [aidl] n. (많은 사랑을 받는 대상인) 우상
If you refer to someone such as a film, pop, or sports star as an idol, you mean that they are greatly admired or loved by their fans.

wicked [wíkid] a. 못된, 사악한; 아주 좋은; 짓궂은 (wickedly ad. 심술궂게)
You use wicked to describe someone or something that is very bad and deliberately harmful to people.

Chapters 16~18

1. **What could Jack-Jack's Super suit do?**

   A. It could shoot bullets.

   B. It could withstand a lot of friction.

   C. It could handle extremely high heat.

   D. It could stretch into any shape.

2. **How could Helen find out Bob's current location?**

   A. By hitting a button on a device

   B. By talking to the receptionist at Insuricare

   C. By calling his personal number

   D. By using her Super power to track him down

3. What information did Mr. Incredible NOT see in Syndrome's control room?

A. Gazerbeam had been terminated.

B. Frozone had been arrested.

C. Elastigirl had not yet been found.

D. The Omnidroid was going to be unleashed.

4. How did Vi react when she saw her Super suit?

A. She was disappointed and embarrassed.

B. She was excited and proud.

C. She was uninterested but grateful.

D. She was hesitant but curious.

5. What did Syndrome assume about Mr. Incredible?

A. He worked for the government.

B. He knew how to fly a government plane.

C. He had contacted someone for help.

D. He had tried to block a homing signal.

Check Your Reading Speed

1분에 몇 단어를 읽는지 리딩 속도를 측정해보세요.

$$\frac{\text{901 words}}{\text{reading time (\qquad) sec}} \times 60 = (\qquad) \text{ WPM}$$

Build Your Vocabulary

⁑ **downstairs** [daunstéərz] **ad.** 아래층으로; **n.** 아래층
If you go downstairs in a building, you go down a staircase toward the ground floor.

lab [læb] **n.** (= laboratory) 실험실, 연구실
A lab is the same as a laboratory, which is a building or a room where scientific experiments, analyses, and research are carried out.

복습 **project** [prádʒekt] **n.** 계획, 프로젝트; **v.** (빛 · 영상 등을) 비추다; 발사하다, 내뿜다; 계획하다
A project is a task that requires a lot of time and effort.

confiscate [kánfəskèit] **v.** 몰수하다, 압수하다
If you confiscate something from someone, you take it away from them, usually as a punishment.

복습 **darling** [dá:rliŋ] **n.** 자기, 얘야; **a.** (대단히) 사랑하는; 굉장히 멋진
You call someone darling if you love them or like them very much.

⋆ **consume** [kənsú:m] **v.** 소모하다; 먹다; (강렬한 감정이) 사로잡다
To consume an amount of fuel, energy, or time means to use it up.

복습 **enthusiastic** [inθù:ziǽstik] **a.** 열렬한, 열광적인 (enthusiasm **n.** 열정, 열의)
Enthusiasm is great eagerness to be involved in a particular activity which you like and enjoy or which you think is important.

⋆ **elegant** [éligənt] **a.** 품위 있는, 우아한, 고상한
If you describe a person or thing as elegant, you mean that they are pleasing and graceful in appearance or style.

복습 **bold** [bould] **a.** 선명한, 굵은; 용감한, 대담한
A bold color or pattern is very bright and noticeable.

복습 **turn out** idiom ~인 것으로 드러나다; 되어 가다; 나타나다
If things turn out, they are discovered or they prove to be the case finally and surprisingly.

★★ **useless** [jú:slis] a. 소용없는, 쓸모 없는
If something is useless, it does not achieve anything helpful or good.

복습 **go on** idiom 말을 계속하다; (어떤 상황이) 계속되다; 자자, 어서
To go on means to continue speaking after a short pause.

★★ **rapid** [rǽpid] a. (속도가) 빠른; (행동이) 민첩한 (rapidly ad. 빠르게, 신속히)
A rapid movement is one that is very fast.

★ **execute** [éksikjù:t] v. (동작을) 해내다; 실행하다
If you execute a difficult action or movement, you successfully perform it.

★ **elaborate** [ilǽbərət] a. 정교한; v. (더) 자세히 말하다; (계획·사상 등을) 정교하게 만들어 내다
You use elaborate to describe something that is very complex because it has a lot of different parts.

복습 **security** [sikjúərəti] n. 보안, 경비; 경비 담당 부서; 안도감, 안심
Security refers to all the measures that are taken to protect a place, or to ensure that only people with permission enter it or leave it.

★★ **measure** [méʒər] n. 조치, 정책; 척도; v. 측정하다; 판단하다
When someone, usually a government or other authority, takes measures to do something, they carry out particular actions in order to achieve a particular result.

복습 **flash** [flæʃ] n. 순간; (잠깐) 반짝임; 뉴스 속보; v. 휙 내보이다; 휙 움직이다; (잠깐) 번쩍이다 (in a flash idiom 순식간에)
If you say that something happens in a flash, you mean that it happens suddenly and lasts only a very short time.

복습 **ceiling** [sí:liŋ] n. 천장
A ceiling is the horizontal surface that forms the top part or roof inside a room.

복습 **panel** [pænl] n. 판; (자동차 등의) 계기판; 패널, 자문단
A panel is a flat rectangular piece of wood or other material that forms part of a larger object such as a door.

복습 **reveal** [riví:l] v. (보이지 않던 것을) 드러내 보이다; (비밀 등을) 밝히다
If you reveal something that has been out of sight, you uncover it so that people can see it.

★ **sight** [sait] **n.** (pl.) (총 · 망원경 등의) 조준기; 광경, 모습; 보기; **v.** 갑자기 보다
The sights of a weapon such as a rifle are the part which helps you aim it more accurately.

train on **idiom** (총 · 카메라 · 불빛 등을) ~로 향하게 하다
If you train a gun, camera, or light on someone or something, you point it at them.

★ **hasty** [héisti] **a.** 서두른; 성급한 (hastily **ad.** 급히, 서둘러서)
A hasty movement, action, or statement is sudden, and often done in reaction to something that has just happened.

★ **retreat** [ritríːt] **v.** 멀어져 가다, 물러가다; 빠져나가다; 후퇴하다; **n.** 후퇴, 철수; 휴양지
If you retreat, you move away from something or someone.

복습 **design** [dizáin] **v.** 설계하다; 고안하다; **n.** 설계; 계획, 의도
When someone designs a garment, building, machine, or other object, they plan it and make a detailed drawing of it from which it can be built or made.

복습 **settle** [setl] **v.** 자리를 잡다; (서서히) 가라앉다; 결정하다
If you settle yourself somewhere or settle somewhere, you sit down or make yourself comfortable.

복습 **be about to** **idiom** 막 ~하려는 참이다
If you are about to do something, you are going to do it immediately.

★ **dim** [dim] **v.** (빛의 밝기가) 낮아지다, 어둑해지다; **a.** (빛이) 어둑한; (형체가) 흐릿한
If you dim a light or if it dims, it becomes less bright.

★★ **cheerful** [ʧíərfəl] **a.** 발랄한, 쾌활한 (cheerfully **ad.** 쾌활하게, 명랑하게)
Someone who is cheerful is happy and shows this in their behavior.

★★ **feature** [fíːʧər] **n.** 특색, 특징; 특집; **v.** 특별히 포함하다, 특징으로 삼다
(featureless **a.** 특색 없는)
If you say that something is featureless, you mean that it has no interesting features or characteristics.

mannequin [mǽnəkin] **n.** (상점의) 마네킹
A mannequin is a life-sized model of a person which is used to display clothes, especially in shop windows.

복습 **tiny** [táini] **a.** 아주 작은
Something or someone that is tiny is extremely small.

복습 **emerge** [imə́:rdʒ] v. 나오다, 모습을 드러내다; (어려움 등을) 헤쳐 나오다
To emerge means to come out from an enclosed or dark space such as a room or a vehicle, or from a position where you could not be seen.

★ **chamber** [ʧéimbər] n. (특정 목적용) -실(室); 회의실; (지하의) 공간
A chamber is a room designed and equipped for a particular purpose.

roomy [rú:mi] a. 널찍한
If you describe a piece of clothing as roomy, you mean that you like it because it is large and fits loosely.

erupt [irʌ́pt] v. 분출되다; (강한 감정을) 터뜨리다
When a volcano erupts, it throws out a lot of hot, melted rock called lava, as well as ash and steam.

복습 **flame** [fleim] n. 불길, 불꽃; 격정; v. 활활 타오르다; 시뻘게지다
A flame is a hot bright stream of burning gas that comes from something that is burning.

★ **withstand** [wiðstǽnd] v. 견뎌 내다, 이겨 내다
If something or someone withstands a force or action, they survive it or do not give in to it.

★★ **temperature** [témpərəʧər] n. 온도, 기온; 체온
The temperature of something is a measure of how hot or cold it is.

복습 **replace** [ripléis] v. 대신하다, 대체하다; 교체하다
If you replace one thing or person with another, you put something or someone else in their place to do their job.

barrage [bərá:ʒ] n. 일제 엄호 사격; (질문 등의) 세례
A barrage is continuous firing on an area with large guns and tanks.

machine-gun [məʃí:n-gʌn] n. 기관총; v. 기관총으로 쏘다
A machine-gun is a gun which fires a lot of bullets one after the other very quickly.

복습 **fire** [faiər] n. 발사, 총격; 화재, 불; v. (엔진이) 점화되다; 해고하다; 발사하다
You can use fire to refer to the shots fired from a gun or guns.

복습 **bullet** [búlit] n. 총알
A bullet is a small piece of metal with a pointed or rounded end, which is fired out of a gun.

★★ **proof** [pru:f] a. 견딜 수 있는; n. 증거, 증명 (bulletproof a. 방탄이 되는)
Something that is bulletproof prevents bullets from going through it.

washable [wáʃəbl] a. 물에 빨아도 되는, 물빨래가 가능한
Washable clothes or materials can be washed in water without being damaged.

in heaven's name idiom 도대체
You can use 'in heaven's name' in questions to add emphasis in a way that shows that you are very angry or surprised.

복습 **favor** [féivər] v. 편들다; 선호하다; n. 지지, 인정; 호의, 친절
If you favor someone, you treat them better or in a kinder way than you treat other people.

복습 **cover** [kʌ́vər] v. 다루다; 가리다; (보험으로) 보장하다; 덮다; n. 위장, 속임수; 몸을 숨길 곳; 덮개
If you cover a particular topic, you discuss it in a lecture, course, or book.

복습 **stare** [stɛər] v. 빤히 쳐다보다, 응시하다; n. 빤히 쳐다보기, 응시
If you stare at someone or something, you look at them for a long time.

복습 **fabulous** [fǽbjuləs] a. 기막히게 좋은; 엄청난, 굉장한
If you describe something as fabulous, you are emphasizing that you like it a lot or think that it is very good.

★ **exit** [égzit] v. 나가다, 떠나다; 퇴장하다; n. (고속도로의) 출구; (공공건물의) 출구; 퇴장
If you exit from a room or building, you leave it.

★ **accelerate** [æksélərèit] v. 속도를 높이다, 가속화되다
When a moving vehicle accelerates, it goes faster and faster.

복습 **blur** [blə:r] v. 흐릿해지다; 모호해지다; n. 흐릿한 형체
When a thing blurs or when something blurs it, you cannot see it clearly because its edges are no longer distinct.

★ **friction** [fríkʃən] n. 마찰, 압력
Friction is the force that makes it difficult for things to move freely when they are touching each other.

tricky [tríki] a. 까다로운; 교묘한
If you describe a task or problem as tricky, you mean that it is difficult to do or deal with.

복습 **sturdy** [stə́:rdi] a. 튼튼한, 견고한; 건장한; 확고한
Someone or something that is sturdy looks strong and is unlikely to be easily injured or damaged.

★ **material** [mətíəriəl] **n.** 직물, 천; 재료; 소재; **a.** 물질적인; 중요한
Material is cloth.

복습 **match** [mæʧ] **v.** 어울리다; 일치하다; 맞먹다; **n.** 똑같은 것; 경쟁 상대; 성냥
If something of a particular color or design matches another thing, they have the same color or design, or have a pleasing appearance when they are used together.

emblazon [imbléizn] **v.** (상징 · 문구 등을) 선명히 새기다
If something is emblazoned with a design, words, or letters, they are clearly drawn, printed, or sewn on it.

복습 **stun** [stʌn] **v.** 어리벙벙하게 하다; 깜짝 놀라게 하다; 기절시키다
If you are stunned by something, you are extremely shocked or surprised by it and are therefore unable to speak or do anything.

복습 **stretch** [streʧ] **v.** (길이 · 폭 등을) 늘이다; 펼쳐지다; 기지개를 켜다; **n.** (길게) 뻗은 구간; 기간
When something soft or elastic stretches or is stretched, it becomes longer or bigger as well as thinner, usually because it is pulled.

복습 **injure** [índʒər] **v.** 부상을 입히다; (평판 · 자존심 등을) 해치다
If you injure a person or animal, you damage some part of their body.

★ **retain** [ritéin] **v.** 계속 유지하다; 보유하다
To retain something means to continue to have that thing.

복습 **clamp** [klæmp] **v.** 꽉 잡다; 죔쇠로 고정시키다; **n.** 죔쇠
To clamp something in a particular place means to put it or hold it there firmly and tightly.

복습 **twist** [twist] **v.** 휘다, 구부리다; (고개 · 몸 등을) 돌리다; **n.** (손으로) 돌리기; (고개 · 몸 등을) 돌리기
If you twist something, you turn it to make a spiral shape, for example by turning the two ends of it in opposite directions.

★ **virtual** [vəːrʧuəl] **a.** 사실상의; 가상의 (virtually **ad.** 사실상, 거의)
You can use virtually to indicate that something is so nearly true that for most purposes it can be regarded as true.

indestructible [ìndistrʌ́ktəbl] **a.** (쉽게) 파괴할 수 없는
If something is indestructible, it is very strong and cannot be destroyed.

★ **breathe** [briːð] **v.** 통풍이 잘되다; 호흡하다, 숨을 쉬다
Clothes that can breathe are made from cloth with very small holes that allow air in.

★★ **contain** [kəntéin] v. ~이 들어 있다; (감정을) 억누르다
If something such as a box, bag, room, or place contains things, those things are inside it.

homing [hóumiŋ] a. 자동 유도 장치를 단; 귀소성이 있는
A weapon or piece of equipment that has a homing system is able to guide itself to a target or to give out a signal that guides people to it.

복습 **device** [diváis] n. 장치, 기구; 폭발물; 방법
A device is an object that has been invented for a particular purpose, for example for recording or measuring something.

★ **precise** [prisáis] a. 정확한, 정밀한; 엄밀한, 꼼꼼한
You use precise to emphasize that you are referring to an exact thing, rather than something vague.

복습 **location** [loukéiʃən] n. 장소, 위치
A location is the place where something happens or is situated.

★ **retire** [ritáiər] v. 물러나다, 은퇴하다 (retired a. 은퇴한)
When older people retire, they leave their job and usually stop working completely.

★ **underground** [ʌ̀ndərgráund] a. 비밀의; 지하의; ad. 지하에
Underground groups and activities are secret because their purpose is to oppose the government and they are illegal.

복습 **resume** [rizúːm] v. 재개하다; 자기 위치로 돌아가다
If you resume an activity or if it resumes, it begins again.

복습 **assume** [əsúːm] v. (사실일 것으로) 추정하다; (특질 · 양상을) 띠다
If you assume that something is true, you imagine that it is true, sometimes wrongly.

복습 **stammer** [stǽmər] v. 말을 더듬다; n. 말 더듬기
If you stammer, you speak with difficulty, hesitating and repeating words or sounds.

★ **tilt** [tilt] v. 기울이다, (뒤로) 젖히다; (의견 · 상황 등이) 기울어지다; n. 기울어짐, 젖혀짐
If you tilt part of your body, usually your head, you move it slightly upward or to one side.

receptionist [risépʃənist] n. (호텔 · 사무실 · 병원 등의) 접수 담당자
In an office or hospital, the receptionist is the person whose job is to answer the telephone, arrange appointments, and deal with people when they first arrive.

복습 **employ** [implɔ́i] v. 고용하다 (employment n. (개인의) 고용)
Employment is the fact of employing someone.

복습 **terminate** [tə́:rmənèit] v. 끝내다, 종료하다; 살해하다; 종점에 닿다
When you terminate something or when it terminates, it ends completely.

expressionless [ikspréʃənlis] a. 표정이 없는, 감정이 없는
If you describe someone's face as expressionless, you mean that they are not showing their feelings.

idiot [ídiət] n. 바보, 멍청이
If you call someone an idiot, you are showing that you think they are very stupid or have done something very stupid.

복습 **get in shape** idiom 좋은 몸매를 유지하다
If you get in shape, you become strong or fit.

복습 **sigh** [sai] v. 한숨을 쉬다, 한숨짓다; 탄식하듯 말하다; n. 한숨
When you sigh, you let out a deep breath, as a way of expressing feelings such as disappointment, tiredness, or pleasure.

복습 **relive** [rì:lív] v. (특히 상상 속에서) 다시 체험하다
If you relive something that has happened to you in the past, you remember it and imagine that you are experiencing it again.

복습 **impatient** [impéiʃənt] a. 짜증난, 안달하는; 어서 ~하고 싶어 하는
If you are impatient, you are annoyed because you have to wait too long for something.

pull oneself together idiom 기운을 되찾다, 냉정해지다
If you pull yourself together, you force yourself to stop behaving in a nervous, frightened, or uncontrolled way.

복습 **remind** [rimáind] v. 상기시키다, 다시 한 번 알려 주다
If someone reminds you of a fact or event that you already know about, they say something which makes you think about it.

⋆ **confront** [kənfrʌ́nt] v. (문제나 곤란한 상황에) 맞서다; 직면하다
If you confront a difficult situation or issue, you accept the fact that it exists and try to deal with it.

Check Your Reading Speed

1분에 몇 단어를 읽는지 리딩 속도를 측정해보세요.

$$\frac{\text{368 words}}{\text{reading time (}\quad\text{) sec}} \times 60 = (\quad) \text{ WPM}$$

Build Your Vocabulary

복습 **calculate** [kǽlkjulèit] v. 추정하다, 추산하다; 계산하다, 산출하다
If you calculate the effects of something, especially a possible course of action, you think about them in order to form an opinion or decide what to do.

★★★ **base** [beis] n. (군사) 기지; (사물의) 맨 아래 부분; 기초, 토대; v. ~에 근거지를 두다
A military base is a place which part of the armed forces works from.

unseen [ʌnsíːn] a. 눈에 띄지 않는; 처음 보는
You can use unseen to describe things which people cannot see.

★★ **arm** [aːrm] v. 무장하다; 폭발하게 하다; n. 무기, 화기; 팔 (disarm v. 무장 해제시키다)
To disarm a person or group means to take away all their weapons.

복습 **control** [kəntróul] n. 통제, 제어; (기계·차량의) 제어 장치; v. 지배하다; 조정하다
If you have control of something or someone, you are able to make them do what you want them to do.

catch hold of idiom ~을 잡다
Hold is used in expressions such as grab hold of, catch hold of, and get hold of, to indicate that you close your hand tightly around something, for example to stop something moving or falling.

복습 **pod** [pad] n. (우주선·선박의 본체에서) 분리 가능한 부분; (콩이 들어 있는) 꼬투리
A pod is a detachable or self-contained unit on an aircraft, spacecraft, vehicle, or vessel, having a particular function.

복습 **streak** [striːk] v. 전속력으로 가다; 줄무늬를 넣다; n. 줄무늬
If something or someone streaks somewhere, they move there very quickly.

복습 **jungle** [dʒʌŋgl] n. 밀림 (지대), 정글
A jungle is a forest in a tropical country where large numbers of tall trees and plants grow very close together.

복습 **guard** [ga:rd] **n.** 경비 요원; 경비, 감시; 보호물; **v.** 지키다, 보호하다
A guard is a specially organized group of people, such as soldiers or policemen, who protect or watch someone or something.

복습 **zoom** [zu:m] **v.** 쌩 하고 가다; 급등하다; **n.** (빠르게) 쌩 하고 지나가는 소리
If you zoom somewhere, you go there very quickly.

compound [kámpaund] **n.** (큰 건물이나 시설 등의) 구내; 복합체; **a.** 합성의
A compound is an enclosed area of land that is used for a particular purpose.

복습 **facility** [fəsíləti] **n.** 시설; 기관; 기능, 특징
Facilities are buildings, pieces of equipment, or services that are provided for a particular purpose.

* **passage** [pǽsidʒ] **n.** 통로, 복도; 통행, 통과
A passage is a long narrow space with walls or fences on both sides, which connects one place or room with another.

복습 **lava** [lá:və] **n.** 용암
Lava is the very hot liquid rock that comes out of a volcano.

* **statue** [stǽʧu:] **n.** 조각상
A statue is a large sculpture of a person or an animal, made of stone or metal.

* **shield** [ʃi:ld] **n.** 보호 장치; 방패; **v.** 보호하다, 가리다; (기계 등에) 보호 장치를 두르다
Something or someone which is a shield against a particular danger or risk provides protection from it.

복습 **part** [pa:rt] **v.** (두 사물 · 부분이) 갈라지다; (~와) 헤어지다; **n.** 일부, 약간; 부분
If things that are next to each other part or if you part them, they move in opposite directions, so that there is a space between them.

복습 **struggle** [strʌgl] **v.** 애쓰다; 몸부림치다, 허우적거리다; 힘겹게 나아가다; **n.** 투쟁, 분투; 몸부림
If you struggle to do something, you try hard to do it, even though other people or things may be making it difficult for you to succeed.

복습 **duck** [dʌk] **v.** (머리나 몸을) 휙 수그리다; 급히 움직이다; **n.** [동물] 오리
If you duck, you move your head or the top half of your body quickly downward to avoid something that might hit you, or to avoid being seen.

복습 **rush** [rʌʃ] **v.** 급히 움직이다; 서두르다; **n.** (감정이 갑자기) 치밀어 오름; 혼잡; 기쁨, 흥분
If you rush somewhere, you go there quickly.

복습 **elaborate** [ilǽbərət] a. 정교한; v. (더) 자세히 말하다; (계획 · 사상 등을) 정교하게 만들어 내다
You use elaborate to describe something that is very complex because it has a lot of different parts.

복습 **leash** [liːʃ] v. 속박하다, 억제하다; 가죽끈으로 매다; n. 가죽 끈; 통제
(unleash v. 풀어놓다; 해방하다)
If you say that someone or something unleashes a powerful force, feeling, activity, or group, you mean that they suddenly start it or send it somewhere.

★★ **improve** [imprúːv] v. 개선하다, 향상시키다
If something improves or if you improve it, it gets better.

★ **status** [stéitəs] n. 상황; 신분, 자격
The status of something is its state of affairs at a particular time.

★ **lure** [luər] v. 꾀다, 유혹하다; n. 유혹, 매력
To lure someone means to trick them into a particular place or to trick them into doing something that they should not do.

do in idiom 죽이다; 기진맥진하게 하다
To do someone in means to kill them.

복습 **evil** [íːvəl] a. 사악한, 악랄한; 유해한; 악마의; n. 악
If you describe someone as evil, you mean that they are very wicked by nature and take pleasure in doing things that harm other people.

mastermind [mǽstərmaind] n. (계획 등의) 지도자; (나쁜 짓의) 주모자;
v. 교묘히 지휘하다, 배후에서 조종하다
The mastermind behind a difficult or complicated plan, often a criminal one, is the person who is responsible for planning and organizing it.

★★ **subject** [sʌ́bdʒikt] n. 연구 대상; (논의 등의) 주제; a. ~에 달려 있는; v. 종속시키다
In an experiment or piece of research, the subject is the person or animal that is being tested or studied.

★★★ **perfect** [pə́ːrfikt] v. 완벽하게 하다; a. 완벽한
If you perfect something, you improve it so that it becomes as good as it can possibly be.

복습 **terminate** [tə́ːrmənèit] v. 살해하다; 끝내다, 종료하다; 종점에 닿다
If you terminate someone, you murder them.

복습 **location** [loukéiʃən] n. 장소, 위치
A location is the place where something happens or is situated.

복습 **relieve** [rilíːv] v. 안도하다; (불쾌감 · 고통 등을) 없애 주다; 완화하다 (relief n. 안도, 안심)
If you feel a sense of relief, you feel happy because something unpleasant has not happened or is no longer happening.

short-lived [ʃɔːrt-lívd] a. 오래가지 못하는, 단명하는
Something that is short-lived does not last very long.

복습 **homing** [hóumiŋ] a. 자동 유도 장치를 단; 귀소성이 있는
A weapon or piece of equipment that has a homing system is able to guide itself to a target or to give out a signal that guides people to it.

복습 **go off** idiom (경보기 등이) 울리다; 폭발하다; 발사되다
If something like an alarm goes off, it starts making a noise as a signal or warning.

복습 **alarm** [əláːrm] n. 경보 장치; 자명종; 불안, 공포; v. 불안하게 하다; 경보장치를 달다
An alarm is an automatic device that warns you of danger, for example by ringing a bell.

turret [tʌ́rit] n. (전함 · 탱크 등의) 회전 포탑; (성 꼭대기의) 작은 탑
The turret on a tank or warship is the part where the guns are fixed, which can be turned in any direction.

★ **sticky** [stíki] a. 끈적거리는, 끈적끈적한; 힘든, 불쾌한
A sticky substance is soft, or thick and liquid, and can stick to other things.

★ **foam** [foum] n. 거품; v. 거품을 일으키다
Foam consists of a mass of small bubbles that are formed when air and a liquid are mixed together.

engulf [ingʌ́lf] v. 완전히 에워싸다, 휩싸다; (강한 감정 등이) 사로잡다
If one thing engulfs another, it completely covers or hides it, often in a sudden and unexpected way.

high-heeled [hai-híːld] a. 굽 높은, 하이힐의
High-heeled shoes are women's shoes that have high heels.

Check Your Reading Speed

1분에 몇 단어를 읽는지 리딩 속도를 측정해보세요.

$$\frac{\text{900 words}}{\text{reading time (\qquad) sec}} \times 60 = (\qquad) \text{ WPM}$$

Build Your Vocabulary

leftover [léftòuvər] **n.** 남은 음식; **a.** 나머지의, 남은
You can refer to food that has not been eaten after a meal as leftovers.

복습 **charge** [ʧa:rdʒ] **n.** 책임, 담당; 요금; **v.** 급히 가다, 달려가다; (요금 · 값을) 청구하다
If you are in charge in a particular situation, you are the most senior person and have control over something or someone.

복습 **closet** [klázit] **n.** 벽장
A closet is a piece of furniture with doors at the front and shelves inside, which is used for storing things.

복습 **pack** [pæk] **v.** (짐을) 싸다; 가득 채우다; **n.** 무리, 집단; 묶음
When you pack a bag, you put clothes and other things into it, because you are leaving a place or going on holiday.

복습 **suit** [su:t] **n.** (특정한 활동 때 입는) 옷; 정장; 소송; **v.** ~에게 편리하다; 어울리다
A particular type of suit is a piece of clothing that you wear for a particular activity.

복습 **stuff** [stʌf] **v.** 쑤셔 넣다; 채워 넣다; **n.** 것, 물건
If you stuff something somewhere, you push it there quickly and roughly.

do a double take **idiom** 깜짝 놀라며 다시 보다, 놀라서 재확인하다
If you do a double take, you look again in surprise at someone or something.

복습 **immediate** [imí:diət] **a.** 즉각적인; 당면한; 아주 가까이에 있는 (immediately **ad.** 즉시, 즉각)
If something happens immediately, it happens without any delay.

* **outfit** [áutfit] **n.** 한 벌의 옷, 복장; 장비; **v.** (복장 · 장비를) 갖추어 주다
An outfit is a set of clothes.

intrigue [intríːg] v. 강한 흥미를 불러일으키다; 음모를 꾸미다; n. 음모; 흥미로움
(intrigued a. 아주 흥미로워하는)
If you are intrigued by something, especially something strange, it interests you and you want to know more about it.

⁑ **blind** [blaind] n. (창문에 치는) 블라인드; v. (잠시) 앞이 안 보이게 하다;
a. 눈이 먼; 앞이 안 보이는; 눈치 채지 못하는
A blind is a roll of cloth or paper which you can pull down over a window as a covering.

복습 **nab** [næb] v. 움켜쥐다; 붙잡다, 체포하다
If you nab something, you take it suddenly.

복습 **yell** [jel] v. 고함치다, 소리 지르다; n. 고함, 외침
If you yell, you shout loudly, usually because you are excited, angry, or in pain.

⁑ **pilot** [páilət] n. 조종사, 비행사
A pilot is a person who is trained to fly an aircraft.

복습 **jet** [dʒet] n. 제트기; 분출; v. 급속히 움직이다; 분출하다
A jet is an aircraft that is powered by jet engines.

복습 **notice** [nóutis] n. 통지, 예고; 신경 씀, 알아챔; v. 알아채다, 인지하다; 주의하다
(short notice n. 촉박한 통보)
If something is short notice, you are told about it only a short time before it happens.

call in a solid idiom 은혜를 갚게 하다
If you call in a solid, you ask someone to help you because you helped them in the past.

mouthpiece [máuθpiːs] n. (전화기의) 송화구
The mouthpiece of a telephone is the part that you speak into.

* **plead** [pliːd] v. 애원하다; 옹호하다, 주장하다
If you plead with someone to do something, you ask them in an intense, emotional way to do it.

복습 **matter-of-fact** [mætər-əv-fǽkt] a. 사무적인; 사실의, 실제적인
(matter-of-factly ad. 무미건조하게, 사무적으로)
If you describe a person as matter-of-fact, you mean that they show no emotions such as enthusiasm, anger, or surprise, especially in a situation where you would expect them to be emotional.

복습 **visible** [vízəbl] a. (눈에) 보이는, 알아볼 수 있는; 뚜렷한 (invisible a. 보이지 않는)
If you describe something as invisible, you mean that it cannot be seen, for example because it is transparent, hidden, or very small.

복습 **headset** [hédsèt] n. (마이크가 붙은) 헤드폰
A headset is a small pair of headphones that you can use for listening to a radio or recorded music, or for using a telephone.

복습 **track** [træk] v. 추적하다, 뒤쫓다; n. (기차) 선로; 경주로, 트랙; 자국
To track someone or something means to follow their movements by means of a special device, such as a satellite or radar.

복습 **homing** [hóumiŋ] a. 자동 유도 장치를 단; 귀소성이 있는
A weapon or piece of equipment that has a homing system is able to guide itself to a target or to give out a signal that guides people to it.

복습 **device** [diváis] n. 장치, 기구; 폭발물; 방법
A device is an object that has been invented for a particular purpose, for example for recording or measuring something.

복습 **volcano** [valkéinou] n. 화산 (volcanic a. 화산의)
Volcanic means coming from or created by volcanoes.

복습 **land** [lænd] v. (땅 · 표면에) 내려앉다, 착륙하다; 놓다, 두다; n. 육지, 땅; 지역 (landing n. 착륙)
A landing is an act of bringing an aircraft or spacecraft down to the ground.

★ **request** [rikwést] v. 요청하다, 요구하다; n. 요구 사항; 요청, 신청
If you request something, you ask for it politely or formally.

vector [véktər] n. (비행기의) 진로; [수학] 벡터
A vector is the course or direction of an airplane.

overreact [òuvəriǽkt] v. 과잉 반응하다
If you say that someone overreacts to something, you mean that they have and show more of an emotion than is necessary or appropriate.

복습 **autopilot** [ɔ́:toupàilət] n. (항공기 · 배의) 자동 조종 장치
An automatic pilot or an autopilot is a device in an aircraft that automatically keeps it on a particular course.

★ **prison** [prizn] n. 교도소, 감옥
A prison is a building where criminals are kept as punishment or where people accused of a crime are kept before their trial.

복습 **chamber** [ʧéimbər] n. (특정 목적용) -실(室); 회의실; (지하의) 공간
A chamber is a room designed and equipped for a particular purpose.

★★ **bind** [baind] v. (bound-bound) 묶다; 결속시키다; 굳다, 뭉치다
If you bind something or someone, you tie rope, string, tape, or other material around them so that they are held firmly.

★ **restraint** [ristréint] n. (움직임을 제한하는) 안전장치; 규제; 통제, 제한
Restraints are devices that hold you and physically controls your movements, often to protect your safety.

★ **suspend** [səspénd] v. (움직이지 않고) 떠 있다; 매달다, 걸다; 중단하다
If something is suspended from a high place, it is hanging from that place.

복습 **ray** [rei] n. 광선; 약간, 소량
Rays of light are narrow beams of light.

복습 **technology** [teknálədʒi] n. (과학) 기술; 기계, 장비
Technology refers to methods, systems, and devices which are the result of scientific knowledge being used for practical purposes.

복습 **triumphant** [traiʌ́mfənt] a. 의기양양한; 크게 성공한, 큰 승리를 거둔
Someone who is triumphant has gained a victory or succeeded in something and feels very happy about it.

★ **capture** [kǽpʧər] v. 포로로 잡다, 억류하다; n. 생포; 구금, 억류
If you capture someone or something, you catch them, especially in a war.

idolize [áidəlàiz] v. 숭배하다
If you idolize someone, you admire them very much.

★★ **trick** [trik] v. 속이다, 속임수를 쓰다; n. 속임수; 솜씨, 재주; 요령
If someone tricks you, they deceive you, often in order to make you do something.

복습 **probe** [proub] n. 탐침, 탐색침; (철저한) 조사; v. 조사하다; (길고 가느다란 기구로) 살피다
A probe is a long thin instrument that doctors and dentists use to examine parts of the body.

★★ **bone** [boun] n. 뼈
Your bones are the hard parts inside your body which together form your skeleton.

geek out idiom 흥분하다
To geek out means to behave in a very enthusiastic way about something that you are interested in and know a lot about but that other people might find boring.

★ **sour** [sauər] v. 안 좋아지다, 틀어지다; (우유가) 상하다; a. 불쾌한, 기분이 언짢은; 신, 시큼한
If a friendship, situation, or attitude sours or if something sours it, it becomes less friendly, enjoyable, or hopeful.

복습 **ruin** [ru:in] v. 엉망으로 만들다; 폐허로 만들다; n. 붕괴, 몰락; 파멸
To ruin something means to severely harm, damage, or spoil it.

★★ **ride** [raid] n. 길, 여정; (차량 · 자전거 등을) 타고 달리기; v. (차량 · 자전거 등을) 타다
A ride is a journey on a horse or bicycle, or in a vehicle.

lame [leim] a. 변변찮은, 설득력이 없는; 절름발이의, 다리를 저는
If you describe something, for example an excuse, argument, or remark, as lame, you mean that it is poor or weak.

★ **contact** [kántækt] v. 연락하다; n. 연락, 접촉
If you contact someone, you telephone them, write to them, or go to see them in order to tell or ask them something.

복습 **nod** [nad] n. (고개를) 끄덕임; v. (고개를) 끄덕이다, 까딱하다
A nod is a movement up and down with the head.

복습 **jolt** [dʒoult] n. 충격; 덜컥 하고 움직임; v. 갑자기 거칠게 움직이다; (~하도록) 충격을 주다
A jolt is a sudden strong increase in energy.

★ **electricity** [ilektrísəti] n. 전기, 전력
Electricity is a form of energy that can be carried by wires and is used for heating and lighting, and to provide power for machines.

wince [wins] v. (통증 · 당혹감으로) 움찔하고 놀라다
If you wince, the muscles of your face tighten suddenly because you have felt a pain or because you have just seen, heard, or remembered something unpleasant.

★ **refer** [rifə́:r] v. 언급하다, 입 밖에 내다; 지시하다, 나타내다; 참조하게 하다
If you refer to a particular subject or person, you talk about them or mention them.

snoop [snu:p] v. 기웃거리다, 염탐하다; n. 염탐꾼; 염탐
If someone snoops around a place, they secretly look around it in order to find out things.

복습 **signal** [sígnəl] n. 신호; 징조; v. (동작 · 소리로) 신호를 보내다; 암시하다
A signal is a gesture, sound, or action which is intended to give a particular message to the person who sees or hears it.

복습 **painful** [péinfəl] a. 고통스러운; (마음이) 괴로운 (painfully ad. 아플 정도로; 극도로)
If a part of your body is painful, it hurts because it is injured or because there is something wrong with it.

복습 **government** [gʌ́vərnmənt] n. 정부, 정권; 행정, 통치
The government of a country is the group of people who are responsible for governing it.

★★ **permission** [pəːrmíʃən] n. 허락, 허가, 승인
If someone is given permission to do something, they are allowed to do it.

★ **rage** [reidʒ] n. 격렬한 분노; v. 몹시 화를 내다; 맹렬히 계속되다
Rage is strong anger that is difficult to control.

grimace [gríməs] v. 얼굴을 찡그리다; n. 찡그린 표정
If you grimace, you twist your face in an ugly way because you are annoyed, disgusted, or in pain.

★ **transmit** [trænsmít] v. 전송하다, 송신하다; 전염시키다; 전도하다 (transmission n. 전송, 송신)
A transmission is a program or signal that is broadcast or sent out.

복습 **snap** [snæp] v. 탁 하고 움직이다; 급히 움직이다; 날카롭게 말하다; 툭 부러지다; n. 탁 하는 소리
If you snap something into a particular position, or if it snaps into that position, it moves quickly into that position, with a sharp sound.

malicious [məlíʃəs] a. 악의적인, 적의 있는 (maliciously ad. 심술궂게)
If you describe someone's words or actions as malicious, you mean that they are intended to harm people or their reputation, or cause them embarrassment and upset.

복습 **greet** [griːt] v. 인사하다; 환영하다; 반응을 보이다 (greeting n. 인사)
A greeting is something friendly that you say or do when you meet someone.

★ **launch** [lɔːntʃ] n. 발사; 개시, 진수; v. 시작하다; 발사하다
A launch is the act of sending a missile, space vehicle, satellite, or other object into the air or into space.

console [kánsoul] ① n. 콘솔, 제어반, 계기반 ② v. 위로하다, 위안을 주다
A console is a panel with a number of switches or knobs that is used to operate a machine.

복습 **helpless** [hélplis] a. 무력한, 속수무책인
If you are helpless, you do not have the strength or power to do anything useful or to control or protect yourself.

1. Where was Jack-Jack?

A. At home with a babysitter

B. In his room by himself

C. On the plane with his family

D. At a nearby relative's house

2. How did the Parr family get from the ocean to land?

A. Helen made a boat out of pieces of the plane.

B. Vi created a force field to push everyone toward land.

C. Dash kicked his legs in the water at high speed.

D. Everyone held on to a monopod flying by.

3. In the cave, what did Helen tell Dash and Vi to do?

A. Search for their father in the cave

B. Fight as many guards as possible

C. Find a way out of the jungle

D. Use their powers if necessary

4. Why did Vi feel sorry?

A. She had not realized how important her family was.

B. She had not tried to save her family from the missile.

C. She had not stopped Dash from getting on the plane.

D. She had not practiced using her powers enough.

5. Why did Elastigirl need a key card?

A. It would enable her to escape from the lair.

B. It would enable her to find Mr. Incredible.

C. It would enable her to launch a rocket.

D. It would enable her to drive a monopod.

Check Your Reading Speed

1분에 몇 단어를 읽는지 리딩 속도를 측정해보세요.

$$\frac{\text{600 words}}{\text{reading time (\qquad) sec}} \times 60 = (\qquad) \text{ WPM}$$

Build Your Vocabulary

복습 **toss** [tɔ:s] **v.** (가볍게) 던지다; (고개를) 홱 쳐들다; **n.** 던지기
If you toss something somewhere, you throw it there lightly, often in a rather careless way.

복습 **passenger** [pǽsəndʒər] **n.** 승객 (passenger seat **n.** (자동차의) 조수석)
A passenger in a vehicle such as a bus, boat, or plane is a person who is traveling in it, but who is not driving it or working on it.

복습 **materialize** [mətíəriəlàiz] **v.** (갑자기) 나타나다; (예상 · 계획대로) 실현되다
(rematerialize **v.** 다시 나타나다)
If a person or thing materializes, they suddenly appear, after they have been invisible or in another place.

⋆⋆ **fault** [fɔ:lt] **n.** 잘못, 책임; 결점
If a bad or undesirable situation is your fault, you caused it or are responsible for it.

⋆⋆ **blame** [bleim] **v.** ~을 탓하다, ~의 책임으로 보다; **n.** 책임; 탓
If you blame a person or thing for something bad, you believe or say that they are responsible for it or that they caused it.

복습 **interrupt** [ìntərʌ́pt] **v.** (말 · 행동을) 방해하다; 중단시키다; 차단하다
If you interrupt someone who is speaking, you say or do something that causes them to stop.

⋆ **pop** [pap] **v.** 불쑥 나타나다; 펑 하는 소리가 나다; 눈이 휘둥그레지다; **n.** 펑 (하는 소리)
If you pop somewhere, you go there for a short time.

⋆ **sneak** [sni:k] **v.** 살금살금 가다; 몰래 하다; **a.** 기습적인
If you sneak somewhere, you go there very quietly on foot, trying to avoid being seen or heard.

take off **idiom** 날아오르다; (서둘러) 떠나다
If an aircraft takes off, it leaves the ground and starts flying.

★ **sarcastic** [sa:rkǽstik] **a.** 빈정대는, 비꼬는; 풍자적인 (sarcastically **ad.** 비꼬는 투로)
Someone who is sarcastic says or does the opposite of what they really mean in order to mock or insult someone.

sitter [sítər] **n.** (= babysitter) 아이를 봐 주는 사람
A sitter is the same as a babysitter who is someone you pay to come to your house and look after your children while you are not there, especially in the evening.

★★ **responsible** [rispánsəbl] **a.** 책임감 있는; (~을) 책임지고 있는 (irresponsible **a.** 무책임한)
If you describe someone as irresponsible, you are criticizing them because they do things without properly considering their possible consequences.

★★★ **anxious** [ǽŋkʃəs] **a.** 염려하는; 열망하는, 간절히 바라는; 불안해 보이는 (anxiously **ad.** 걱정스럽게)
If you are anxious, you are nervous or worried about something.

복습 **dial** [dáiəl] **v.** 다이얼을 돌리다, 전화를 걸다; **n.** (시계 · 계기 등의) 문자반
If you dial or if you dial a number, you turn the dial or press the buttons on a telephone in order to phone someone.

babysit [béibisit] **v.** (부모가 외출한 동안) 아이를 봐 주다 (babysitter **n.** 아이를 봐 주는 사람)
If you babysit for someone or babysit their children, you look after their children while they are out.

★ **uncertain** [ʌnsə́:rtn] **a.** 자신 없는; 확신이 없는, 잘 모르는; 불확실한 (uncertainly **ad.** 자신 없게, 머뭇거리며)
If you are uncertain about something, you do not know what you should do, what is going to happen, or what the truth is about something.

★★ **leading** [lí:diŋ] **a.** 가장 중요한, 선두적인; (시합에서) 선두의
The leading person or thing in a particular area is the one which is most important or successful.

복습 **expert** [ékspə:rt] **n.** 전문가; **a.** 숙련된; 전문가의, 전문적인
An expert is a person who is very skilled at doing something or who knows a lot about a particular subject.

복습 **handle** [hændl] **v.** (사람 · 작업 등을) 처리하다; 들다, 옮기다; **n.** 손잡이
If you say that someone can handle a problem or situation, you mean that they have the ability to deal with it successfully.

dish out idiom 주다
To dish out means to give or say things to people without thinking about them carefully.

coo [kuː] v. 정답게 소곤거리다; 구구 울다; n. 구구 (하고 새가 우는 소리)
When someone coos, they speak in a very soft, quiet voice which is intended to sound attractive.

cockpit [kákpit] n. (비행기 · 우주선 등의) 조종석, 조종실
In an airplane or racing car, the cockpit is the part where the pilot or driver sits.

★ **widen** [waidn] v. 넓어지다; (정도 · 범위 등이) 커지다
If your eyes widen, they open more.

복습 **trail** [treil] n. 자국, 흔적; 자취; v. 끌다; 뒤쫓다, 추적하다
A trail is a series of marks or other signs of movement or other activities left by someone or something.

복습 **missile** [mísəl] n. 미사일
A missile is a tube-shaped weapon that travels long distances through the air and explodes when it reaches its target.

복습 **grab** [græb] v. (와락 · 단단히) 붙잡다; 급히 ~하다; n. 와락 잡아채려고 함
If you grab something, you take it or pick it up suddenly and roughly.

복습 **headset** [hédsèt] n. (마이크가 붙은) 헤드폰
A headset is a small pair of headphones that you can use for listening to a radio or recorded music, or for using a telephone.

복습 **rocket** [rákit] n. 로켓 추진 미사일; 로켓; v. 로켓처럼 가다, 돌진하다; 급증하다
A rocket is a missile containing explosive that is powered by gas.

복습 **roar** [rɔːr] v. 굉음을 내며 질주하다; 고함치다; 웅웅거리다; n. 함성; 울부짖는 듯한 소리
If something, usually a vehicle, roars somewhere, it goes there very fast, making a loud noise.

★★ **friendly** [fréndli] n. (pl.) 우호적인 사람, 자기편; a. 우호적인; 상냥한; (행동이) 친절한
Friendlies are some people who show no hostility.

복습 **engage** [ingéidʒ] v. 교전을 시작하다; 약속하다; 관여하다; 기계 부품이 맞물리다
(disengage v. 철수하다; 떼어 내다)
If an army disengages, it stops fighting in an area.

복습 **frantic** [frǽntik] a. (두려움 · 걱정으로) 제정신이 아닌; 정신없이 서두는
If you are frantic, you are behaving in a wild and uncontrolled way because you are frightened or worried.

복습 **glance** [glæns] n. 흘낏 봄; v. 흘낏 보다; 대충 훑어보다
A glance is a quick look at someone or something.

복습 **fasten** [fæsn] v. 매다, 채우다; (단단히) 잠그다; 고정시키다
When you fasten something, you close it by means of buttons or a strap, or some other device.

* **panic** [pǽnik] v. (panicked-panicked) 어쩔 줄 모르다, 공황 상태에 빠지다; n. 극심한 공포, 공황; 허둥지둥함
If you panic or if someone panics you, you suddenly feel anxious or afraid, and act quickly and without thinking carefully.

* **buckle** [bʌkl] v. 버클로 잠그다; 찌그러지다; n. 버클, 잠금장치
When you buckle a belt or strap, you fasten it.

복습 **dive** [daiv] n. 급강하; (물속으로) 뛰어들기; v. 급히 움직이다; (물속으로) 뛰어들다; 급강하하다
A dive is a quick sudden movement toward the ground from the air.

복습 **slam** [slæm] v. 세게 치다, 놓다; 쾅 닫다; n. 쾅 하고 닫기; 탕 하는 소리
If one thing slams into or against another, it crashes into it with great force.

복습 **ceiling** [síːliŋ] n. 천장
A ceiling is the horizontal surface that forms the top part or roof inside a room.

복습 **smoke** [smouk] v. 질주하다; (담배를) 피우다; 연기를 내뿜다; n. 연기
To smoke means to go or proceed at high speed.

yank [jæŋk] v. 홱 잡아당기다; n. 홱 잡아당기기
If you yank someone or something somewhere, you pull them there suddenly and with a lot of force.

복습 **nose** [nouz] n. (항공기 · 우주선 등의) 앞부분; 코; v. 천천히 조심스럽게 나아가다
The nose of a vehicle such as a car or airplane is the front part of it.

* **skim** [skim] v. (표면을) 스치듯 하며 지나가다; 훑어보다; 걷어 내다
If something skims a surface, it moves quickly along just above it.

복습 **wave** [weiv] n. 물결; (손 · 팔을) 흔들기; (열 · 소리 · 빛 등의) -파; v. (손 · 팔을) 흔들다; 손짓하다
A wave is a raised mass of water on the surface of water, especially the sea, which is caused by the wind or by tides making the surface of the water rise and fall.

⋆ **whirl** [hwəːrl] **v.** 빙그르르 돌다; (마음 · 생각 등이) 혼란스럽다; **n.** 빙빙 돌기
If something or someone whirls around or if you whirl them around, they move around or turn around very quickly.

복습 **force** [fɔːrs] **n.** 작용력; 힘; 영향력; **v.** 억지로 ~하다; ~를 강요하다
Force is the power or strength which something has.

복습 **field** [fiːld] **n.** ~장; 경기장; 들판, 밭
A magnetic, gravitational, or electric field is the area in which that particular force is strong enough to have an effect.

복습 **protest** [próutest] **v.** 항의하다, 이의를 제기하다; **n.** 항의; 시위
If you protest against something or about something, you say or show publicly that you object to it.

복습 **prison** [prizn] **n.** 교도소, 감옥
A prison is a building where criminals are kept as punishment or where people accused of a crime are kept before their trial.

⋆⋆ **cell** [sel] **n.** 감방; (작은) 칸; (= cell phone) 휴대 전화
A cell is a small room in which a prisoner is locked.

복습 **transmit** [trænsmít] **v.** 전송하다, 송신하다; 전염시키다; 전도하다
(transmission **n.** 전송, 송신)
A transmission is a program or signal that is broadcast or sent out.

call off **idiom** ~을 철수시키다
If you call something off, you decide to stop something that is already happening.

복습 **close in** **idiom** (~에) 접근하다
To close in someone or close in on someone means to move nearer to them, especially in order to surround them and stop them from escaping.

⋆ **leap** [liːp] **v.** (서둘러) ~하다; 뛰다, 뛰어오르다; **n.** 높이뛰기, 도약; 급증
If you leap somewhere, you move there suddenly and quickly.

⋆ **register** [rédʒistər] **v.** 기록하다, 나타내다; 기억하다; (이름을) 등록하다; **n.** 기록부, 명부
When something registers on a scale or measuring instrument, it shows on the scale or instrument.

⋆ **grieve** [griːv] **v.** 비통해하다; 대단히 슬프게 하다 (grief **n.** 비탄, 비통)
Grief is a feeling of extreme sadness.

⋆ **horror** [hɔ́:rər] **n.** 공포, 경악; ~의 참상
Horror is a feeling of great shock, fear, and worry caused by something extremely unpleasant.

Check Your Reading Speed

1분에 몇 단어를 읽는지 리딩 속도를 측정해보세요.

$$\frac{\text{922 words}}{\text{reading time (}\qquad\text{) sec}} \times 60 = (\qquad) \text{ WPM}$$

Build Your Vocabulary

★ **confirm** [kənfə́:rm] v. 사실임을 보여주다, 확인해 주다; 더 분명히 해 주다
If you confirm something that has been stated or suggested, you say that it is true because you know about it.

복습 **target** [tá:rgit] n. (공격의) 표적; 목표; v. (공격 · 비판의) 목표로 삼다
A target is something at which someone is aiming a weapon or other object.

복습 **crush** [krʌʃ] v. 좌절시키다; 으스러뜨리다; 밀어 넣다; n. 홀딱 반함
If you are crushed by something, it upsets you a great deal.

get over idiom ~을 극복하다
If you get over something, you start to feel happy or well again after something bad has happened to you.

★ **recall** [rikɔ́:l] v. 기억해 내다, 상기하다; 다시 불러들이다; n. 회상; (제품의) 회수
When you recall something, you remember it and tell others about it.

복습 **burst** [bə:rst] n. (갑자기) ~을 함; 파열, 폭발; v. 갑자기 ~하다; 불쑥 움직이다
A burst of something is a sudden short period of it.

복습 **rage** [reidʒ] n. 격렬한 분노; v. 몹시 화를 내다; 맹렬히 계속되다
Rage is strong anger that is difficult to control.

복습 **lunge** [lʌndʒ] v. 달려들다, 돌진하다; n. 돌진
If you lunge in a particular direction, you move in that direction suddenly and clumsily.

★ **release** [rilí:s] v. 풀어 주다; 놓아 주다; (감정을) 발산하다; n. 풀어 줌; 발표, 공개
If a person or animal is released from somewhere where they have been locked up or looked after, they are set free or allowed to go.

⋆ **growl** [graul] v. 으르렁거리듯 말하다; 으르렁거리다; n. 으르렁거리는 소리
If someone growls something, they say something in a low, rough, and angry voice.

복습 **panel** [pænl] n. (자동차 등의) 계기판; 판; 패널, 자문단
A control panel or instrument panel is a board or surface which contains switches and controls to operate a machine or piece of equipment.

복습 **suspend** [səspénd] v. (움직이지 않고) 떠 있다; 매달다, 걸다; 중단하다
If something is suspended from a high place, it is hanging from that place.

복습 **squeeze** [skwi:z] v. (꼭) 쥐다; (좁은 곳에) 비집고 들어가다; n. (손으로 꼭) 쥐기
If you squeeze something, you press it firmly, usually with your hands.

toothpick [tú:θpìk] n. 이쑤시개
A toothpick is a small stick which you use to remove food from between your teeth.

복습 **smug** [smʌg] a. 의기양양한, 우쭐해하는 (smugly ad. 잘난 체하며)
If you say that someone is smug, you are criticizing the fact they seem very pleased with how good, clever, or lucky they are.

복습 **hesitate** [hézətèit] v. 망설이다, 주저하다; 거리끼다
If you hesitate, you do not speak or act for a short time, usually because you are uncertain, embarrassed, or worried about what you are going to say or do.

복습 **grit** [grit] v. 이를 갈다; 잔모래를 뿌리다; n. 투지, 기개; 모래
If you grit your teeth, you press your upper and lower teeth tightly together, usually because you are angry about something.

outgrow [àutgróu] v. (outgrew-outgrown) ~보다 크게 성장하다; (옷 등이) 커져 맞지 않다
If you outgrow a particular way of behaving or thinking, you change and become more mature, so that you no longer behave or think in that way.

⋆ **disgust** [disgʌ́st] n. 혐오감, 역겨움; v. 혐오감을 유발하다, 역겹게 하다
Disgust is a feeling of very strong dislike or disapproval.

⋆ **meanwhile** [mí:nwàil] ad. (다른 일이 일어나고 있는) 그동안에
Meanwhile means while a particular thing is happening.

복습 **missile** [mísəl] n. 미사일
A missile is a tube-shaped weapon that travels long distances through the air and explodes when it reaches its target.

복습 **explode** [iksplóud] v. 폭발하다; (갑자기 강한 감정을) 터뜨리다 (explosion **n.** 폭발)
An explosion is a sudden, violent burst of energy, for example one caused by a bomb.

disperse [dispə́:rs] v. 흩어지다; 해산하다
When something disperses or when you disperse it, it spreads over a wide area.

복습 **emerge** [imə́:rdʒ] v. 나오다, 모습을 드러내다; (어려움 등을) 헤쳐 나오다
To emerge means to come out from an enclosed or dark space such as a room or a vehicle, or from a position where you could not be seen.

복습 **blast** [blæst] **n.** 폭발; (한 줄기의) 강한 바람; **v.** 확 뿌리다; 폭발시키다; 빠르게 가다
A blast is a big explosion, especially one caused by a bomb.

furl [fə:rl] v. (돛 · 깃발을) 걷다; (우산을) 접다 (unfurl **v.** 펼쳐지다)
If you unfurl something rolled or folded such as an umbrella, sail, or flag, you open it, so that it is spread out.

plummet [plʌ́mit] v. 곤두박질치다, 급락하다
If someone or something plummets, they fall very fast toward the ground, usually from a great height.

복습 **stretch** [stretʃ] v. (길이 · 폭 등을) 늘이다; 펼쳐지다; 기지개를 켜다; **n.** (길게) 뻗은 구간; 기간
When something soft or elastic stretches or is stretched, it becomes longer or bigger as well as thinner, usually because it is pulled.

parachute [pǽrəʃù:t] **n.** 낙하산; **v.** 낙하산을 타고 뛰어내리다
A parachute is a device which enables a person to jump from an aircraft and float safely to the ground.

복습 **midair** [midέər] **n.** 공중, 상공
If something happens in midair, it happens in the air, rather than on the ground.

break one's fall **idiom** ~가 떨어지는 것을 막다
To break someone's fall means to stop someone who is falling from hitting the ground directly, so that they hurt themselves less than they would have done.

★ **splash** [splæʃ] v. 첨벙거리다; (물 등을) 끼얹다; **n.** 첨벙 하는 소리; (어디에 떨어지는) 방울
If you splash about or splash around in water, you hit or disturb the water in a noisy way, causing some of it to fly up into the air.

복습 **surface** [sə́:rfis] **n.** 수면, 표면, 지면; 외관; **v.** 수면으로 올라오다; (갑자기) 나타나다
The surface of something is the flat top part of it or the outside of it.

sputter [spʌ́tər] **v.** (분노 · 충격으로) 식식거리며 말하다; 털털거리는 소리를 내다
If you sputter, you speak or say something in a confused way, often while taking short quick breaths, for example because you are shocked or angry.

afloat [əflóut] **a.** (물에) 뜬
If someone or something is afloat, they remain partly above the surface of water and do not sink.

복습 **panic** [pǽnik] **v.** 어쩔 줄 모르다, 공황 상태에 빠지다; **n.** 극심한 공포, 공황; 허둥지둥함
If you panic or if someone panics you, you suddenly feel anxious or afraid, and act quickly and without thinking carefully.

★ **overtake** [òuvərtéik] **v.** 압도하다; 불시에 닥치다; 앞지르다, 추월하다
If a feeling overtakes you, it affects you very strongly.

★ **tread** [tred] **v.** (발을) 디디다; 밟아서 뭉개다; **n.** 걸음걸이; 발소리
(tread water **idiom** 선헤엄을 치다)
If someone who is in deep water treads water, they float in an upright position by moving their legs slightly.

★★ **survive** [sərváiv] **v.** 살아남다, 생존하다
If a person or living thing survives in a dangerous situation such as an accident or an illness, they do not die.

get a grip **idiom** 정신을 바짝 차리다
If you get a grip on yourself, you make an effort to control or improve your behavior or work.

so help me **idiom** 맹세코, 진정으로
You can say 'so help me' when you are making a serious promise, especially in a court of law.

★★★ **ground** [graund] **v.** (벌로) 외출하지 못하게 하다; 좌초되다; **n.** 땅바닥, 지면
When parents ground a child, they forbid them to go out and enjoy themselves for a period of time, as a punishment.

복습 **nod** [nad] **v.** (고개를) 끄덕이다, 까딱하다; **n.** (고개를) 끄덕임
If you nod, you move your head downward and upward to show that you are answering 'yes' to a question, or to show agreement, understanding, or approval.

★★ **range** [reindʒ] **n.** 거리, 범위; 산맥, 산줄기; **v.** 포함하다; 배열하다
The range of something is the maximum area in which it can reach things or detect things.

bob [bab] **v.** 위아래로 움직이다; (고개를) 까닥거리다; **n.** (머리 · 몸을) 까닥거림
If something bobs, it moves up and down, like something does when it is floating on water.

복습 **base** [beis] **v.** ~에 근거지를 두다; **n.** (사물의) 맨 아래 부분; 기초, 토대; (군사) 기지 (based **a.** (~에) 기반을 둔)
If you base one thing on another thing, the first thing develops from the second thing.

⋆ **bet** [bet] **n.** 짐작, 추측; 내기; **v.** (~이) 틀림없다; (내기 등에) 돈을 걸다
If you tell someone that something is a good bet, you are suggesting that it is the thing or course of action that they should choose.

복습 **amaze** [əméiz] **v.** (대단히) 놀라게 하다; 경악하게 하다 (amazed **a.** 놀란)
If something amazes you, it surprises you very much.

on board **idiom** 승선한, 탑승한
When you are on board a train, ship, or aircraft, you are on it or in it.

trooper [trú:pər] **n.** 용감한 사람; 기병; 포병
A trooper is a reliable and uncomplaining person.

복습 **hug** [hʌg] **v.** 껴안다, 포옹하다; **n.** 포옹
When you hug someone, you put your arms around them and hold them tightly.

복습 **exhaust** [igzɔ́:st] **v.** 기진맥진하게 하다; 다 써 버리다; **n.** (자동차 등의) 배기가스 (exhausted **a.** 기진맥진한)
If something exhausts you, it makes you so tired, either physically or mentally, that you have no energy left.

복습 **weary** [wíəri] **a.** 지친, 피곤한; ~에 싫증난; **v.** 지치게 하다; ~에 싫증나다 (wearily **ad.** 지쳐서)
If you are weary, you are very tired.

복습 **cave** [keiv] **n.** 동굴
A cave is a large hole in the side of a cliff or hill, or one that is under the ground.

⋆ **huddle** [hʌdl] **v.** 모이다; 몸을 움츠리다; **n.** 모여 서 있는 것; 혼잡
If people huddle together or huddle round something, they stand, sit, or lie close to each other, usually because they all feel cold or frightened.

battered [bǽtərd] **a.** 오래 써서 낡은; 박살난
Something that is battered is old and in poor condition because it has been used a lot.

복습 **mask** [mæsk] **n.** 마스크; 가면; **v.** 가면을 쓰다; (감정 · 냄새 · 사실 등을) 가리다
A mask is a piece of cloth or other material, which you wear over your face so that people cannot see who you are, or so that you look like someone or something else.

복습 **identity** [aidéntəti] **n.** 신원, 신분, 정체; 독자성
Your identity is who you are.

★★ **valuable** [vǽljuəbl] **a.** 소중한, 귀중한; 가치가 큰, 값비싼
If you describe something or someone as valuable, you mean that they are very useful and helpful.

★★ **possess** [pəzés] **v.** 소유하다, 소지하다; (자질 · 특징을) 지니다 (possession **n.** 소유물, 소지품)
Your possessions are the things that you own or have with you at a particular time.

복습 **sigh** [sai] **v.** 한숨을 쉬다, 한숨짓다; 탄식하듯 말하다; **n.** 한숨
When you sigh, you let out a deep breath, as a way of expressing feelings such as disappointment, tiredness, or pleasure.

count on **idiom** 기대하다, 의지하다
If you count on someone, you have confidence in them because you know that they will do what you want.

복습 **tear** [tiər] ① **n.** 눈물 ② **v.** 뜯어 내다; 찢다, 뜯다; 부리나케 가다; **n.** 찢어진 곳, 구멍
Tears are the drops of salty liquid that come out of your eyes when you are crying.

복습 **confident** [kánfədənt] **a.** 자신감 있는; 확신하는
If a person or their manner is confident, they feel sure about their own abilities, qualities, or ideas.

복습 **tilt** [tilt] **v.** 기울이다, (뒤로) 젖히다; (의견 · 상황 등이) 기울어지다; **n.** 기울어짐, 젖혀짐
If you tilt part of your body, usually your head, you move it slightly upward or to one side.

★★★ **doubt** [daut] **n.** 의심, 의혹, 의문; **v.** 확신하지 못하다, 의심하다, 의문을 갖다
If you have doubt or doubts about something, you feel uncertain about it and do not know whether it is true or possible.

★ **luxury** [lʌ́kʃəri] **n.** 호화로움, 사치; 드문 호사
A luxury is a pleasure which you do not often have the opportunity to enjoy.

★ **afford** [əfɔ́:rd] **v.** (~을 살 · 할) 여유가 되다; 제공하다
If you say that you cannot afford to do something or allow it to happen, you mean that you must not do it or must prevent it from happening because it would be harmful or embarrassing to you.

복습 **realize** [rí:əlàiz] **v.** 깨닫다, 알아차리다; 실현하다, 달성하다
If you realize that something is true, you become aware of that fact or understand it.

복습 **cell** [sel] **n.** 감방; (작은) 칸; (= cell phone) 휴대 전화
A cell is a small room in which a prisoner is locked.

★ **rub** [rʌb] **v.** (손 · 손수건 등을 대고) 문지르다; (두 손 등을) 맞비비다; **n.** 문지르기, 비비기
If you rub a part of your body, you move your hand or fingers backward and forward over it while pressing firmly.

★★ **value** [vǽlju:] **v.** 소중하게 생각하다; (가치 · 가격을) 평가하다; **n.** 가치; 중요성, 유용성
If you value something or someone, you think that they are important and you appreciate them.

복습 **wave** [weiv] **v.** 손짓하다; (손 · 팔을) 흔들다; **n.** 물결; (손 · 팔을) 흔들기; (열 · 소리 · 빛 등의) -파
If you wave or wave your hand, you move your hand from side to side in the air, usually in order to say hello or goodbye to someone.

★ **disregard** [dìsrigá:rd] **v.** 무시하다, 경시하다; **n.** 무시, 경시
If you disregard something, you ignore it or do not take account of it.

복습 **accuse** [əkjú:z] **v.** 비난하다, 고발하다 (accusingly **ad.** 비난하듯)
If you look at someone with an accusing expression or speak to them in an accusing tone of voice, you are showing that you think they have done something wrong.

bluff [blʌf] **n.** 허세, 엄포; **v.** 허세를 부리다 (call one's bluff **idiom** 엄포를 알아차리다)
If you call someone's bluff, you tell them to do what they have been threatening to do, because you are sure that they will not really do it.

복습 **shrug** [ʃrʌg] **v.** (어깨를) 으쓱하다; **n.** 어깨를 으쓱하기
If you shrug, you raise your shoulders to show that you are not interested in something or that you do not know or care about something.

★ **gamble** [gæmbl] **v.** 모험을 하다; 돈을 걸다, 도박을 하다; **n.** 도박, 모험
If you gamble on something, you take a risky action or decision in the hope of gaining money, success, or an advantage over other people.

Check Your Reading Speed

1분에 몇 단어를 읽는지 리딩 속도를 측정해보세요.

$$\frac{292 \text{ words}}{\text{reading time (} \quad \text{) sec}} \times 60 = (\quad) \text{ WPM}$$

Build Your Vocabulary

복습 **fluid** [flu:id] **a.** 부드러운, 우아한; 가변적인; **n.** 유체(流體), 유동체 (fluidly **ad.** 우아하게)
Fluid movements or lines or designs are smooth and graceful.

★ **dense** [dens] **a.** 빽빽한, 밀집한; (앞이 안 보이게) 짙은, 자욱한
Something that is dense contains a lot of things or people in a small area.

복습 **jungle** [dʒʌŋgl] **n.** 밀림 (지대), 정글
A jungle is a forest in a tropical country where large numbers of tall trees and plants grow very close together.

★ **occasional** [əkéiʒənəl] **a.** 가끔의, 때때로의 (occasionally **ad.** 때때로, 가끔)
Occasional means happening sometimes, but not regularly or often.

복습 **outstretched** [àutstréʧt] **a.** 쭉 뻗은
If a part of the body of a person or animal is outstretched, it is stretched out as far as possible.

복습 **make one's way** **idiom** 나아가다, 가다
When you make your way somewhere, you walk or travel there.

복습 **clearing** [klíəriŋ] **n.** (숲 속의) 빈터
A clearing is a small area in a forest where there are no trees or bushes.

복습 **glint** [glint] **n.** 반짝임; (눈이 강하게) 번득임; **v.** 반짝거리다; (눈이 강하게) 번득이다
A glint is a quick flash of light.

★ **hum** [hʌm] **n.** 윙윙거리는 소리; **v.** 윙윙거리다; 왁자지껄하다
Hum is a low continuous noise made by a machine or a lot of people talking.

복습 **pod** [pad] **n.** (우주선 · 선박의 본체에서) 분리 가능한 부분; (콩이 들어 있는) 꼬투리
A pod is a detachable or self-contained unit on an aircraft, spacecraft, vehicle, or vessel, having a particular function.

distance [dístəns] **n.** 먼 곳; 거리; **v.** (~에) 관여하지 않다 (in the distance **idiom** 저 멀리)
If you can see something in the distance, you can see it, far away from you.

streak [stri:k] **v.** 전속력으로 가다; 줄무늬를 넣다; **n.** 줄무늬
If something or someone streaks somewhere, they move there very quickly.

grip [grip] **v.** 꽉 잡다, 움켜잡다; (마음 · 흥미 · 시선을) 끌다; **n.** 꽉 붙잡음, 움켜쥠; 통제, 지배
If you grip something, you take hold of it with your hand and continue to hold it firmly.

vehicle [ví:ikl] **n.** 차량, 운송 수단; 수단, 매개체
A vehicle is a machine such as a car, bus, or truck which has an engine and is used to carry people from place to place.

yank [jæŋk] **v.** 홱 잡아당기다; **n.** 홱 잡아당기기
If you yank someone or something somewhere, you pull them there suddenly and with a lot of force.

dangle [dæŋgl] **v.** 매달리다; (무엇을 들고) 달랑거리다
If something dangles from somewhere or if you dangle it somewhere, it hangs or swings loosely.

swing [swiŋ] **v.** 휙 움직이다; (전후 · 좌우로) 흔들다; 방향을 바꾸다; **n.** 흔들기; 휘두르기
If something swings in a particular direction or if you swing it in that direction, it moves in that direction with a smooth, curving movement.

slice [slais] **v.** (하늘 · 물 등을) 가르듯이 달리다; 베다; **n.** (얇게 썬) 조각; 부분, 몫
To slice through something means to pass through it very easily.

canopy [kǽnəpi] **n.** 숲의 우거진 윗부분; (늘어뜨린) 덮개
A canopy is a layer of something that spreads out and covers an area, for example the branches and leaves that spread out at the top of trees in a forest.

determine [ditə́:rmin] **v.** ~을 하기로 결정하다; 알아내다, 밝히다
(determined **a.** 단단히 결심한)
If you are determined to do something, you have made a firm decision to do it and will not let anything stop you.

hang on **idiom** 꽉 붙잡다; 잠깐 기다려, 멈춰 봐
If you hang on to something, you hold tightly to it.

squint [skwint] **v.** 눈을 가늘게 뜨고 보다; 사시이다; **n.** 사시; 잠깐 봄
If you squint at something, you look at it with your eyes partly closed.

복습 **speed** [spi:d] v. 빨리 가다; 더 빠르게 하다; n. 속도
If you speed somewhere, you move or travel there quickly, usually in a vehicle.

★ **tower** [táuər] v. (~보다) 매우 높다; 솟다; n. 탑 (towering a. 우뚝 솟은, 높이 치솟은)
If you describe something such as a mountain or cliff as towering, you mean that it is very tall and therefore impressive.

복습 **plunge** [plʌndʒ] v. (갑자기) 거꾸러지다; 급락하다; n. (갑자기) 떨어져 내림; 급락
If something or someone plunges in a particular direction, especially into water, they fall, rush, or throw themselves in that direction.

복습 **massive** [mǽsiv] a. (육중하면서) 거대한; 엄청나게 심각한
Something that is massive is very large in size, quantity, or extent.

복습 **launch** [lɔ:ntʃ] n. 발사; 개시, 진수; v. 시작하다; 발사하다
A launch is the act of sending a missile, space vehicle, satellite, or other object into the air or into space.

복습 **pad** [pæd] n. (우주선) 발사대; (메모지 등의) 묶음; 패드; v. 소리 안 나게 걷다; 완충재를 대다 (launchpad n. 발사대)
A launchpad or launching pad is a platform from which rockets, missiles, or satellites are launched.

drop in idiom 잠깐 들르다
To drop in means to pay a short, informal visit to someone, often without arranging this in advance.

★ **investigate** [invéstəgèit] v. 수사하다, 조사하다, 살피다; 연구하다
If someone, especially an official, investigates an event, situation, or claim, they try to find out what happened or what is the truth.

★ **corridor** [kɔ́:ridər] n. 복도; 통로
A corridor is a long passage in a building or train, with doors and rooms on one or both sides.

복습 **guard** [ga:rd] n. 경비 요원; 경비, 감시; 보호물; v. 지키다, 보호하다
A guard is a specially organized group of people, such as soldiers or policemen, who protect or watch someone or something.

복습 **slide** [slaid] v. 슬며시 넣다; 미끄러지듯이 움직이다; n. 떨어짐; 미끄러짐
When something slides somewhere or when you slide it there, it moves there smoothly over or against something.

★ **reader** [rí:dər] **n.** 판독기, 판독 장치
A reader is a device or piece of software used for reading or obtaining data stored on tape, cards, or other media.

복습 **whoosh** [hwu:ʃ] **n.** 쉭 하는 소리; **v.** (아주 빠르게) 휙 하고 지나가다
People sometimes say 'whoosh' when they are emphasizing the fact that something happens very suddenly or very fast.

★ **access** [ǽkses] **v.** 들어가다; 접근하다; **n.** 입장, 접근
If you access a place, you get to and enter that place.

lair [lɛər] **n.** 은신처; (야생 동물의) 집, 굴
Someone's lair is the particular room or hiding place that they go to, especially when they want to get away from other people.

복습 **trap** [træp] **v.** (위험한 장소에) 가두다; (함정으로) 몰아넣다; **n.** 함정; 덫
If you are trapped somewhere, something falls onto you or blocks your way and prevents you from moving or escaping.

★★ **separate** [sépərèit] **a.** 별개의; 분리된; **v.** 분리하다, 나누다; 갈라지다
If you refer to separate things, you mean several different things, rather than just one thing.

복습 **doorway** [dɔ́:rwèi] **n.** 출입구
A doorway is a space in a wall where a door opens and closes.

torso [tɔ́:rsou] **n.** 몸통, 동체; 토르소(몸통만으로 된 조각상)
Your torso is the main part of your body, and does not include your head, arms, and legs.

elasticity [ilæstísəti] **n.** 탄성, 탄력성
The elasticity of a material or substance is its ability to return to its original shape, size, and condition after it has been stretched.

복습 **punch** [pʌnʧ] **v.** 주먹으로 치다; (자판 · 번호판 등을) 치다; **n.** 주먹으로 한 대 침
If you punch someone or something, you hit them hard with your fist.

복습 **conscious** [kánʃəs] **a.** 의식이 있는; 자각하는; 의도적인 (unconscious **a.** 의식을 잃은)
Someone who is unconscious is in a state similar to sleep, usually as the result of a serious injury or a lack of oxygen.

복습 **free** [fri:] **v.** (freed-freed) (갇히거나 걸린 데서) 풀어 주다; **a.** 자유로운; 무료의
If you free someone or something, you remove them from the place in which they have been trapped or become fixed.

set off idiom 출발하다
If you set off, you begin a journey.

Chapters 22~24

1. What did the robotic bird in the jungle do?

A. It chased Dash and Vi.

B. It uncovered Dash and Vi's identities.

C. It attacked a velocipod.

D. It set off an alarm.

2. What did Mirage do for Mr. Incredible?

A. She gave him access to the control panel.

B. She told him that his family was still alive.

C. She revealed details about Syndrome's plan.

D. She led him to Elastigirl.

3. What did Dash NOT do in the jungle?

A. Steer a velocipod into a wall

B. Fall off the edge of a cliff

C. Swing around on vines

D. Punch a guard at high speed

4. What happened when Violet became invisible?

A. A guard followed the sound of her voice.

B. A guard saw her footprints.

C. A guard hit her with his gun.

D. A guard gave up looking for her.

5. How did Dash and Violet escape together?

A. Dash picked up Violet and ran past the guards.

B. Dash picked up Violet and they tumbled down a hill.

C. Violet made a force field and Dash ran inside of it.

D. Violet made a force field and they floated away in it.

Check Your Reading Speed

1분에 몇 단어를 읽는지 리딩 속도를 측정해보세요.

$$\frac{\text{411 words}}{\text{reading time (} \quad \text{) sec}} \times 60 = (\quad) \text{ WPM}$$

Build Your Vocabulary

복습 **stare** [stεər] **v.** 빤히 쳐다보다, 응시하다; **n.** 빤히 쳐다보기, 응시
If you stare at someone or something, you look at them for a long time.

복습 **generate** [dʒénərèit] **v.** 발생시키다, 만들어 내다
To generate a form of energy or power means to produce it.

복습 **bubble** [bʌbl] **n.** 거품; (감정의) 약간; **v.** (감정이) 차오르다; 거품이 일다
Bubbles are small balls of air or gas in a liquid.

jeopardy [dʒépərdi] **n.** 위험
If someone or something is in jeopardy, they are in a dangerous situation where they might fail, be lost, or be destroyed.

복습 **roll one's eyes** **idiom** 눈을 굴리다
If you roll your eyes or if your eyes roll, they move round and upward to show you are bored or annoyed.

★ **annoy** [ənɔ́i] **v.** 짜증나게 하다; 귀찮게 하다 (annoyed **a.** 짜증이 난, 약이 오른)
If you are annoyed, you are fairly angry about something.

★ **grumble** [grʌmbl] **v.** 투덜거리다, 불평하다; **n.** 투덜댐; 불평
If someone grumbles, they complain about something in a bad-tempered way.

복습 **flame** [fleim] **v.** 활활 타오르다; 시뻘게지다; **n.** 불길, 불꽃; 격정 (flaming **a.** 불타는)
Flaming is used to describe something that is burning and producing a lot of flames.

복습 **distance** [dístəns] **n.** 먼 곳; 거리; **v.** (~에) 관여하지 않다 (in the distance **idiom** 저 멀리)
If you can see something in the distance, you can see it, far away from you.

복습 **yell** [jel] **v.** 고함치다, 소리 지르다; **n.** 고함, 외침
If you yell, you shout loudly, usually because you are excited, angry, or in pain.

warp [wɔːrp] **a.** 초광속의, 워프의; **v.** (원래의 모습을 잃고) 휘다
If someone or something moves at warp speed, they move at an extremely high speed.

복습 **glow** [glou] **n.** (은은한) 불빛; 홍조; **v.** 빛나다, 타다; (얼굴이) 상기되다
A glow is a dull, steady light, for example the light produced by a fire when there are no flames.

복습 **race** [reis] **v.** 쏜살같이 가다; 경주하다; **n.** 경주; 경쟁; 인종, 종족
If you race somewhere, you go there as quickly as possible.

outrun [àutrʌ́n] **v.** (outran-outrun) ~보다 더 빨리 달리다; 넘어서다, 웃돌다
If you outrun someone, you run faster than they do, and therefore are able to escape from them or to arrive somewhere before they do.

fireball [fáiərbɔːl] **n.** 불덩이, 화구
A fireball is a ball of fire, for example one at the center of a nuclear explosion.

복습 **in time** **idiom** 제때에, 시간 맞춰, 늦지 않게
If you are in time for a particular event, you are not too late for it.

복습 **roar** [rɔːr] **v.** 굉음을 내며 질주하다; 고함치다; 웅웅거리다; **n.** 함성; 울부짖는 듯한 소리
If something, usually a vehicle, roars somewhere, it goes there very fast, making a loud noise.

복습 **exhaust** [igzɔ́ːst] **n.** (자동차 등의) 배기가스; **v.** 기진맥진하게 하다; 다 써 버리다
The exhaust or the exhaust pipe is the pipe which carries the gas out of the engine of a vehicle.

exotic [igzátik] **a.** 이국적인; 외국의
Something that is exotic is unusual and interesting, usually because it comes from or is related to a distant country.

복습 **stiff** [stif] **a.** 뻣뻣한; 딱딱한, 경직된; 심한; **ad.** 몹시, 극심하게
If you are stiff, your muscles or joints hurt when you move, because of illness or because of too much exercise.

★ **identify** [aidéntəfài] **v.** (신원 등을) 확인하다; 찾다, 발견하다 (identification **n.** 신원 확인, 식별)
If someone asks you for some identification, they want to see something such as a driving licence, which proves who you are.

복습 **rub** [rʌb] **v.** (손 · 손수건 등을 대고) 문지르다; (두 손 등을) 맞비비다; **n.** 문지르기, 비비기
If you rub a part of your body, you move your hand or fingers backward and forward over it while pressing firmly.

⋆ **brilliant** [bríljənt] a. 아주 밝은, 눈부신; 훌륭한; (재능이) 뛰어난 (brilliantly ad. 눈부시게)
A brilliant color is extremely bright.

복습 **robotic** [roubátik] a. 로봇식의; 로봇 같은
Robotic equipment can perform certain tasks automatically.

⋆ **perch** [pəːrʧ] v. (무엇의 꼭대기나 끝에) 위치하다; n. 높은 자리
To perch somewhere means to be on the top or edge of something.

복습 **nearby** [nìərbái] a. 인근의, 가까운 곳의; ad. 가까운 곳에
If something is nearby, it is only a short distance away.

복습 **mesmerize** [mézməràiz] v. 마음을 사로잡다, 완전 넋을 빼놓다
If you are mesmerized by something, you are so interested in it or so attracted to it that you cannot think about anything else.

복습 **thrill** [θril] v. 열광시키다, 정말 신나게 하다; n. 흥분, 설렘; 전율 (thrilled a. 아주 흥분한, 신이 난)
If someone is thrilled, they are extremely pleased about something.

nudge [nʌdʒ] v. (살짝) 쿡 찌르다; 조금씩 밀면서 가다; n. (팔꿈치로 살짝) 쿡 찌르기
If you nudge someone, you push them gently, usually with your elbow, in order to draw their attention to something.

복습 **tilt** [tilt] v. 기울이다, (뒤로) 젖히다; (의견 · 상황 등이) 기울어지다; n. 기울어짐, 젖혀짐
If you tilt part of your body, usually your head, you move it slightly upward or to one side.

⋆ **enchant** [inʧǽnt] v. 황홀하게 하다; 마법을 걸다 (enchanted a. 황홀해하는)
If you are enchanted by someone or something, they cause you to have feelings of great delight or pleasure.

복습 **frown** [fraun] v. 얼굴을 찡그리다; 눈살을 찌푸리다; n. 찡그림, 찌푸림
When someone frowns, their eyebrows become drawn together, because they are annoyed or puzzled.

⋆ **mechanical** [məkǽnikəl] a. 기계와 관련된; (행동이) 기계적인
(mechanically ad. 기계적으로)
A mechanical device has parts that move when it is working, often using power from an engine or from electricity.

swivel [swívəl] v. 돌리다, 회전시키다; (몸 · 눈 · 고개를) 홱 돌리다; n. 회전 고리
If something swivels or if you swivel it, it turns around a central point so that it is facing in a different direction.

⋆ **beak** [bi:k] n. (새의) 부리
A bird's beak is the hard curved or pointed part of its mouth.

⋆ **shrill** [ʃril] a. 새된, 날카로운; v. 날카로운 소리를 내다
A shrill sound is high-pitched and unpleasant.

복습 **electronic** [ilektránik] a. 전자의, 전자 장비와 관련된
An electronic device has transistors or silicon chips which control and change the electric current passing through the device.

복습 **alarm** [əlá:rm] n. 경보 장치; 자명종; 불안, 공포; v. 불안하게 하다; 경보장치를 달다
An alarm is an automatic device that warns you of danger, for example by ringing a bell.

복습 **hesitate** [hézətèit] v. 망설이다, 주저하다; 거리끼다
If you hesitate, you do not speak or act for a short time, usually because you are uncertain, embarrassed, or worried about what you are going to say or do.

Check Your Reading Speed

1분에 몇 단어를 읽는지 리딩 속도를 측정해보세요.

$$\frac{\text{287 words}}{\text{reading time (\qquad) sec}} \times 60 = (\qquad)\ \text{WPM}$$

Build Your Vocabulary

silhouette [siluét] n. 외형, 윤곽, 실루엣; v. 실루엣으로 나타내다
The silhouette of something is the outline that it has, which often helps you to recognize it.

* **slender** [sléndər] a. 호리호리한, 날씬한
A slender person is attractively thin and graceful.

복습 **control** [kəntróul] n. (기계 · 차량의) 제어 장치; 통제, 제어; v. 지배하다; 조정하다
A control is a device such as a switch or lever which you use in order to operate a machine or other piece of equipment.

switch off idiom ~을 끄다
If you switch off something such as a light or a machine, or if it switches off, it stops working.

복습 **ray** [rei] n. 광선; 약간, 소량
Rays of light are narrow beams of light.

** **knee** [ni:] n. 무릎; v. 무릎으로 치다
Your knee is the place where your leg bends.

복습 **grab** [græb] v. (와락 · 단단히) 붙잡다; 급히 ~하다; n. 와락 잡아채려고 함
If you grab something, you take it or pick it up suddenly and roughly.

** **throat** [θróut] n. 목; 목구멍; 좁은 통로
Your throat is the front part of your neck.

복습 **gasp** [gæsp] v. 헉 하고 숨을 쉬다; 숨을 제대로 못 쉬다; n. 헉 하는 소리를 냄
When you gasp, you take a short quick breath through your mouth, especially when you are surprised, shocked, or in pain.

* **fury** [fjúəri] n. (격렬한) 분노, 격분; 흥분 상태
Fury is violent or very strong anger.

⁑ **lash** [læʃ] v. 심하게 나무라다; 후려치다, 채찍으로 때리다; n. 채찍, 끈; 속눈썹
If someone lashes you or lashes into you, they speak very angrily to you, criticizing you or saying you have done something wrong.

복습 **survive** [sərváiv] v. 살아남다, 생존하다
If a person or living thing survives in a dangerous situation such as an accident or an illness, they do not die.

복습 **crash** [kræʃ] n. (자동차 · 항공기) 사고; 요란한 소리; v. 부딪치다; 충돌하다; 굉음을 내다
A crash is an accident in which a moving vehicle hits something and is damaged or destroyed.

astound [əstáund] v. 경악시키다, 큰 충격을 주다 (astounded a. 경악한, 몹시 놀란)
If you are astounded by something, you are very shocked or surprised that it could exist or happen.

overjoyed [òuvərdʒɔ́id] a. 매우 기뻐하는
If you are overjoyed, you are extremely pleased about something.

복습 **doorway** [dɔ́:rwèi] n. 출입구
A doorway is a space in a wall where a door opens and closes.

복습 **be about to** idiom 막 ~하려는 참이다
If you are about to do something, you are going to do it immediately.

⋆ **fist** [fist] n. 주먹
Your hand is referred to as your fist when you have bent your fingers in toward the palm in order to hit someone, to make an angry gesture, or to hold something.

⁑ **faithful** [féiθfəl] a. 믿을 수 있는; 충실한, 성실한 (unfaithful a. 바람을 피우는)
If someone is unfaithful to their lover or to the person they are married to, they have a sexual relationship with someone else.

⋆ **creep** [kri:p] n. 너무 싫은 사람; v. 살금살금 움직이다; 기다
If you describe someone as a creep, you mean that you dislike them a great deal, especially because they are insincere and flatter people.

복습 **protest** [próutest] v. 항의하다, 이의를 제기하다; n. 항의; 시위
If you protest against something or about something, you say or show publicly that you object to it.

⋆ **betray** [bitréi] v. 배신하다, 배반하다; (원칙 등을) 저버리다
If you betray someone who loves or trusts you, your actions hurt and disappoint them.

복습 **jaw** [dʒɔ:] **n.** 턱
Your jaw is the lower part of your face below your mouth.

★ **trigger** [trígə:r] **v.** 작동시키다; 촉발시키다; **n.** (총의) 방아쇠
To trigger a bomb or system means to cause it to work.

★ **alert** [ələ́:rt] **n.** 경계경보; **a.** 경계하는; 기민한; **v.** (위험 등을) 알리다
The alert is a warning that something dangerous has happened or is going to happen.

복습 **security** [sikjúərəti] **n.** 경비 담당 부서; 보안, 경비; 안도감, 안심
Security refers to all the measures that are taken to protect a place, or to ensure that only people with permission enter it or leave it.

복습 **upset** [ʌpsét] **a.** 속상한, 마음이 상한; **v.** 속상하게 하다; (계획 · 상황 등이) 잘못되게 하다
If you are upset, you are unhappy or disappointed because something unpleasant has happened to you.

★ **suspect** [səspékt] **v.** 의심하다; 수상쩍어 하다; **n.** 용의자
If you suspect that something dishonest or unpleasant has been done, you believe that it has probably been done.

stow away **idiom** (배 · 비행기 등을) 몰래 타다
If someone stows away, they hide in a vehicle, ship, or plane in order to travel without permission.

★★ **strike** [straik] **v.** 인상을 주다; (세게) 치다, 부딪치다; **n.** 공격; 치기, 때리기
(strike a tone **idiom** ~의 감정을 나타내다)
To strike a tone means to express and communicate a particular opinion or feeling about something.

★★ **proper** [prápər] **a.** 적절한, 제대로 된; 올바른, 정당한
The proper thing is the one that is correct or most suitable.

복습 **tone** [toun] **n.** 어조, 말투; (글 등의) 분위기; 음색
Someone's tone is a quality in their voice which shows what they are feeling or thinking.

Check Your Reading Speed

1분에 몇 단어를 읽는지 리딩 속도를 측정해보세요.

$$\frac{\text{888 words}}{\text{reading time (\qquad) sec}} \times 60 = (\qquad) \text{ WPM}$$

Build Your Vocabulary

복습 **blind** [blaind] a. 앞이 안 보이는; 눈이 먼; 눈치 채지 못하는; n. (창문에 치는) 블라인드; v. (잠시) 앞이 안 보이게 하다 (blindly ad. 앞이 안 보이는 채)
If you do something blindly, you do it without noticing what is around you, for example because you are excited or upset.

out of breath idiom 숨을 헐떡이며, 숨이 차서
If you are out of breath, you are breathing very quickly and with difficulty because you have been doing something energetic.

복습 **stop in one's tracks** idiom 갑자기 딱 멈추다
If you stop in your tracks or stop dead in your tracks, you suddenly stop moving because you are very surprised, impressed, or frightened.

복습 **arm** [a:rm] v. 무장하다; 폭발하게 하다; n. 무기, 화기; 팔 (armed a. 무장한, 무기를 가진)
Someone who is armed is carrying a weapon, usually a gun.

* **terrify** [térəfài] v. (몹시) 무섭게 하다 (terrified a. (몹시) 무서워하는, 겁이 난)
If something terrifies you, it makes you feel extremely frightened.

복습 **bolt** [boult] v. 달아나다; 빗장을 지르다; n. (물 등의) 분출; 볼트
If a person or animal bolts, they suddenly start to run very fast, often because something has frightened them.

복습 **lightning** [láitniŋ] a. 아주 빨리; 급작스럽게; n. 번개, 번갯불
Lightning describes things that happen very quickly or last for only a short time.

복습 **trail** [treil] n. 자국, 흔적; 자취; v. 끌다; 뒤쫓다, 추적하다
(hot on one's trail idiom 바짝 뒤쫓아)
If you are hot on someone's or something's trail, you are very close behind them, and about to catch them.

★ **vine** [vain] **n.** 덩굴식물; 포도나무
A vine is a plant that grows up or over things, especially one which produces grapes.

undergrowth [ʌ́ndərgrouθ] **n.** 덤불, 관목
Undergrowth consists of bushes and plants growing together under the trees in a forest.

복습 **dense** [dens] **a.** 빽빽한, 밀집한; (앞이 안 보이게) 짙은, 자욱한
Something that is dense contains a lot of things or people in a small area.

복습 **force** [fɔ:rs] **v.** 억지로 ~하다; ~를 강요하다; **n.** 작용력; 힘; 영향력
If a situation or event forces you to do something, it makes it necessary for you to do something that you would not otherwise have done.

stick to **idiom** ~을 (바꾸지 않고) 지키다
If you stick to something, you keep using or doing one particular thing and not change to anything else.

복습 **narrow** [nǽrou] **a.** 좁은; **v.** (눈을) 찌푸리다; 좁히다
Something that is narrow measures a very small distance from one side to the other, especially compared to its length or height.

복습 **rocket** [rákit] **v.** 로켓처럼 가다, 돌진하다; 급증하다; **n.** 로켓; 로켓 추진 미사일
If something such as a vehicle rockets somewhere, it moves there very quickly.

★ **swarm** [swɔ:rm] **n.** (곤충의) 떼, 무리; 군중; **v.** 많이 모여들다; 무리를 지어 다니다
A swarm of bees or other insects is a large group of them flying together.

★★ **choke** [ʧouk] **v.** 숨이 막히다; (목소리가) 잠기다; 채우다; **n.** 숨이 막힘
When you choke or when something chokes you, you cannot breathe properly or get enough air into your lungs.

복습 **smash** [smæʃ] **v.** (세게) 부딪치다; 박살내다; 부서지다; **n.** 박살내기; 요란한 소리
If something smashes or is smashed against something solid, it moves very fast and with great force against it.

windshield [wíndʃi:ld] **n.** (자동차 등의) 앞 유리
The windshield of a car or other vehicle is the glass window at the front through which the driver looks.

복습 **tumble** [tʌmbl] **v.** 굴러떨어지다; 폭삭 무너지다; **n.** (갑자기) 굴러떨어짐; 폭락
If someone or something tumbles somewhere, they fall there with a rolling or bouncing movement.

복습 **rub** [rʌb] v. (손 · 손수건 등을 대고) 문지르다; (두 손 등을) 맞비비다; n. 문지르기, 비비기
If you rub an object or a surface, you move a cloth backward and forward over it in order to clean or dry it.

★ **spatter** [spǽtəːr] v. (액체 방울 등이) 튀다; 후두두 떨어지다; n. (액체 등이) 튀는 것
If a liquid spatters a surface or you spatter a liquid over a surface, drops of the liquid fall on an area of the surface.

★ **sleeve** [sliːv] n. (옷의) 소매, 소맷자락
The sleeves of a coat, shirt, or other item of clothing are the parts that cover your arms.

복습 **sputter** [spʌ́tər] v. (분노 · 충격으로) 식식거리며 말하다; 털털거리는 소리를 내다
If you sputter, you speak or say something in a confused way, often while taking short quick breaths, for example because you are shocked or angry.

복습 **spit** [spit] v. (~을) 뱉다; ~에서 나오다; n. 침; (침 등을) 뱉기
If you spit liquid or food somewhere, you force a small amount of it out of your mouth.

복습 **burst** [bəːrst] v. (burst-burst) 불쑥 움직이다; 갑자기 ~하다; n. (갑자기) ~을 함; 파열, 폭발
To burst into or out of a place means to enter or leave it suddenly with a lot of energy or force.

복습 **tear** [tɛər] ① v. 부리나케 가다; 뜯어 내다; 찢다, 뜯다; n. 찢어진 곳, 구멍 ② n. 눈물
If you tear somewhere, you move there very quickly, often in an uncontrolled or dangerous way.

복습 **zoom** [zuːm] v. 쌩 하고 가다; 급등하다; n. (빠르게) 쌩 하고 지나가는 소리
If you zoom somewhere, you go there very quickly.

복습 **swing** [swiŋ] v. (swung-swung) 휙 움직이다; (전후 · 좌우로) 흔들다; 방향을 바꾸다; n. 흔들기; 휘두르기
If something swings in a particular direction or if you swing it in that direction, it moves in that direction with a smooth, curving movement.

★ **arc** [aːrk] n. 둥근 (활) 모양; 호, 원호; v. 활 모양을 그리다
An arc is a smoothly curving line or movement.

veer [viər] v. 방향을 홱 틀다; (성격을) 바꾸다
If something veers in a certain direction, it suddenly moves in that direction.

복습 **immediate** [imíːdiət] a. 즉각적인; 당면한; 아주 가까이에 있는 (immediately ad. 즉시, 즉각)
If something happens immediately, it happens without any delay.

propel [prəpél] **v.** 나아가게 하다; 몰고 가다
To propel something in a particular direction means to cause it to move in that direction.

복습 **snap** [snæp] **v.** 툭 부러지다; 탁 하고 움직이다; 급히 움직이다; 날카롭게 말하다; **n.** 탁 하는 소리
If something snaps or if you snap it, it breaks suddenly, usually with a sharp cracking noise.

복습 **realize** [ríːəlàiz] **v.** 깨닫다, 알아차리다; 실현하다, 달성하다
If you realize that something is true, you become aware of that fact or understand it.

edge [edʒ] **n.** 끝, 가장자리; 우위; **v.** 조금씩 움직이다; 테두리를 두르다
The edge of something is the place or line where it stops, or the part of it that is furthest from the middle.

cliff [klif] **n.** 절벽, 낭떠러지
A cliff is a high area of land with a very steep side, especially one next to the sea.

thud [θʌd] **n.** 쿵 (하는 소리); **v.** 쿵 치다; (심장이) 쿵쿵거리다
A thud is a dull sound, such as that which a heavy object makes when it hits something soft.

복습 **land** [lænd] **v.** (땅 · 표면에) 내려앉다, 착륙하다; 놓다, 두다; **n.** 육지, 땅; 지역
When someone or something lands, they come down to the ground after moving through the air or falling.

복습 **hood** [hud] **n.** (자동차 등의) 덮개; (외투 등에 달린) 모자
The hood of a car is the metal cover over the engine at the front.

복습 **duck** [dʌk] **v.** (머리나 몸을) 휙 수그리다; 급히 움직이다; **n.** [동물] 오리
If you duck, you move your head or the top half of your body quickly downward to avoid something that might hit you, or to avoid being seen.

sock [sak] **v.** 세게 치다, 강타하다; **n.** 양말
If you sock someone, you hit them with your fist.

복습 **jaw** [dʒɔː] **n.** 턱
Your jaw is the lower part of your face below your mouth.

복습 **knock** [nak] **v.** 치다, 부딪치다; (문 등을) 두드리다; **n.** 문 두드리는 소리; 부딪침
To knock someone into a particular position or condition means to hit them very hard so that they fall over or become unconscious.

복습 **slam** [slæm] v. 세게 치다, 놓다; 쾅 닫다; n. 쾅 하고 닫기; 탕 하는 소리
If one thing slams into or against another, it crashes into it with great force.

vaporize [véipəràiz] v. 증발하다; 증발시키다
If a liquid or solid vaporizes or if you vaporize it, it changes into vapor or gas.

☆ **branch** [bræntʃ] n. 나뭇가지; 지사, 분점; v. 갈라지다, 나뉘다
The branches of a tree are the parts that grow out from its trunk and have leaves, flowers, or fruit growing on them.

flail [fleil] v. 마구 움직이다; (팔다리를) 마구 흔들다
If your arms or legs flail or if you flail them about, they wave about in an energetic but uncontrolled way.

복습 **enormous** [inɔ́:rməs] a. 막대한, 거대한
Something that is enormous is extremely large in size or amount.

복습 **survive** [sərváiv] v. 살아남다, 생존하다
If a person or living thing survives in a dangerous situation such as an accident or an illness, they do not die.

whoop [hu:p] n. 와 하는 함성; v. (기쁨 · 흥분 등으로) 와 하고 함성을 지르다
A whoop is a loud, excited shout, especially showing your enjoyment of or agreement with something.

☆ **victory** [víktəri] n. 승리
A victory is a success in a struggle, war, or competition.

복습 **nearby** [nìərbái] a. 인근의, 가까운 곳의; ad. 가까운 곳에
If something is nearby, it is only a short distance away.

복습 **lagoon** [ləgú:n] n. 석호(潟湖)
A lagoon is an area of calm sea water that is separated from the ocean by a line of rock or sand.

복습 **charge** [ʧa:rdʒ] v. 급히 가다, 달려가다; (요금 · 값을) 청구하다; n. 책임, 담당; 요금
If you charge toward someone or something, you move quickly and aggressively toward them.

복습 **skim** [skim] v. (표면을) 스치듯 하며 지나가다; 훑어보다; 걷어 내다
If something skims a surface, it moves quickly along just above it.

복습 **surface** [sə́:rfis] n. 수면, 표면, 지면; 외관; v. 수면으로 올라오다; (갑자기) 나타나다
The surface of something is the flat top part of it or the outside of it.

복습 **blast** [blæst] v. 빠르게 가다; 확 뿌리다; 폭발시키다; n. 폭발; (한 줄기의) 강한 바람
If someone or something blasts in a particular direction, they move very quickly and loudly in that direction.

★ **weave** [wiːv] v. 이리저리 빠져 나가다, 누비며 가다; (옷감 등을) 짜다; n. (직물을) 짜는 법
If you weave your way somewhere, you move between and around things as you go there.

복습 **volcano** [valkéinou] n. 화산 (volcanic a. 화산의)
Volcanic means coming from or created by volcanoes.

jut [dʒʌt] v. 돌출하다, 튀어나오다; 내밀다
If something juts out, it sticks out above or beyond a surface.

★ **dart** [daːrt] v. 쏜살같이 움직이다; 흘깃 쳐다보다; n. (작은) 화살; 쏜살같이 달림
If a person or animal darts somewhere, they move there suddenly and quickly.

복습 **cave** [keiv] n. 동굴
A cave is a large hole in the side of a cliff or hill, or one that is under the ground.

복습 **frantic** [frǽntik] a. (두려움 · 걱정으로) 제정신이 아닌; 정신없이 서두는 (frantically ad. 미친 듯이)
If you are frantic, you are behaving in a wild and uncontrolled way because you are frightened or worried.

복습 **relieve** [rilíːv] v. 안도하다; (불쾌감 · 고통 등을) 없애 주다; 완화하다 (relieved a. 안도하는)
If you are relieved, you feel happy because something unpleasant has not happened or is no longer happening.

복습 **boom** [buːm] n. 쾅 (하는 소리); v. 쾅 하는 소리를 내다; 굵은 목소리로 말하다
A boom is a deep loud sound that continues for some time, for example the noise of thunder or an explosion.

★ **collide** [kəláid] v. 충돌하다, 부딪치다; (의견 등이) 상충하다
If two or more moving people or objects collide, they crash into one another.

복습 **scan** [skæn] v. (유심히) 살피다; (빛 · 레이더 등이) 훑다; 정밀 촬영하다; n. 정밀 검사
When you scan a place or group of people, you look at it carefully, usually because you are looking for something or someone.

★ **rifle** [raifl] n. 라이플총, 소총; v. 샅샅이 뒤지다; 훔치다
A rifle is a gun with a long barrel.

복습 **sign** [sain] n. 기색, 흔적; 표지판; 몸짓; v. 서명하다; 신호를 보내다
If there is a sign of something, there is something which shows that it exists or is happening.

복습 **visible** [vízəbl] a. (눈에) 보이는, 알아볼 수 있는; 뚜렷한 (invisible a. 보이지 않는)
If you describe something as invisible, you mean that it cannot be seen, for example because it is transparent, hidden, or very small.

★★★ **club** [klʌb] v. (곤봉 등으로) 때리다; n. 클럽, 동호회; 곤봉
To club a person or animal means to hit them hard with a thick heavy stick or a similar weapon.

★★ **command** [kəmǽnd] v. 명령하다, 지시하다; 지휘하다; n. 명령; 지휘, 통솔
If someone in authority commands you to do something, they tell you that you must do it.

복습 **fire** [faiər] v. 발사하다; (엔진이) 점화되다; 해고하다; n. 화재, 불; 발사, 총격
If someone fires a gun or a bullet, or if they fire, a bullet is sent from a gun that they are using.

복습 **leash** [liːʃ] v. 속박하다, 억제하다; 가죽끈으로 매다; n. 가죽 끈; 통제
(unleash v. 풀어놓다; 해방하다)
If you say that someone or something unleashes a powerful force, feeling, activity, or group, you mean that they suddenly start it or send it somewhere.

복습 **barrage** [bərá:ʒ] n. 일제 엄호 사격; (질문 등의) 세례
A barrage is continuous firing on an area with large guns and tanks.

복습 **bullet** [búlit] n. 총알
A bullet is a small piece of metal with a pointed or rounded end, which is fired out of a gun.

footprint [fútprìnt] n. (사람 · 동물의) 발자국
A footprint is a mark in the shape of a foot that a person or animal makes in or on a surface.

복습 **splash** [splæʃ] n. 첨벙 하는 소리; (어디에 떨어지는) 방울; v. 첨벙거리다; (물 등을) 끼얹다
A splash is the sound made when something hits water or falls into it.

★ **ripple** [ripl] v. 잔물결을 이루다; (감정 등이) 파문처럼 번지다; n. 잔물결, 파문 (모양의 것)
When the surface of an area of water ripples or when something ripples it, a number of little waves appear on it.

★★ **mass** [mæs] n. 덩어리; (많은 사람 · 사물의) 무리; a. 대량의, 대규모의
A mass of something is a large amount of it.

★ **handful** [hǽndfùl] **n.** 줌, 움큼; 몇 안 되는 수
A handful of something is the amount of it that you can hold in your hand.

★ **outline** [áutlàin] **n.** 윤곽; **v.** 윤곽을 보여주다; 개요를 서술하다
The outline of something is its general shape, especially when it cannot be clearly seen.

murky [mə́:rki] **a.** (진흙 등으로) 흐린, 탁한
Murky water or fog is so dark and dirty that you cannot see through it.

★★★ **aim** [eim] **n.** 겨냥, 조준; 목적; **v.** 겨누다; 목표하다
When you take aim, you point a weapon or object at someone or something, before firing or throwing it.

make a run for **idiom** ~를 향해 달려가다
If you make a run for something, you run toward something trying to reach it.

throttle [θratl] **n.** (자동차 등의 연료) 조절판; **v.** 목을 조르다 (full throttle **idiom** 전속력으로)
If you do something at full throttle, you do it with as much speed and energy as you can.

복습 **stun** [stʌn] **v.** 어리벙벙하게 하다; 깜짝 놀라게 하다; 기절시키다
If you are stunned by something, you are extremely shocked or surprised by it and are therefore unable to speak or do anything.

복습 **trigger** [trígə:r] **n.** (총의) 방아쇠; **v.** 작동시키다; 촉발시키다
The trigger of a gun is a small lever which you pull to fire it.

복습 **click** [klik] **v.** 딸깍 하는 소리를 내다; 분명해지다; **n.** 딸깍 (하는 소리)
If something clicks or if you click it, it makes a short, sharp sound.

복습 **leap** [li:p] **v.** (서둘러) ~하다; 뛰다, 뛰어오르다; **n.** 높이뛰기, 도약; 급증
If you leap somewhere, you move there suddenly and quickly.

복습 **field** [fi:ld] **n.** ~장; 경기장; 들판, 밭
A magnetic, gravitational, or electric field is the area in which that particular force is strong enough to have an effect.

복습 **amaze** [əméiz] **v.** (대단히) 놀라게 하다; 경악하게 하다 (amazed **a.** 놀란)
If something amazes you, it surprises you very much.

★★ **float** [flout] **v.** (물 위나 공중에서) 떠가다; (물에) 뜨다; **n.** 부표
Something that floats in or through the air hangs in it or moves slowly and gently through it.

복습 **midair** [midέər] **n.** 공중, 상공
If something happens in midair, it happens in the air, rather than on the ground.

복습 **suspend** [səspénd] **v.** (움직이지 않고) 떠 있다; 매달다, 걸다; 중단하다
If something is suspended from a high place, it is hanging from that place.

ricochet [ríkəʃéi] **v.** ~에 맞고 튀어 나오다; **n.** (어떤 것에 맞고) 튀어 나옴
When a bullet ricochets, it hits a surface and bounces away from it.

복습 **enthusiastic** [inθù:ziǽstik] **a.** 열렬한, 열광적인 (enthusiastically **ad.** 열광적으로)
If you are enthusiastic about something, you show how much you like or enjoy it by the way that you behave and talk.

복습 **wheel** [hwi:l] **n.** 바퀴; (자동차 등의) 핸들; **v.** (바퀴 달린 것을) 밀다
A wheel is a circular object which forms a part of a machine, usually a moving part.

복습 **rumble** [rʌmbl] **v.** 덜커덩거리며 나아가다; 웅웅거리는 소리를 내다; **n.** 우르렁거리는 소리
If a vehicle rumbles somewhere, it moves slowly forward while making a low continuous noise.

⋆ **hillside** [hílsàid] **n.** (작은 산 · 언덕의) 비탈, 산비탈
A hillside is the sloping side of a hill.

1. How did Syndrome capture the Incredibles in the jungle?

A. He knocked them over with a velocipod.

B. He disintegrated their force field with a remote control.

C. He used his immobi-ray to trap them.

D. He called out to his guards to surround them.

2. What was Syndrome planning to do in Metroville?

A. Make the people believe he was a Super

B. Destroy the people with his Omnidroid

C. Show the people that he was the best inventor ever

D. Convince the people that heroes were not real

3. What did Vi realize about the rocket in the launching bay?

A. It could be flown just like a plane.

B. It could get to the city as fast as a jet.

C. It could not be accessed without the correct password.

D. It could go to the same place as the previously launched rocket.

4. What did Lucius do when he saw the Omnidroid?

A. He searched for a weapon to use against it.

B. He thought of a way to defeat it.

C. He started looking for his Super suit.

D. He told his wife to cancel their dinner plans.

5. What did NOT happen after Syndrome fake-punched the Omnidroid?

A. Syndrome sent a signal to the Omnidroid's arm through a remote.

B. The people watching were suspicious of Syndrome's abilities.

C. The Omnidroid's arm fell off and landed in the street.

D. The Omnidroid realized that Syndrome was trying to control it.

Check Your Reading Speed

1분에 몇 단어를 읽는지 리딩 속도를 측정해보세요.

$$\frac{\text{397 words}}{\text{reading time (}\qquad\text{) sec}} \times 60 = (\qquad) \text{ WPM}$$

Build Your Vocabulary

복습 **jungle** [dʒʌŋgl] **n.** 밀림 (지대), 정글
A jungle is a forest in a tropical country where large numbers of tall trees and plants grow very close together.

side by side idiom 나란히; 함께
If two people or things are side by side, they are next to each other.

★ **apologize** [əpálədʒàiz] **v.** 사과하다
When you apologize to someone, you say that you are sorry that you have hurt them or caused trouble for them.

복습 **exclaim** [ikskléim] **v.** 소리치다, 외치다
If you exclaim, you cry out suddenly in surprise, strong emotion, or pain.

godforsaken [gádfərseikən] **a.** 황폐한, 쓸쓸한
If you say that somewhere is a godforsaken place, you dislike it a lot because you find it very boring and depressing.

pick a fight idiom (~에게) 싸움을 걸다
If someone picks a fight with you, they deliberately start a fight or an argument with you.

복습 **explode** [iksplóud] **v.** 폭발하다; (갑자기 강한 감정을) 터뜨리다 (explosion **n.** 폭발)
An explosion is a sudden, violent burst of energy, for example one caused by a bomb.

복습 **echo** [ékou] **v.** (소리가) 울리다; 그대로 따라 하다; **n.** (소리의) 울림, 메아리; 반복
If a sound echoes, it is reflected off a surface and can be heard again after the original sound has stopped.

복습 **barely** [bɛ́ərli] **ad.** 간신히, 가까스로; 거의 ~아니게
You use barely to say that something is only just true or only just the case.

복습 **chase** [ʧeis] v. 뒤쫓다, 추적하다; 추구하다; n. 추적, 추격; 추구함
If you chase someone, or chase after them, you run after them or follow them quickly in order to catch or reach them.

복습 **pod** [pad] n. (우주선 · 선박의 본체에서) 분리 가능한 부분; (콩이 들어 있는) 꼬투리
A pod is a detachable or self-contained unit on an aircraft, spacecraft, vehicle, or vessel, having a particular function.

복습 **burst** [bəːrst] v. (burst-burst) 불쑥 움직이다; 갑자기 ~하다; n. (갑자기) ~을 함; 파열, 폭발
To burst into or out of a place means to enter or leave it suddenly with a lot of energy or force.

⋆ **flatten** [flætn] v. 납작하게 하다; 때려눕히다
If you flatten something or if it flattens, it becomes flat or flatter.

dough [dou] n. 밀가루 반죽; 돈
Dough is a fairly firm mixture of flour, water, and sometimes also fat and sugar. It can be cooked to make bread, pastry, and biscuits.

rolling pin [róuliŋ pin] n. (반죽을 미는) 밀방망이
A rolling pin is a cylinder that you roll backward and forward over uncooked pastry in order to make the pastry flat.

disintegrate [disíntəgrèit] v. 해체하다, 산산조각 나다; 붕괴되다
If an object or substance disintegrates, it breaks into many small pieces or parts and is destroyed.

복습 **hug** [hʌg] v. 껴안다, 포옹하다; n. 포옹
When you hug someone, you put your arms around them and hold them tightly.

복습 **stretch** [streʧ] v. (길이 · 폭 등을) 늘이다; 펼쳐지다; 기지개를 켜다; n. (길게) 뻗은 구간; 기간
When something soft or elastic stretches or is stretched, it becomes longer or bigger as well as thinner, usually because it is pulled.

복습 **guard** [gaːrd] n. 경비 요원; 경비, 감시; 보호물; v. 지키다, 보호하다
A guard is a specially organized group of people, such as soldiers or policemen, who protect or watch someone or something.

⋆ **harmony** [háːrməni] n. 조화, 화합; 화음
If people are living in harmony with each other, they are living together peacefully rather than fighting or arguing.

★ **plow** [plau] v. 충돌하다, 들이받다; (밭을) 경작하다; n. 쟁기
To plow into someone or something means to crash into them with force, especially because you are moving or driving too quickly or in a careless or uncontrolled way.

★ **coil** [kɔil] v. (고리 모양으로) 감다, 휘감다; n. 고리; 전선
If you coil something, you wind it into a series of loops or into the shape of a ring.

복습 **pilot** [páilət] n. 조종사, 비행사
A pilot is a person who is trained to fly an aircraft.

whiplash [hwíplæʃ] v. 채찍질하다; 아프게 하다; n. 채찍질
To whiplash means to beat, hit, or throw someone or something with or as if with a whiplash.

out cold idiom 의식을 잃고, 기절하여, 깊이 잠들어 있는
If someone is out cold, they are unconscious or sleeping very heavily.

복습 **emerge** [imə́:rdʒ] v. 나오다, 모습을 드러내다; (어려움 등을) 헤쳐 나오다
To emerge means to come out from an enclosed or dark space such as a room or a vehicle, or from a position where you could not be seen.

★ **litter** [lítər] v. 흐트러져 어지럽히다; (쓰레기 등을) 버리다; n. 쓰레기
If a number of things litter a place, they are scattered untidily around it or over it.

복습 **admire** [ædmáiər] v. 감탄하며 바라보다; 존경하다, 칭찬하다 (admiration n. 감탄, 존경)
Admiration is a feeling of great liking and respect for a person or thing.

★ **react** [riǽkt] v. 반응하다; 반응을 보이다
When you react to something that has happened to you, you behave in a particular way because of it.

복습 **blur** [blə:r] n. 흐릿한 형체; v. 흐릿해지다; 모호해지다
A blur is a shape or area which you cannot see clearly because it has no distinct outline or because it is moving very fast.

복습 **match** [mæʧ] n. 경쟁 상대; 똑같은 것; 성냥; v. 어울리다; 일치하다; 맞먹다
If one person or thing is no match for another, they are unable to compete successfully with the other person or thing.

time out [táim aut] int. 잠깐 중지!; 기다려!; n. (경기 중간의) 타임아웃
You use 'time out' to tell people to stop what they are doing, especially when they are having a disagreement.

motionless [móuʃənlis] a. 움직이지 않는, 가만히 있는
Someone or something that is motionless is not moving at all.

복습 **midair** [midέər] n. 공중, 상공
If something happens in midair, it happens in the air, rather than on the ground.

복습 **cross** [krɔːs] v. 서로 겹치게 놓다; 반대하다; (가로질러) 건너다; n. 십자 기호
If you cross your arms, legs, or fingers, you put one of them on top of the other.

⋆ **assess** [əsés] v. (특성·자질 등을) 재다; 평가하다, 가늠하다
When you assess a person, thing, or situation, you consider them in order to make a judgment about them.

복습 **scene** [siːn] n. 현장; 장면, 광경; 풍경
The scene of an event is the place where it happened.

⋆ **amuse** [əmjúːz] v. 즐겁게 하다, 재미있게 하다 (amused a. 재미있어 하는)
If you are amused by something, it makes you want to laugh or smile.

복습 **narrow** [nǽrou] v. (눈을) 찌푸리다; 좁히다; a. 좁은
If your eyes narrow or if you narrow your eyes, you almost close them, for example because you are angry or because you are trying to concentrate on something.

jackpot [dʒǽkpɑ̀t] n. 거액의 상금, 대박 (hit the jackpot idiom 대박을 터뜨리다)
If you hit the jackpot, you have a great success, for example by winning a lot of money or having a piece of good luck.

relish [réliʃ] v. (대단히) 즐기다; n. (큰) 즐거움
If you relish something, you get a lot of enjoyment from it.

Check Your Reading Speed

1분에 몇 단어를 읽는지 리딩 속도를 측정해보세요.

$$\frac{\text{644 words}}{\text{reading time (\qquad) sec}} \times 60 = (\qquad) \text{ WPM}$$

Build Your Vocabulary

복습 **prison** [prizn] n. 교도소, 감옥
A prison is a building where criminals are kept as punishment or where people accused of a crime are kept before their trial.

복습 **chamber** [ʧéimbər] n. (특정 목적용) -실(室); 회의실; (지하의) 공간
A chamber is a room designed and equipped for a particular purpose.

★ **captive** [kǽptiv] a. 사로잡힌, 억류된; 마음을 빼앗긴; n. 포로
A captive person or animal is being kept imprisoned or enclosed.

복습 **ray** [rei] n. 광선; 약간, 소량
Rays of light are narrow beams of light.

복습 **side by side** idiom 나란히; 함께
If two people or things are side by side, they are next to each other.

newscast [njú:zkæst] n. 뉴스 방송
A newscast is a news program that is broadcast on the radio or on television.

복습 **crowd** [kraud] n. 사람들, 군중; v. 가득 메우다; 바싹 붙어 서다
A crowd is a large group of people who have gathered together, for example to watch or listen to something interesting, or to protest about something.

★★ **gather** [gǽðər] v. (사람들이) 모이다; (여기저기 있는 것을) 모으다
If people gather somewhere or if someone gathers people somewhere, they come together in a group.

smolder [smóuldər] v. (서서히) 타다; (속으로) 들끓다
If something smolders, it burns slowly, producing smoke but not flames.

★ **craft** [kræft] n. 항공기; 공예; 기술, 기교; v. 공예품을 만들다; 공들여 만들다
You can refer to a boat, a spacecraft, or an aircraft as a craft.

복습 **react** [riǽkt] **v.** 반응하다; 반응을 보이다 (reaction **n.** 반응, 반작용)
Your reaction to something that has happened or something that you have experienced is what you feel, say, or do because of it.

* **destruction** [distrʌ́kʃən] **n.** 파괴, 파멸; 말살
Destruction is the action or process of causing so much damage to something that it no longer exists or cannot be repaired.

복습 **dramatic** [drəmǽtik] **a.** 감격적인, 인상적인; 극적인; 과장된 (dramatically **ad.** 극적으로)
A dramatic action, event, or situation is exciting and impressive.

복습 **damage** [dǽmidʒ] **n.** 손상, 피해; 훼손; **v.** 손상을 주다, 피해를 입히다, 훼손하다
Damage is physical harm that is caused to an object.

* **throng** [θrɔːŋ] **n.** 군중, 인파; **v.** 떼 지어 모이다
A throng is a large crowd of people.

save the day **idiom** 곤경을 면하게 하다; 궁지를 벗어나다
If you save the day, you do something that prevents a situation from becoming unpleasant, embarrassing, or unsuccessful.

복습 **defeat** [difíːt] **v.** 물리치다; 좌절시키다; 이해가 안 되다; **n.** 패배
If you defeat someone, you win a victory over them in a battle, game, or contest.

cynical [sínikəl] **a.** 빈정대는, 냉소적인, 비꼬는 (cynically **ad.** 냉소적으로)
If you describe someone as cynical, you mean they believe that people always act selfishly.

* **precious** [préʃəs] **a.** 소중한; 귀중한, 값비싼; **ad.** 정말 거의 없는
If something is precious to you, you regard it as important and do not want to lose it.

복습 **heroic** [hiróuik] **n.** (pl.) 영웅적 행동; **a.** 영웅적인, 용감무쌍한; 영웅의
Heroics are actions involving bravery, courage, or determination.

복습 **spectacular** [spektǽkjulər] **a.** 극적인; 장관을 이루는; **n.** 화려한 쇼
Something that is spectacular is very impressive or dramatic.

cackle [kækl] **v.** (불쾌하게) 낄낄 웃다, 키득거리다; **n.** 낄낄거림
If someone cackles, they laugh in a loud unpleasant way, often at something bad that happens to someone else.

복습 **invent** [invént] **v.** 발명하다; (사실이 아닌 것을) 지어내다 (invention **n.** 발명품)
An invention is a machine, device, or system that has been invented by someone.

복습 **exit** [égzit] v. 나가다, 떠나다; 퇴장하다; n. (고속도로의) 출구; (공공건물의) 출구; 퇴장
If you exit from a room or building, you leave it.

복습 **triumph** [tráiəmf] n. 승리감, 환희; 업적, 승리; v. 승리를 거두다, 이기다
Triumph is a feeling of great satisfaction and pride resulting from a success or victory.

hang one's head idiom 낙담하다; 부끄러워 고개를 숙이다
If you hang your head, you are ashamed and discouraged.

복습 **fault** [fɔːlt] n. 잘못, 책임; 결점
If a bad or undesirable situation is your fault, you caused it or are responsible for it.

lousy [láuzi] a. 형편없는; (아주) 안 좋은, 엉망인
If you describe someone as lousy, you mean that they are very bad at something they do.

복습 **blind** [blaind] a. 눈치 채지 못하는; 앞이 안 보이는; 눈이 먼; n. (창문에 치는) 블라인드; v. (잠시) 앞이 안 보이게 하다
If you say that someone is blind to a fact or a situation, you mean that they ignore it or are unaware of it, although you think that they should take notice of it or be aware of it.

복습 **notice** [nóutis] v. 알아채다, 인지하다; 주의하다; n. 신경 씀, 알아챔; 통지, 예고
If you notice something or someone, you become aware of them.

복습 **suspend** [səspénd] v. (움직이지 않고) 떠 있다; 매달다, 걸다; 중단하다
If something is suspended from a high place, it is hanging from that place.

복습 **panel** [pænl] n. (자동차 등의) 계기판; 판; 패널, 자문단
A control panel or instrument panel is a board or surface which contains switches and controls to operate a machine or piece of equipment.

obsess [əbsés] v. 집착하게 하다; (~에 대해) 끙끙거리며 걱정하다 (obsessed a. 집착하는)
If someone is obsessed with a person or thing, they keep thinking about them and find it difficult to think about anything else.

복습 **value** [vǽljuː] v. (가치 · 가격을) 평가하다; 소중하게 생각하다; n. 가치; 중요성, 유용성 (undervalue v. 과소평가하다, 경시하다)
If you undervalue something or someone, you fail to recognize how valuable or important they are.

복습 **be lost in** idiom ~에 빠져 있다
If you are lost in something, you are too interested in it, or concentrating so hard on it, that you do not notice other things around you.

★ **confess** [kənfés] v. 고백하다, 인정하다; 자백하다 (confession n. 고백, 인정)
Confession is the act of admitting that you have done something that you are ashamed of or embarrassed about.

복습 **interrupt** [ìntərʌ́pt] v. (말 · 행동을) 방해하다; 중단시키다; 차단하다
If you interrupt someone who is speaking, you say or do something that causes them to stop.

be caught up in idiom ~에 열중하다; ~에 휘말려 들다
If you are caught up in something, you are completely absorbed in an activity or your own feelings.

★ **adventure** [ædvénʧər] n. 모험; 모험심
If someone has an adventure, they become involved in an unusual, exciting, and rather dangerous journey or series of events.

dissipate [dísəpèit] v. 소멸하다; (시간 · 돈 등을) 낭비하다
When something dissipates or when you dissipate it, it becomes less or becomes less strong until it disappears or goes away completely.

★ **swear** [swɛər] v. 맹세하다; 욕을 하다
If you swear to do something, you promise in a serious way that you will do it.

복습 **progress** [prágres] n. 진전; 진행; 나아감; v. 진전을 보이다; (앞으로) 나아가다
Progress is the process of gradually improving or getting nearer to achieving or completing something.

wind down idiom 긴장을 풀다; (서서히) 종료되다
If you wind down, you relax after a period of excitement or worry.

복습 **switch** [swiʧ] n. 스위치; 전환; v. 전환하다, 바꾸다
A switch is a small control for an electrical device which you use to turn the device on or off.

복습 **beam** [bi:m] n. 빛줄기; 기둥; v. 활짝 웃다; 비추다
A beam is a line of energy, radiation, or particles sent in a particular direction.

flicker [flíkər] v. (불 · 빛 등이) 깜박거리다; 움직거리다; n. (빛의) 깜박거림; 움직거림
If a light or flame flickers, it shines unsteadily.

복습 **race** [reis] v. 쏜살같이 가다; 경주하다; n. 경주; 경쟁; 인종, 종족
If you race somewhere, you go there as quickly as possible.

복습 **corridor** [kɔ́:ridər] n. 복도; 통로
A corridor is a long passage in a building or train, with doors and rooms on one or both sides.

★★ **aircraft** [ɛ́ərkræft] n. 항공기
An aircraft is a vehicle which can fly, for example an aeroplane or a helicopter.

복습 **hangar** [hǽŋər] n. 격납고
A hangar is a large building in which aircraft are kept.

pry [prai] v. ~을 비틀어 열다; 힘들여 입수하다; 엿보다; n. 지레; 엿보기; 탐색
If you pry something open or pry it away from a surface, you force it open or away from a surface.

복습 **swarm** [swɔ:rm] n. 군중; (곤충의) 떼, 무리; v. 많이 모여들다; 무리를 지어 다니다
A swarm of people is a large group of them moving about quickly.

복습 **cheer** [ʧiər] n. 환호(성), 응원; v. 환호성을 지르다, 환호하다
A cheer is a loud shout of happiness or approval.

★ **mobile** [móubəl] a. 이동하는, 이동식의; 움직임이 자유로운
You use mobile to describe something large that can be moved easily from place to place.

복습 **command** [kəmǽnd] n. 지휘, 통솔; 명령; v. 명령하다, 지시하다; 지휘하다
In the armed forces, a command is a group of officers who are responsible for organizing and controlling part of an army, navy, or air force.

복습 **vehicle** [ví:ikl] n. 차량, 운송 수단; 수단, 매개체
A vehicle is a machine such as a car, bus, or truck which has an engine and is used to carry people from place to place.

복습 **bay** [bei] n. 구역, 구간; 만(灣)
A bay is a partly enclosed area, inside or outside a building, that is used for a particular purpose.

복습 **celebrate** [séləbrèit] v. 기념하다, 축하하다
If you celebrate, you do something enjoyable because of a special occasion or to mark someone's success.

⁑ **whistle** [hwisl] **v.** 휘파람을 불다; 기적을 울리다; **n.** 휘파람 (소리); (기차 · 배 등의) 기적, 경적
When you whistle or when you whistle a tune, you make a series of musical notes by forcing your breath out between your lips, or your teeth.

복습 **jet** [dʒet] **n.** 제트기; 분출; **v.** 급속히 움직이다; 분출하다
A jet is an aircraft that is powered by jet engines.

head start [hed stá:rt] **n.** (남보다 일찍 시작해서 갖게 되는) 유리함
If you have a head start on other people, you have an advantage over them in something such as a competition or race.

복습 **launch** [lɔ:ntʃ] **v.** 발사하다; 시작하다; **n.** 발사; 개시, 진수
To launch a rocket, missile, or satellite means to send it into the air or into space.

⁎ **coordinate** [kouɔ́:rdənət] **n.** 좌표; **v.** 조직화하다; (몸의 움직임을) 조정하다
The coordinates of a point on a map or graph are the two sets of numbers or letters that you need in order to find that point.

복습 **bet** [bet] **v.** (~이) 틀림없다; (내기 등에) 돈을 걸다; **n.** 내기; 짐작, 추측
You use expressions such as 'I bet,' 'I'll bet,' and 'you can bet' to indicate that you are sure something is true.

복습 **loudspeaker** [láudspì:kər] **n.** 확성기
A loudspeaker is a piece of equipment that converts electric signals to audible sound.

⁎ **monitor** [mánətər] **v.** 감시하다; 추적 관찰하다; **n.** (텔레비전 · 컴퓨터의) 화면; 감시 장치
If you monitor something, you regularly check its development or progress, and sometimes comment on it.

⁂ **station** [stéiʃən] **n.** 구역, 부서; 위치, 장소; 역; **v.** 배치하다
A station is a place or building where a specified activity or service is based.

Check Your Reading Speed

1분에 몇 단어를 읽는지 리딩 속도를 측정해보세요.

$$\frac{\text{315 words}}{\text{reading time (\quad) sec}} \times 60 = (\quad)\ \text{WPM}$$

Build Your Vocabulary

복습 **engage** [ingéidʒ] v. 약속하다; 교전을 시작하다; 관여하다; 기계 부품이 맞물리다 (engagement n. 약속)
An engagement is an arrangement that you have made to do something at a particular time.

dresser [drésə] n. 서랍장; 화장대
A dresser is a chest of drawers, usually with a mirror on the top.

* **drawer** [drɔ:r] n. 서랍
A drawer is part of a desk, chest, or other piece of furniture that is shaped like a box and is designed for putting things in.

복습 **suit** [su:t] n. (특정한 활동 때 입는) 옷; 정장; 소송; v. ~에게 편리하다; 어울리다
A particular type of suit is a piece of clothing that you wear for a particular activity.

put away idiom 치우다
To put away something means to put it in the place where you usually keep it when you are not using it.

복습 **firm** [fə:rm] a. 단호한, 확고한; 단단한 (firmly ad. 단호히)
If you describe someone as firm, you mean they behave in a way that shows that they are not going to change their mind, or that they are the person who is in control.

greater good idiom 대의, 공공의 이익
The greater good means a general advantage that you can only gain by losing or harming something that is considered less important.

in hand idiom (일 등을) 처리하는, 다루는
If a situation is in hand, it is under control.

hunk [hʌŋk] **n.** 큰 덩어리, 두꺼운 조각
A hunk of something is a large piece of it.

★ **fake** [feik] **v.** ~인 척하다; **a.** 가짜의, 거짓된; 모조의; **n.** 모조품
If someone fakes something, they try to make it look valuable or genuine, although in fact it is not.

복습 **punch** [pʌnʧ] **n.** 주먹으로 한 대 침; **v.** (자판 · 번호판 등을) 치다; 주먹으로 치다
A punch is the action of hitting someone or something with your fist.

복습 **remote** [rimóut] **n.** (= remote control) 리모콘; 원격 조종; **a.** 외진, 외딴; 원격의; 먼
Remote control is a system of controlling a machine or a vehicle from a distance by using radio or electronic signals.

복습 **wrist** [rist] **n.** 손목
Your wrist is the part of your body between your hand and your arm which bends when you move your hand.

복습 **signal** [sígnəl] **n.** 신호; 징조; **v.** (동작 · 소리로) 신호를 보내다; 암시하다
A signal is a gesture, sound, or action which is intended to give a particular message to the person who sees or hears it.

socket [sákit] **n.** 푹 들어간 곳, 구멍; 콘센트
You can refer to any hollow part or opening in a structure which another part fits into as a socket.

복습 **crash** [kræʃ] **v.** 부딪치다; 충돌하다; 굉음을 내다; **n.** (자동차 · 항공기) 사고; 요란한 소리
If something crashes somewhere, it moves and hits something else violently, making a loud noise.

go wild **idiom** 미쳐 날뛰다
If someone or something goes wild, they behave in a very excited uncontrolled way.

revel in **idiom** ~을 한껏 즐기다
If you revel in something, you enjoy it very much.

복습 **appreciate** [əprí:ʃièit] **v.** 고마워하다; 진가를 알아보다 (appreciation **n.** 감사)
Your appreciation for something that someone does for you is your gratitude for it.

복습 **control** [kəntróul] **n.** 통제, 제어; (기계 · 차량의) 제어 장치; **v.** 지배하다; 조정하다
If you have control of something or someone, you are able to make them do what you want them to do.

★ **external** [ikstə́:rnəl] a. 외부에서 작용하는; 외면의; n. 외부
External means happening or existing in the world in general and affecting you in some way.

복습 **process** [práses] v. (공식적으로) 처리하다; 가공하다; n. 과정, 절차; 공정
When people process information, they put it through a system or into a computer in order to deal with it.

crunch [krʌntʃ] v. (많은 양의 정보를) 고속으로 처리하다; 으드득거리다; n. 으드득거리는 소리
To crunch numbers means to do a lot of calculations using a calculator or computer.

복습 **conclude** [kənklú:d] v. 결론을 내리다; 끝내다, 마치다
If you conclude that something is true, you decide that it is true using the facts you know as a basis.

복습 **boot** [bu:t] n. 목이 긴 신발, 부츠; v. 세게 차다; (컴퓨터를) 부팅하다
Boots are shoes that cover your whole foot and the lower part of your leg.

careen [kərí:n] v. 위태롭게 달리다, 흔들리면서 질주하다
To careen somewhere means to rush forward in an uncontrollable way.

복습 **conscious** [kánʃəs] a. 의식이 있는; 자각하는; 의도적인 (unconscious a. 의식을 잃은)
Someone who is unconscious is in a state similar to sleep, usually as the result of a serious injury or a lack of oxygen.

thrash [θræʃ] v. ~을 세게 때리다; 격파하다; 몸부림치다
If a person or thing thrashes something, or thrashes at something, they hit it continually in a violent or noisy way.

★ **interfere** [ìntərfíər] v. 방해하다; 간섭하다, 개입하다 (interference n. 간섭, 방해)
Interference by a person or group is their unwanted or unnecessary involvement in something.

Chapters 28~30

1. What happened when the Incredibles first reached Metroville?

A. They drove the mobile command vehicle on the freeway.

B. They steered the landing craft to the Omnidroid's exact location.

C. They fell from the sky and landed in an empty parking lot.

D. They used Helen as a parachute and floated gently to the ground.

2. Why did Bob want to fight the Omnidroid alone?

A. He did not want to put his family in danger.

B. He wanted to demonstrate how strong he was.

C. He figured it would be easy to defeat the robot.

D. He thought it would be faster to find the robot on his own.

3. How did Frozone help?

A. He shot ice at the Omnidroid's laser beam.

B. He moved Dash away from the Omnidroid.

C. He found the remote that controlled the Omnidroid.

D. He punched the Omnidroid and broke its arm.

4. How was the Omnidroid finally destroyed?

A. By the Supers' powers

B. By chunks of ice

C. By a button on the remote

D. By its own claw

5. Why did Kari call Helen?

A. She was not sure where Jack-Jack was.

B. She felt like Jack-Jack missed his family.

C. She noticed something odd about Jack-Jack.

D. She was scared because someone kidnapped Jack-Jack.

Check Your Reading Speed

1분에 몇 단어를 읽는지 리딩 속도를 측정해보세요.

$$\frac{\text{349 words}}{\text{reading time (\qquad) sec}} \times 60 = (\qquad) \text{ WPM}$$

Build Your Vocabulary

복습 **land** [lænd] v. (땅 · 표면에) 내려앉다, 착륙하다; 놓다, 두다; n. 육지, 땅; 지역 (landing n. 착륙)
A landing is an act of bringing an aircraft or spacecraft down to the ground.

복습 **craft** [kræft] n. 항공기; 공예; 기술, 기교; v. 공예품을 만들다; 공들여 만들다
You can refer to a boat, a spacecraft, or an aircraft as a craft.

복습 **rocket** [rákit] n. 로켓; 로켓 추진 미사일; v. 로켓처럼 가다, 돌진하다; 급증하다
A rocket is a space vehicle that is shaped like a long tube.

복습 **mobile** [móubəl] a. 이동하는, 이동식의; 움직임이 자유로운
You use mobile to describe something large that can be moved easily from place to place.

복습 **command** [kəmǽnd] n. 지휘, 통솔; 명령; v. 명령하다, 지시하다; 지휘하다
In the armed forces, a command is a group of officers who are responsible for organizing and controlling part of an army, navy, or air force.

van [væn] n. 승합차; 밴
A van is a small or medium-sized road vehicle with one row of seats at the front and a space for carrying goods behind.

복습 **wheel** [hwi:l] n. (자동차 등의) 핸들; 바퀴; v. (바퀴 달린 것을) 밀다
The wheel of a car or other vehicle is the circular object that is used to steer it. For example, if someone is at the wheel of a car, they are driving it.

복습 **impatient** [impéiʃənt] a. 짜증난, 안달하는; 어서 ~하고 싶어 하는 (impatiently ad. 성급하게)
If you are impatient, you are annoyed because you have to wait too long for something.

복습 **lean** [li:n] v. 기울이다, (몸을) 숙이다; ~에 기대다; a. 군살이 없는, 호리호리한
When you lean in a particular direction, you bend your body in that direction.

max [mæks] **a.** (= maximum) (크기 · 빠르기 등이) 최대의; **n.** (양 · 규모 · 속도 등의) 최고
If you say that someone does something to the maximum, you are emphasizing that they do it to the greatest degree possible.

⋆ **elastic** [ilǽstik] **a.** 탄력 있는, 신축성이 있는
Something that is elastic is able to stretch easily and then return to its original shape.

복습 **attach** [ətǽʧ] **v.** 붙이다, 첨부하다; 연관되다
If you attach something to an object, you join it or fasten it to the object.

⋆ **strap** [stræp] **v.** 끈으로 묶다; 붕대를 감다; **n.** 끈, 줄, 띠
If you strap something somewhere, you fasten it there with a strap.

⋆⋆ **rough** [rʌf] **a.** (길 등이) 험한; (행동이) 거친; 개략적인
If you describe something as rough, you mean that it is uncomfortable, and with difficult conditions.

복습 **poke** [pouk] **v.** 쑥 내밀다; (손가락 등으로) 쿡 찌르다; **n.** (손가락 등으로) 찌르기
If you poke your head through an opening or if it pokes through an opening, you push it through, often so that you can see something more easily.

복습 **release** [rilíːs] **v.** 놓아 주다; 풀어 주다; (감정을) 발산하다; **n.** 풀어 줌; 발표, 공개
If you release someone or something, you stop holding them.

복습 **engage** [ingéidʒ] **v.** 기계 부품이 맞물리다; 약속하다; 교전을 시작하다; 관여하다
(disengage v. 떼어 내다; 철수하다)
If you disengage something, or if it disengages, it becomes separate from something which it has been attached to.

복습 **streak** [striːk] **v.** 전속력으로 가다; 줄무늬를 넣다; **n.** 줄무늬
If something or someone streaks somewhere, they move there very quickly.

freeway [fríːwèi] **n.** 고속도로
A freeway is a major road that has been specially built for fast travel over long distances.

복습 **pavement** [péivmənt] **n.** 노면; 인도, 보도
The pavement is the hard surface of a road.

복습 **shower** [ʃáuər] **n.** 빗발침, 쏟아짐; 소나기; **v.** (작은 조각들을) 쏟아 붓다; 샤워를 하다
You can refer to a lot of things that are falling as a shower of them.

복습 **spark** [spa:rk] **n.** 불꽃, 불똥; (전류의) 스파크; **v.** 촉발시키다; 불꽃을 일으키다
A spark is a tiny bright piece of burning material that flies up from something that is burning.

복습 **struggle** [strʌgl] **v.** 애쓰다; 몸부림치다, 허우적거리다; 힘겹게 나아가다; **n.** 투쟁, 분투; 몸부림
If you struggle to do something, you try hard to do it, even though other people or things may be making it difficult for you to succeed.

★★ **maintain** [meintéin] **v.** 유지하다; 주장하다; 지속하다
If you maintain something, you continue to have it, and do not let it stop or grow weaker.

복습 **brake** [breik] **n.** 브레이크, 제동 장치; 제동; **v.** 브레이크를 밟다; 속도를 줄이다
(hit the brakes **idiom** 브레이크를 걸다)
Brakes are devices in a vehicle that make it go slower or stop.

복습 **smoke** [smouk] **v.** 연기를 내뿜다; 질주하다; (담배를) 피우다; **n.** 연기
If something is smoking, smoke is coming from it.

★ **steer** [stiər] **v.** (보트·자동차 등을) 조종하다; (특정 방향으로) 움직이다
When you steer a car, boat, or plane, you control it so that it goes in the direction that you want.

★★ **traffic** [trǽfik] **n.** 차량들, 교통; 수송
Traffic refers to all the vehicles that are moving along the roads in a particular area.

★★ **financial** [finǽnʃəl] **a.** 금융의, 재정의
Financial means relating to or involving money.

★★ **district** [dístrikt] **n.** 지구, 지역, 구역
A district is an area of a town or country which has been given official boundaries for the purpose of administration.

복습 **exit** [égzit] **n.** (고속도로의) 출구; (공공건물의) 출구; 퇴장; **v.** 나가다, 떠나다; 퇴장하다
An exit on a motorway or highway is a place where traffic can leave it.

★ **avenue** [ǽvənju:] **n.** (도시의) 거리, -가; (나아갈) 길, 방안
Avenue is sometimes used in the names of streets.

복습 **passenger** [pǽsəndʒər] **n.** 승객 (passenger seat **n.** (자동차의) 조수석)
A passenger in a vehicle such as a bus, boat, or plane is a person who is traveling in it, but who is not driving it or working on it.

★★ **lane** [léin] n. (도로의) 차선; 좁은 길, 골목, 작은 길
A lane is a part of a main road which is marked by the edge of the road and a painted line, or by two painted lines.

복습 **bullet** [búlit] n. 총알
A bullet is a small piece of metal with a pointed or rounded end, which is fired out of a gun.

★ **downtown** [dauntáun] n. 도심지; 상업 지구; ad. 시내에
Downtown places are in or toward the center of a large town or city, where the shops and places of business are.

복습 **yell** [jel] v. 고함치다, 소리 지르다; n. 고함, 외침
If you yell, you shout loudly, usually because you are excited, angry, or in pain.

복습 **furious** [fjúəriəs] a. 몹시 화가 난; 맹렬한
Someone who is furious is extremely angry.

복습 **insist** [insíst] v. 고집하다, 주장하다, 우기다
If you insist that something should be done, you say so very firmly and refuse to give in about it.

복습 **signal** [sígnəl] n. 신호; 징조; v. (동작 · 소리로) 신호를 보내다; 암시하다
A signal is a gesture, sound, or action which is intended to give a particular message to the person who sees or hears it.

swerve [swə:rv] v. (갑자기) 방향을 바꾸다
If a vehicle or other moving thing swerves or if you swerve it, it suddenly changes direction, often in order to avoid hitting something.

guardrail [gá:rdreil] n. (도로의) 가드레일
A guardrail is a railing that is placed along the edge of something such as a staircase, path, or boat, so that people can hold onto it or so that they do not fall over the edge.

Check Your Reading Speed

1분에 몇 단어를 읽는지 리딩 속도를 측정해보세요.

$$\frac{\text{976 words}}{\text{reading time (\quad\quad) sec}} \times 60 = (\quad\quad\quad) \text{ WPM}$$

Build Your Vocabulary

복습 **struggle** [strʌgl] v. 애쓰다; 몸부림치다, 허우적거리다; 힘겹게 나아가다; n. 투쟁, 분투; 몸부림
If you struggle to do something, you try hard to do it, even though other people or things may be making it difficult for you to succeed.

복습 **van** [væn] n. 승합차; 밴
A van is a small or medium-sized road vehicle with one row of seats at the front and a space for carrying goods behind.

복습 **careen** [kəríːn] v. 위태롭게 달리다, 흔들리면서 질주하다
To careen somewhere means to rush forward in an uncontrollable way.

복습 **brake** [breik] n. 브레이크, 제동 장치; 제동; v. 브레이크를 밟다; 속도를 줄이다
(hit the brakes idiom 브레이크를 걸다)
Brakes are devices in a vehicle that make it go slower or stop.

복습 **blow** [blou] v. (blew-blown) (타이어가) 터지다; (비밀을) 누설하다; (바람 · 입김에) 날리다; n. 강타
If a tire blows, or if you blow it, it bursts.

복습 **vehicle** [víːikl] n. 차량, 운송 수단; 수단, 매개체
A vehicle is a machine such as a car, bus, or truck which has an engine and is used to carry people from place to place.

⋆ **overturn** [òuvərtə́ːrn] v. 뒤집히다, 뒤집다
If something overturns or if you overturn it, it turns upside down or on its side.

복습 **tumble** [tʌmbl] v. 굴러떨어지다; 폭삭 무너지다; n. (갑자기) 굴러떨어짐; 폭락
If someone or something tumbles somewhere, they fall there with a rolling or bouncing movement.

come to rest idiom 멈추다
If something comes to rest, it finally stops moving.

복습 **spot** [spat] n. (특정한) 곳; (작은) 점; v. 발견하다, 찾다, 알아채다
You can refer to a particular place as a spot.

super-duper [su:pər-djú:pər] a. 아주 훌륭한, 월등히 좋은
Super-duper means very excellent.

복습 **helpless** [hélplis] a. 무력한, 속수무책인 (helplessly ad. 어찌해 볼 수도 없이)
If you are helpless, you do not have the strength or power to do anything useful or to control or protect yourself.

sideline [sáidlain] n. (pl.) (테니스장 등의) 사이드라인; v. 열외로 취급하다
(from the sidelines idiom 옆에서 지켜보는)
If you are on the sidelines or do something from the sidelines, you are not actively involved in something.

not a chance idiom 그럴 가능성은 없다!, 천만에!
If you say 'not a chance,' you mean that there is no possibility of that.

복습 **insist** [insíst] v. 고집하다, 주장하다, 우기다
If you insist that something should be done, you say so very firmly and refuse to give in about it.

⋆ **stern** [stə:rn] a. 엄중한, 근엄한; 심각한 (sternly ad. 엄격하게)
Stern words or actions are very severe.

playtime [pléitàim] n. 놀이 시간
In a school for young children, playtime is the period of time between lessons when they can play outside.

복습 **snap** [snæp] v. 날카롭게 말하다; 탁 하고 움직이다; 급히 움직이다; 툭 부러지다; n. 탁 하는 소리
If someone snaps at you, they speak to you in a sharp, unfriendly way.

복습 **confuse** [kənfjú:z] v. (사람을) 혼란시키다; 혼동하다 (confused a. 혼란스러워하는)
If you are confused, you do not know exactly what is happening or what to do.

복습 **workout** [wə́:rkàut] n. 운동
A workout is a period of physical exercise or training.

복습 **whisper** [hwíspər] v. 속삭이다, 소곤거리다; n. 속삭임, 소곤거리는 소리
When you whisper, you say something very quietly, using your breath rather than your throat, so that only one person can hear you.

복습 **stun** [stʌn] v. 어리벙벙하게 하다; 깜짝 놀라게 하다; 기절시키다
If you are stunned by something, you are extremely shocked or surprised by it and are therefore unable to speak or do anything.

복습 **rage** [reidʒ] **v.** 맹렬히 계속되다; 몹시 화를 내다; **n.** 격렬한 분노
You say that something powerful or unpleasant rages when it continues with great force or violence.

복습 **loom** [lu:m] **v.** (무섭게) 흐릿하게 보이다; (일이) 곧 닥칠 것처럼 보이다
If something looms over you, it appears as a large or unclear shape, often in a frightening way.

pounce [pauns] **v.** (공격하거나 잡으려고 확) 덮치다, 덤비다
If someone pounces on you, they come up toward you suddenly and take hold of you.

복습 **freeze** [fri:z] **v.** (froze-frozen) (두려움 등으로 몸이) 얼어붙다; 얼다; **n.** 동결; 한파
If someone who is moving freezes, they suddenly stop and become completely still and quiet.

복습 **barely** [béərli] **ad.** 거의 ~아니게; 간신히, 가까스로
You use barely to say that something is only just true or only just the case.

복습 **enormous** [inɔ́:rməs] **a.** 막대한, 거대한
Something that is enormous is extremely large in size or amount.

복습 **crush** [krʌʃ] **v.** 으스러뜨리다; 밀어 넣다; 좌절시키다; **n.** 홀딱 반함
To crush something means to press it very hard so that its shape is destroyed or so that it breaks into pieces.

복습 **force** [fɔ:rs] **n.** 작용력; 힘; 영향력; **v.** 억지로 ~하다; ~를 강요하다
Force is the power or strength which something has.

복습 **field** [fi:ld] **n.** ~장; 경기장; 들판, 밭
A magnetic, gravitational, or electric field is the area in which that particular force is strong enough to have an effect.

복습 **project** [prádʒekt] **v.** 발사하다, 내뿜다; (빛 · 영상 등을) 비추다; 계획하다; **n.** 계획, 프로젝트
If you project something, you throw or direct it forward, with force.

* **protective** [prətéktiv] **a.** 보호용의; 보호하려고 하는
Protective means designed or intended to protect something or someone from harm.

복습 **press** [pres] **v.** 누르다; (무엇에) 바짝 대다; 꾹 밀어 넣다; **n.** 언론
If you press something somewhere, you push it firmly against something else.

복습 **knock** [nak] v. 치다, 부딪치다; (문 등을) 두드리다; n. 문 두드리는 소리; 부딪침
If you knock something, you touch or hit it roughly, especially so that it falls or moves.

복습 **vanish** [vǽniʃ] v. 사라지다, 없어지다; 모습을 감추다
If someone or something vanishes, they disappear suddenly or in a way that cannot be explained.

⋆ **wedge** [wedʒ] v. (좁은 틈 사이에) 끼워 넣다; 고정시키다; n. 분열의 원인; 쐐기
If you wedge something somewhere, you fit it there tightly.

복습 **take off** idiom (서둘러) 떠나다; 날아오르다
If you take off, you leave somewhere suddenly or in a hurry.

stay put idiom (있던 자리에) 그대로 있다
If you stay put, you remain in the same place or position.

복습 **lunge** [lʌndʒ] v. 달려들다, 돌진하다; n. 돌진
If you lunge in a particular direction, you move in that direction suddenly and clumsily.

복습 **powerful** [páuərfəl] a. 강력한; 영향력 있는, 유력한
You say that someone's body is powerful when it is physically strong.

복습 **punch** [pʌnʧ] n. 주먹으로 한 대 침; v. (자판 · 번호판 등을) 치다; 주먹으로 치다
A punch is the action of hitting someone or something with your fist.

복습 **instant** [ínstənt] n. 순간, 아주 짧은 동안; a. 즉각적인
An instant is an extremely short period of time.

복습 **flash** [flæʃ] v. (잠깐) 번쩍이다; 휙 내보이다; 휙 움직이다; n. (잠깐) 반짝임; 뉴스 속보; 순간
If a light flashes or if you flash a light, it shines with a sudden bright light, especially as quick, regular flashes of light.

복습 **surface** [sə́:rfis] n. 수면, 표면, 지면; 외관; v. 수면으로 올라오다; (갑자기) 나타나다
The surface of something is the flat top part of it or the outside of it.

복습 **bolt** [boult] n. (물 등의) 분출; 볼트; v. 달아나다; 빗장을 지르다
A bolt of some liquid is a jet or column of it.

⋆ **buddy** [bʌ́di] n. 친구
A buddy is a close friend, usually a male friend of a man.

⋆ **glide** [glaid] v. 미끄러지듯 움직이다; 활공하다; n. 미끄러지는 듯한 움직임
If you glide somewhere, you move silently and in a smooth and effortless way.

* **foe** [fou] n. 적, 원수
Someone's foe is their enemy.

backhand [bǽkhæ̀nd] v. 손등으로 치다; (공을) 백핸드로 치다; n. 백핸드
If you backhand something, you strike it with the back of the hand.

shake off idiom 떨쳐내다
If you shake off something that you do not want such as an illness or a bad habit, you manage to recover from it or get rid of it.

* **momentary** [móuməntèri] a. 순간적인, 잠깐의
Something that is momentary lasts for a very short period of time, for example for a few seconds or less.

복습 **notice** [nóutis] v. 알아채다, 인지하다; 주의하다; n. 신경 씀, 알아챔; 통지, 예고
If you notice something or someone, you become aware of them.

복습 **remote** [rimóut] n. (= remote control) 리모콘; 원격 조종; a. 외진, 외딴; 원격의; 먼
Remote control is a system of controlling a machine or a vehicle from a distance by using radio or electronic signals.

figure out idiom ~을 이해하다, 알아내다; 계산하다, 산출하다
If you figure out someone or something, you come to understand them by thinking carefully.

복습 **grab** [græb] v. (와락 · 단단히) 붙잡다; 급히 ~하다; n. 와락 잡아채려고 함
If you grab something, you take it or pick it up suddenly and roughly.

gadget [gǽdʒit] n. (작은) 기계 장치; 도구
A gadget is a small machine or device which does something useful.

복습 **claw** [klɔː] n. 갈고리 모양의 기계; (동물 · 새의) 발톱; v. (손톱 · 발톱으로) 할퀴다
A claw is a curved end on a tool or machine, used for pulling or picking things up.

복습 **release** [rilíːs] v. 풀어 주다; 놓아 주다; (감정을) 발산하다; n. 풀어 줌; 발표, 공개
If you release someone or something, you stop holding them.

복습 **blur** [bləːr] n. 흐릿한 형체; v. 흐릿해지다; 모호해지다
A blur is a shape or area which you cannot see clearly because it has no distinct outline or because it is moving very fast.

복습 **speed** [spiːd] v. 빨리 가다; 더 빠르게 하다; n. 속도 (speedy a. 빠른, 신속한)
A speedy process, event, or action happens or is done very quickly.

복습 **in time** idiom 제때에, 시간 맞춰, 늦지 않게
If you are in time for a particular event, you are not too late for it.

복습 **trap** [træp] v. (위험한 장소에) 가두다; (함정으로) 몰아넣다; **n.** 함정; 덫
If you are trapped somewhere, something falls onto you or blocks your way and prevents you from moving or escaping.

복습 **burn** [bə:rn] v. 불에 타다; 태우다; 상기되다; **n.** 화상
If something is burning, it is on fire.

복습 **take out** idiom ~을 죽이다, 없애다
If you take out someone or something, you kill or destroy them, or injure or damage them so that they cannot work or be used.

복습 **fling** [fliŋ] v. (flung-flung) (힘껏) 던지다; (머리 · 팔 등을) 휘두르다; **n.** (한바탕) 실컷 즐기기
If you fling something somewhere, you throw it there using a lot of force.

manhole [mǽnhòul] **n.** (도로 등의) 맨홀; 출입 구멍
A manhole is a large hole in a road or path, covered by a metal plate that can be removed.

복습 **cover** [kʌ́vər] **n.** 덮개; 위장, 속임수; 몸을 숨길 곳; **v.** 가리다; (보험으로) 보장하다; 다루다; 덮다
A cover is something which is put over an object, usually in order to protect it.

복습 **beam** [bi:m] **n.** 빛줄기; 기둥; **v.** 활짝 웃다; 비추다
A beam is a line of energy, radiation, or particles sent in a particular direction.

복습 **swoop** [swu:p] **v.** 급강하하다, 위에서 덮치다; 급습하다; **n.** 급강하; 급습
When a bird or airplane swoops, it suddenly moves downward through the air in a smooth curving movement.

복습 **rescue** [réskju:] **v.** 구하다, 구출하다; **n.** 구출, 구조, 구제
If you rescue someone, you get them out of a dangerous or unpleasant situation.

⋆ **thunder** [θʌ́ndər] **v.** 우르릉거리며 질주하다; 천둥이 치다; **n.** 천둥, 우레
If something or someone thunders somewhere, they move there quickly and with a lot of noise.

복습 **turn** [tə:rn] **n.** 차례, 순번; 전환; 돌기, 돌리기; **v.** 돌다; 변하다
If it is your turn to do something, you now have the duty, chance, or right to do it, when other people have done it before you or will do it after you.

vault [vɔ:lt] **v.** 뛰어넘다; **n.** 금고, 보관실; 뛰기, 도약
If you vault something or vault over it, you jump quickly onto or over it, especially by putting a hand on top of it to help you balance while you jump.

복습 **chunk** [ʧʌŋk] **n.** 덩어리; 상당히 많은 양; **v.** 덩어리로 나누다
Chunks of something are thick solid pieces of it.

복습 **spin** [spin] **v.** (spun-spun) (빙빙) 돌다; 돌아서다; **n.** 회전
If something spins or if you spin it, it turns quickly around a central point.

복습 **charge** [ʧa:rdʒ] **v.** 급히 가다, 달려가다; (요금 · 값을) 청구하다; **n.** 책임, 담당; 요금
If you charge toward someone or something, you move quickly and aggressively toward them.

복습 **fire** [faiər] **v.** 발사하다; (엔진이) 점화되다; 해고하다; **n.** 화재, 불; 발사, 총격
If someone fires a gun or a bullet, or if they fire, a bullet is sent from a gun that they are using.

pincer [pínsər] **n.** 집게; (게 · 바닷가재의) 집게발
Pincers consist of two pieces of metal that are hinged in the middle. They are used as a tool for gripping things or for pulling things out.

복습 **seeming** [sí:miŋ] **a.** 외견상의, 겉보기의 (seemingly **ad.** 외견상으로, 겉보기에는)
If something is seemingly the case, you mean that it appears to be the case, even though it may not really be so.

복습 **visible** [vízəbl] **a.** (눈에) 보이는, 알아볼 수 있는; 뚜렷한 (invisible **a.** 보이지 않는)
If you describe something as invisible, you mean that it cannot be seen, for example because it is transparent, hidden, or very small.

* **bear** [bɛər] **v.** (bore-borne) 가다; 견디다; (책임 등을) 떠맡다; (아이를) 낳다; **n.** [동물] 곰
(bear down **idiom** 돌진하다)
To bear down means to move toward someone or something in a determined or threatening way.

복습 **desperate** [déspərət] **a.** 간절히 원하는; 필사적인, 극단적인 (desperately **ad.** 간절히)
If you are desperate for something or desperate to do something, you want or need it very much indeed.

* **combination** [kámbənéiʃən] **n.** 조합, 결합; 연합
A combination of things is a mixture of them.

복습 **pin** [pin] **v.** 꼼짝 못하게 하다; (핀으로) 고정시키다; **n.** 핀
If someone pins you to something, they press you against a surface so that you cannot move.

복습 **realize** [rí:əlàiz] **v.** 깨닫다, 알아차리다; 실현하다, 달성하다
If you realize that something is true, you become aware of that fact or understand it.

복습 **penetrate** [pénətrèit] v. 뚫고 들어가다; 침투하다; 간파하다
If something or someone penetrates a physical object or an area, they succeed in getting into it or passing through it.

복습 **activate** [ǽktəvèit] v. 작동시키다; 활성화시키다
If a device or process is activated, something causes it to start working.

복습 **duck** [dʌk] v. (머리나 몸을) 획 수그리다; 급히 움직이다; n. [동물] 오리
If you duck, you move your head or the top half of your body quickly downward to avoid something that might hit you, or to avoid being seen.

복습 **mass** [mæs] n. (많은 사람 · 사물의) 무리; 덩어리; a. 대량의, 대규모의
A mass of something is a large amount of it.

복습 **spark** [spa:rk] n. 불꽃, 불똥; (전류의) 스파크; v. 촉발시키다; 불꽃을 일으키다
A spark is a tiny bright piece of burning material that flies up from something that is burning.

복습 **explode** [iksplóud] v. 폭발하다; (갑자기 강한 감정을) 터뜨리다 (explosion n. 폭발)
An explosion is a sudden, violent burst of energy, for example one caused by a bomb.

복습 **citizen** [sítəzən] n. 시민; 주민
The citizens of a town or city are the people who live there.

⋆ **circuit** [sə́:rkit] n. (전기) 회로; 순환, 순회
An electrical circuit is a complete route which an electric current can flow around.

복습 **crowd** [kraud] n. 사람들, 군중; v. 가득 메우다; 바싹 붙어 서다
A crowd is a large group of people who have gathered together, for example to watch or listen to something interesting, or to protest about something.

Check Your Reading Speed

1분에 몇 단어를 읽는지 리딩 속도를 측정해보세요.

$$\frac{\text{317 words}}{\text{reading time (\qquad) sec}} \times 60 = (\qquad) \text{ WPM}$$

Build Your Vocabulary

company [kʌ́mpəni] n. 함께 있음; 손님; 회사
When you are in company, you are with a person or group of people.

government [gʌ́vərnmənt] n. 정부, 정권; 행정, 통치
The government of a country is the group of people who are responsible for governing it.

relocate [riːlóukeit] v. 이전하다, 이동하다 (relocation n. 재배치)
If people or businesses relocate or if someone relocates them, they move to a different place.

handle [hændl] v. (사람·작업 등을) 처리하다; 들다, 옮기다; n. 손잡이 (handler n. 담당자)
A handler is someone whose job is to deal with a particular type of object.

debt [det] n. 은혜를 입음, 신세를 짐; 빚, 부채
You use debt in expressions such as I owe you a debt or I am in your debt when you are expressing gratitude for something that someone has done for you.

gratitude [grǽtətjùːd] n. 고마움, 감사
Gratitude is the state of feeling grateful.

make good on idiom (약속 등을) 지키다
If you make good on something, you do what you have said you would do.

hopeful [hóupfəl] a. 희망에 찬, 기대하는; 희망적인 (hopefully ad. 희망을 갖고)
If you do something hopefully, you do it in a way that expresses desire with an expectation of fulfillment.

politician [pàlitíʃən] n. 정치인
A politician is a person whose job is in politics, especially a member of parliament or congress.

복습 **figure out** idiom ~을 이해하다, 알아내다; 계산하다, 산출하다
If you figure out someone or something, you come to understand them by thinking carefully.

★ **assure** [əʃúər] v. 장담하다, 확언하다; 확인하다
If you assure someone that something is true or will happen, you tell them that it is definitely true or will definitely happen, often in order to make them less worried.

take care of idiom ~을 처리하다; ~을 돌보다
To take care of someone or something means to do what is necessary to deal with a person or situation.

복습 **meanwhile** [míːnwàil] ad. (다른 일이 일어나고 있는) 그동안에
Meanwhile means while a particular thing is happening.

복습 **cell** [sel] n. (= cell phone) 휴대 전화; 감방; (작은) 칸
A cell phone or cellular phone is a type of telephone which does not need wires to connect it to a telephone system.

복습 **babysit** [béibisit] v. (부모가 외출한 동안) 아이를 봐 주다 (babysitter n. 아이를 봐 주는 사람)
If you babysit for someone or babysit their children, you look after their children while they are out.

★ **unusual** [ʌnjúːʒuəl] a. 특이한, 흔치 않은, 드문
If something is unusual, it does not happen very often or you do not see it or hear it very often.

복습 **blush** [blʌʃ] v. 얼굴을 붉히다; ~에 부끄러워하다; n. 얼굴이 붉어짐
When you blush, your face becomes redder than usual because you are ashamed or embarrassed.

복습 **battle** [bætl] n. 전투; 싸움; v. 싸우다, 투쟁하다
A battle is a violent fight between groups of people, especially one between military forces during a war.

복습 **guard** [gaːrd] n. 경비 요원; 경비, 감시; 보호물; v. 지키다, 보호하다
A guard is a specially organized group of people, such as soldiers or policemen, who protect or watch someone or something.

복습 **jungle** [dʒʌŋgl] n. 밀림 (지대), 정글
A jungle is a forest in a tropical country where large numbers of tall trees and plants grow very close together.

복습 **go on** idiom 말을 계속하다; (어떤 상황이) 계속되다; 자자, 어서
To go on means to continue speaking after a short pause.

복습 **snag** [snæg] v. 잡아채다, 낚아채다; (날카롭거나 튀어나온 것에) 걸리다; n. 문제; 날카로운 것
If you snag something, you get or catch it by acting quickly.

복습 **whiplash** [hwíplæʃ] v. 채찍질하다; 아프게 하다; n. 채찍질
To whiplash means to beat, hit, or throw someone or something with or as if with a whiplash.

복습 **exclaim** [ikskléim] v. 소리치다, 외치다
If you exclaim, you cry out suddenly in surprise, strong emotion, or pain.

복습 **cover** [kʌ́vər] v. 덮다; 다루다; 가리다; (보험으로) 보장하다; n. 위장, 속임수; 몸을 숨길 곳; 덮개
If you cover something, you place something else over it in order to protect it, hide it, or close it.

weird out idiom 어리둥절해지다, 정신 나가다
If something weirds you out, it is so strange that it makes you feel uncomfortable or worried.

★ **concern** [kənsə́:rn] v. 걱정스럽게 하다; 관련되다; n. 우려, 걱정; 관심사
(concerned a. 걱정하는, 염려하는)
If something concerns you, it worries you.

복습 **lean** [li:n] v. 기울이다, (몸을) 숙이다; ~에 기대다; a. 군살이 없는, 호리호리한
When you lean in a particular direction, you bend your body in that direction.

freak out idiom 기겁을 하다, 질겁하다, 놀라다
If someone freaks out or if something freaks them out, they react very strongly to something that shocks, angers, excites or frightens them.

복습 **replace** [ripléis] v. 대신하다, 대체하다; 교체하다 (replacement n. 교체, 대체)
If you refer to the replacement of one thing by another, you mean that the second thing takes the place of the first.

복습 **sitter** [sítər] n. (= babysitter) 아이를 봐 주는 사람
A sitter is the same as a babysitter who is someone you pay to come to your house and look after your children while you are not there, especially in the evening.

Chapters 31 & 32

1. Why did Syndrome try to take Jack-Jack?

A. To prove he was a good babysitter

B. To prove how weak Jack-Jack was

C. To make Mr. Incredible apologize

D. To make Mr. Incredible suffer

2. What did Jack-Jack do to Syndrome's rocket boots?

A. He put them on his feet.

B. He set them on fire.

C. He tore off pieces of them.

D. He switched off their power source.

3. What ultimately happened to Syndrome?

A. His cape got caught in his jet's turbines.

B. He crashed into the door of his jet.

C. He got hit by Helen's car.

D. His boots made him zoom into the ground.

4. What happened when the debris from the jet exploded?

A. Vi protected the Parr family's home.

B. The Parr family's home was ruined.

C. Everyone in the neighborhood ran out their homes.

D. The entire neighborhood was destroyed.

5. What did NOT change about the Parr family?

A. Dash was allowed to play sports.

B. Bob and Helen watched Dash compete.

C. Vi became more outgoing.

D. Everyone's Super identities were revealed.

Check Your Reading Speed

1분에 몇 단어를 읽는지 리딩 속도를 측정해보세요.

$$\frac{\text{477 words}}{\text{reading time (\quad) sec}} \times 60 = (\quad) \text{ WPM}$$

Build Your Vocabulary

front door [frʌnt dɔ́:r] n. (주택의) 현관
The front door of a house or other building is the main door, which is usually in the wall that faces a street.

복습 **replace** [ripléis] v. 대신하다, 대체하다; 교체하다 (replacement n. 교체, 대체)
If you refer to the replacement of one thing by another, you mean that the second thing takes the place of the first.

복습 **sitter** [sítər] n. (= babysitter) 아이를 봐 주는 사람
A sitter is the same as a babysitter who is someone you pay to come to your house and look after your children while you are not there, especially in the evening.

복습 **favor** [féivər] n. 호의, 친절; 지지, 인정; v. 편들다; 선호하다
If you do someone a favor, you do something for them even though you do not have to.

mentor [méntɔ:r] n. 스승; 조언자; 멘토
A person's mentor is someone who gives them help and advice over a period of time, especially help and advice related to their job.

supportive [səpɔ́:rtiv] a. 지원하는, 도와주는, 힘을 주는
If you are supportive, you are kind and helpful to someone at a difficult or unhappy time in their life.

복습 **encourage** [inkə́:ridʒ] v. 격려하다, 용기를 북돋우다; 부추기다
If you encourage someone, you give them confidence, for example by letting them know that what they are doing is good and telling them that they should continue to do it.

sidekick [sáidkìk] n. 동료, 친구, 조수
Someone's sidekick is a person who accompanies them and helps them, and who you consider to be less intelligent or less important than the other person.

복습 **blast** [blæst] v. 폭발시키다; 빠르게 가다; 확 뿌리다; n. 폭발; (한 줄기의) 강한 바람
If something is blasted into a particular place or state, an explosion causes it to be in that place or state.

복습 **roof** [ru:f] n. 지붕; (터널 · 동굴 등의) 천장; v. 지붕을 씌우다
The roof of a building is the covering on top of it that protects the people and things inside from the weather.

복습 **jet** [dʒet] n. 제트기; 분출; v. 급속히 움직이다; 분출하다
A jet is an aircraft that is powered by jet engines.

★ **hover** [hʌ́vər] v. (허공을) 맴돌다; 서성이다; 주저하다; n. 공중을 떠다님
To hover means to stay in the same position in the air without moving forward or backward.

복습 **activate** [ǽktəvèit] v. 작동시키다; 활성화시키다
If a device or process is activated, something causes it to start working.

복습 **rocket** [rákit] n. 로켓; 로켓 추진 미사일; v. 로켓처럼 가다, 돌진하다; 급증하다
A rocket is an engine that operates by the combustion of its contents, providing thrust as in a jet engine but without depending on the intake of air for combustion.

복습 **boot** [bu:t] n. 목이 긴 신발, 부츠; v. 세게 차다; (컴퓨터를) 부팅하다
Boots are shoes that cover your whole foot and the lower part of your leg.

복습 **zoom** [zu:m] v. 쌩 하고 가다; 급등하다; n. (빠르게) 쌩 하고 지나가는 소리
If you zoom somewhere, you go there very quickly.

★ **hatch** [hæʧ] n. (배 · 항공기의) 출입구; v. 부화하다; (계획 등을) 만들어 내다
A hatch is an opening in the deck of a ship, through which people or cargo can go. You can also refer to the door of this opening as a hatch.

복습 **be about to** idiom 막 ~하려는 참이다
If you are about to do something, you are going to do it immediately.

복습 **duck** [dʌk] v. (머리나 몸을) 휙 수그리다; 급히 움직이다; n. [동물] 오리
If you duck, you move your head or the top half of your body quickly downward to avoid something that might hit you, or to avoid being seen.

복습 **freeze** [fri:z] v. (froze-frozen) (두려움 등으로 몸이) 얼어붙다; 얼다; n. 동결; 한파
If someone who is moving freezes, they suddenly stop and become completely still and quiet.

⋆ **transform** [trænsfɔ́:rm] v. 변형시키다; 완전히 바꿔 놓다
To transform something into something else means to change or convert it into that thing.

⋆ **hideous** [hídiəs] a. 흉측한, 흉물스러운, 끔찍한
If you say that someone or something is hideous, you mean that they are very ugly or unattractive.

⋆ **monster** [mánstər] n. 괴물; a. 기이하게 큰, 거대한
A monster is a large imaginary creature that looks very ugly and frightening.

horrify [hɔ́:rəfài] v. 몸서리치게 하다, 소름끼치게 하다 (horrified a. 겁에 질린, 충격받은)
If someone is horrified, they feel shocked or disgusted, usually because of something that they have seen or heard.

⋆ **cling** [kliŋ] v. 꼭 붙잡다, 매달리다; 들러붙다; 애착을 갖다
If you cling to someone or something, you hold onto them tightly.

복습 **spin** [spin] v. (spun-spun) (빙빙) 돌다; 돌아서다; n. 회전
If something spins or if you spin it, it turns quickly around a central point.

복습 **control** [kəntróul] n. 통제, 제어; (기계 · 차량의) 제어 장치; v. 지배하다; 조정하다
If you have control of something or someone, you are able to make them do what you want them to do.

복습 **rip** [rip] v. (거칠게) 떼어 내다, 뜯어 내다; (갑자기) 찢다; 빠른 속도로 돌진하다; n. (길게) 찢어진 곳
If you rip something away, you remove it quickly and forcefully.

복습 **chunk** [ʧʌŋk] n. 덩어리; 상당히 많은 양; v. 덩어리로 나누다
Chunks of something are thick solid pieces of it.

복습 **helpless** [hélplis] a. 무력한, 속수무책인
If you are helpless, you do not have the strength or power to do anything useful or to control or protect yourself.

복습 **stretch** [streʧ] v. (길이 · 폭 등을) 늘이다; 펼쳐지다; 기지개를 켜다; n. (길게) 뻗은 구간; 기간
When something soft or elastic stretches or is stretched, it becomes longer or bigger as well as thinner, usually because it is pulled.

javelin [dʒǽvlin] n. 던지는 창, 투창
A javelin is a long spear that is used in sports competitions.

복습 **fling** [fliŋ] v. (flung-flung) (힘껏) 던지다; (머리 · 팔 등을) 휘두르다; n. (한바탕) 실컷 즐기기
If you fling something somewhere, you throw it there using a lot of force.

⋆ **soar** [sɔːr] v. (하늘 높이) 날아오르다; 솟구치다
If something such as a bird soars into the air, it goes quickly up into the air.

overshoot [òuvərʃúːt] v. (overshot-overshot) (목표 지점보다) 더 가다; 더 많이 하다
If you overshoot a place that you want to get to, you go past it by mistake.

복습 **dive** [daiv] v. (dove/dived-dived) 급강하하다; 급히 움직이다; (물속으로) 뛰어들다; n. 급강하; (물속으로) 뛰어들기
If an airplane dives, it flies or drops down quickly and suddenly.

⋆ **snatch** [snæʧ] v. 와락 붙잡다, 잡아채다; 간신히 얻다; n. 잡아 뺏음, 강탈; 조각
If you snatch something or snatch at something, you take it or pull it away quickly.

billow [bílou] v. 부풀어 오르다; (연기 · 구름 등이) 피어오르다; n. 자욱하게 피어오르는 것
When something made of cloth billows, it swells out and moves slowly in the wind.

복습 **parachute** [pǽrəʃùːt] n. 낙하산; v. 낙하산을 타고 뛰어내리다
A parachute is a device which enables a person to jump from an aircraft and float safely to the ground.

⋆ **drift** [drift] v. (물 · 공기에) 떠가다; (서서히) 이동하다; n. 표류; 흐름
When something drifts somewhere, it is carried there by the movement of wind or water.

⋆ **regain** [rigéin] v. 되찾다, 회복하다; 되돌아오다
If you regain something that you have lost, you get it back again.

복습 **dock** [dak] v. (배를) 부두에 대다; n. 부두, 선창
When a ship docks or is docked, it is brought into a dock.

복습 **cape** [keip] n. 망토
A cape is a short cloak.

복습 **blow** [blou] v. (바람 · 입김에) 날리다; (비밀을) 누설하다; (타이어가) 터지다; n. 강타
If the wind blows something somewhere or if it blows there, the wind moves it there.

⋆ **beloved** [bilʌ́vid] a. (대단히) 사랑하는; 총애 받는; 인기 많은
A beloved person, thing, or place is one that you feel great affection for.

복습 **knock** [nak] v. 치다, 부딪치다; (문 등을) 두드리다; n. 문 두드리는 소리; 부딪침
To knock someone into a particular position or condition means to hit them very hard so that they fall over or become unconscious.

★★ **balance** [bǽləns] **n.** (몸의) 균형; 균형 (상태); **v.** 균형을 유지하다
(off balance **idiom** 균형을 잃은)
If you are off balance, you are in an unsteady position and about to fall.

★ **tug** [tʌg] **n.** (갑자기 세게) 잡아당김; **v.** (세게) 잡아당기다
A tug is a short strong pull.

복습 **in time** **idiom** 제때에, 시간 맞춰, 늦지 않게
If you are in time for a particular event, you are not too late for it.

★★ **suck** [sʌk] **v.** (특정한 방향으로) 빨아들이다; 빨아 먹다; **n.** 빨기, 빨아 먹기
If something sucks a liquid, gas, or object in a particular direction, it draws it there with a powerful force.

복습 **monologue** [mánəlɔ̀ːg] **n.** 독백; **v.** 독백하다
If you refer to a long speech by one person during a conversation as a monologue, you mean it prevents other people from talking or expressing their opinions.

복습 **burn** [bəːrn] **v.** 불에 타다; 태우다; 상기되다; **n.** 화상
If something is burning, it is on fire.

wreckage [rékidʒ] **n.** 잔해
When something such as a plane, car, or building has been destroyed, you can refer to what remains as wreckage or the wreckage.

복습 **terrify** [térəfài] **v.** (몹시) 무섭게 하다 (terrified **a.** (몹시) 무서워하는, 겁이 난)
If something terrifies you, it makes you feel extremely frightened.

복습 **shriek** [ʃriːk] **v.** (날카롭게) 비명을 지르다; 악을 쓰며 말하다; **n.** (날카로운) 비명
When someone shrieks, they make a short, very loud cry, for example because they are suddenly surprised, are in pain, or are laughing.

복습 **land** [lænd] **v.** (땅 · 표면에) 내려앉다, 착륙하다; 놓다, 두다; **n.** 육지, 땅; 지역
When someone or something lands, they come down to the ground after moving through the air or falling.

복습 **huddle** [hʌdl] **v.** 모이다; 몸을 움츠리다; **n.** 모여 서 있는 것; 혼잡
If people huddle together or huddle round something, they stand, sit, or lie close to each other, usually because they all feel cold or frightened.

debris [dəbríː] **n.** 파편, 잔해; 쓰레기
Debris is pieces from something that has been destroyed or pieces of rubbish or unwanted material that are spread around.

복습 **erupt** [irʌ́pt] v. 분출되다; (강한 감정을) 터뜨리다
When a volcano erupts, it throws out a lot of hot, melted rock called lava, as well as ash and steam.

복습 **massive** [mǽsiv] a. (육중하면서) 거대한; 엄청나게 심각한
Something that is massive is very large in size, quantity, or extent.

복습 **explode** [iksplóud] v. 폭발하다; (갑자기 강한 감정을) 터뜨리다 (explosion n. 폭발)
An explosion is a sudden, violent burst of energy, for example one caused by a bomb.

★ **inch** [inʧ] n. 조금, 약간; v. 조금씩 움직이다
An inch can refer to a very small amount or distance.

복습 **crush** [krʌʃ] v. 으스러뜨리다; 밀어 넣다; 좌절시키다; n. 홀딱 반함
To crush something means to press it very hard so that its shape is destroyed or so that it breaks into pieces.

복습 **powerful** [páuərfəl] a. 강력한; 영향력 있는, 유력한
A powerful machine or substance is effective because it is very strong.

복습 **force** [fɔːrs] n. 작용력; 힘; 영향력; v. 억지로 ~하다; ~를 강요하다
Force is the power or strength which something has.

복습 **field** [fiːld] n. ~장; 경기장; 들판, 밭
A magnetic, gravitational, or electric field is the area in which that particular force is strong enough to have an effect.

복습 **bubble** [bʌbl] n. 거품; (감정의) 약간; v. (감정이) 차오르다; 거품이 일다
Bubbles are small balls of air or gas in a liquid.

복습 **amaze** [əméiz] v. (대단히) 놀라게 하다; 경악하게 하다 (amazed a. 놀란)
If something amazes you, it surprises you very much.

복습 **smolder** [smóuldər] v. (서서히) 타다; (속으로) 들끓다
If something smolders, it burns slowly, producing smoke but not flames.

★ **scratch** [skræʧ] n. 긁힌 자국; 긁는 소리; v. 긁힌 자국을 내다; (가려운 데를) 긁다
Scratches on someone or something are small shallow cuts.

복습 **wicked** [wíkid] a. 아주 좋은; 못된, 사악한; 짓궂은
If you describe someone or something as wicked, you mean that they are rather naughty, but in a way that you find attractive or enjoyable.

복습 **neighborhood** [néibərhùd] **n.** 인근, 근처; (도시의) 지역, 구역; 이웃 사람들
A neighborhood is one of the parts of a town where people live.

복습 **trike** [traik] **n.** 세발자전거
A trike is a child's tricycle.

★ **wow** [wau] **v.** 놀라게 하다; 열광시키다; **int.** 우아, 와 (하고 외치는 소리); **n.** 대성공
If someone or something wows you, they impress you by doing something extremely well.

Check Your Reading Speed

1분에 몇 단어를 읽는지 리딩 속도를 측정해보세요.

$$\frac{\text{318 words}}{\text{reading time (\quad\quad) sec}} \times 60 = (\quad\quad\quad) \text{ WPM}$$

Build Your Vocabulary

복습 **identity** [aidéntəti] **n.** 신원, 신분, 정체; 독자성
Your identity is who you are.

복습 **confident** [kánfədənt] **a.** 자신감 있는; 확신하는 (confidence **n.** 자신(감); 확신)
If you have confidence, you feel sure about your abilities, qualities, or ideas.

track meet [træk mi:t] **n.** 육상 경기 대회
A track meet is a sports competition between two or more teams, involving various different running races and jumping and throwing events.

복습 **stammer** [stǽmər] **v.** 말을 더듬다; **n.** 말 더듬기
If you stammer, you speak with difficulty, hesitating and repeating words or sounds.

복습 **shy** [ʃai] **a.** 수줍음을 많이 타는, 수줍어하는
A shy person is nervous and uncomfortable in the company of other people.

복습 **ease** [i:z] **n.** (근심 · 걱정 없이) 편안함; 쉬움, 용이함; **v.** 편해지다
If you are at ease, you are feeling confident and relaxed, and are able to talk to people without feeling nervous or anxious.

★★★ **stand** [stænd] **n.** (경기장의) 관중석; 가판대, 좌판; **v.** 서다; (어떤 위치에) 세우다
A stand at a sports ground is a large structure where people sit or stand to watch what is happening.

복습 **cheer** [ʧiər] **v.** 환호성을 지르다, 환호하다; **n.** 환호(성), 응원
When people cheer, they shout loudly to show their approval or to encourage someone who is doing something such as taking part in a game.

복습 **yell** [jel] **v.** 고함치다, 소리 지르다; **n.** 고함, 외침
If you yell, you shout loudly, usually because you are excited, angry, or in pain.

복습 **pistol** [pístəl] **n.** 권총, 피스톨
A pistol is a small gun which is held in and fired from one hand.

복습 **fire** [faiər] **v.** 발사하다; (엔진이) 점화되다; 해고하다; **n.** 화재, 불; 발사, 총격
If someone fires a gun or a bullet, or if they fire, a bullet is sent from a gun that they are using.

복습 **pack** [pæk] **n.** 무리, 집단; 묶음; **v.** (짐을) 싸다; 가득 채우다
You can refer to a group of people who go around together as a pack, especially when it is a large group that you feel threatened by.

give up **idiom** 포기하다; 그만두다; 단념하다
If you give up, you stop trying to do something, usually because it is too difficult.

복습 **accelerate** [æksélərèit] **v.** 속도를 높이다, 가속화되다
When a moving vehicle accelerates, it goes faster and faster.

hold back **idiom** ~을 저지하다; (진전·발전을) 저해하다
To hold back means to stop someone or something from moving forward.

복습 **race** [reis] **n.** 경주; 경쟁; 인종, 종족; **v.** 쏜살같이 가다; 경주하다
A race is a competition to see who is the fastest, for example in running, swimming, or driving.

복습 **triumphant** [traiʌ́mfənt] **a.** 의기양양한; 크게 성공한, 큰 승리를 거둔
Someone who is triumphant has gained a victory or succeeded in something and feels very happy about it.

복습 **rumble** [rʌmbl] **n.** 우르렁거리는 소리; **v.** 웅웅거리는 소리를 내다; 덜커덩거리며 나아가다
A rumble is a low continuous noise.

parking lot [pá:rkiŋ lat] **n.** 주차장
A parking lot is an area of ground where people can leave their cars.

★ **swell** [swel] **v.** 불룩해지다; (마음이) 벅차다; **n.** 증가, 팽창
If the amount or size of something swells or if something swells it, it becomes larger than it was before.

★★ **violent** [váiələnt] **a.** 격렬한, 맹렬한; 폭력적인; 지독한 (violently **ad.** 격렬하게, 맹렬히)
If you describe something as violent, you mean that it is said, done, or felt very strongly.

복습 **massive** [mǽsiv] **a.** (육중하면서) 거대한; 엄청나게 심각한
Something that is massive is very large in size, quantity, or extent.

* **drill** [dril] **v.** (드릴로) 구멍을 뚫다; 훈련시키다; **n.** 반복 연습; 송곳
When you drill into something or drill a hole in something, you make a hole in it using a drill.

복습 **surface** [sə́:rfis] **v.** (갑자기) 나타나다; 수면으로 올라오다; **n.** 수면, 표면, 지면; 외관
When someone surfaces, they appear after not being seen for some time, for example because they have been asleep.

복습 **dramatic** [drəmǽtik] **a.** 감격적인, 인상적인; 극적인; 과장된 (dramatically **ad.** 극적으로)
A dramatic action, event, or situation is exciting and impressive.

복습 **villain** [vílən] **n.** 악인, 악한; (이야기 · 연극 등의) 악당
A villain is someone who deliberately harms other people or breaks the law in order to get what they wants.

복습 **claw** [klɔ:] **n.** 갈고리 모양의 기계; (동물 · 새의) 발톱; **v.** (손톱 · 발톱으로) 할퀴다
A claw is a curved end on a tool or machine, used for pulling or picking things up.

복습 **emerge** [imə́:rdʒ] **v.** 나오다, 모습을 드러내다; (어려움 등을) 헤쳐 나오다
To emerge means to come out from an enclosed or dark space such as a room or a vehicle, or from a position where you could not be seen.

behold [bihóuld] **v.** 보다
If you behold someone or something, you see them.

복습 **monologue** [mánəlɔ̀:g] **v.** 독백하다; **n.** 독백
If you monologue, you deliver a monologue or long speech.

복습 **mask** [mæsk] **n.** 마스크; 가면; **v.** 가면을 쓰다; (감정 · 냄새 · 사실 등을) 가리다
A mask is a piece of cloth or other material, which you wear over your face so that people cannot see who you are, or so that you look like someone or something else.

복습 **rip** [rip] **v.** (거칠게) 떼어 내다, 뜯어 내다; (갑자기) 찢다; 빠른 속도로 돌진하다; **n.** (길게) 찢어진 곳
If you rip something away, you remove it quickly and forcefully.

복습 **reveal** [riví:l] **v.** (보이지 않던 것을) 드러내 보이다; (비밀 등을) 밝히다
If you reveal something that has been out of sight, you uncover it so that people can see it.

복습 **suit** [su:t] **n.** (특정한 활동 때 입는) 옷; 정장; 소송; **v.** ~에게 편리하다; 어울리다
A particular type of suit is a piece of clothing that you wear for a particular activity.

수고하셨습니다!

드디어 끝까지 다 읽으셨군요! 축하드립니다! 여러분은 이 책을 통해 총 19,526개의 단어를 읽으셨고, 1,000개 이상의 어휘와 표현들을 공부하셨습니다. 이 책에 나온 어휘는 다른 원서를 읽을 때도 빈번히 만날 수 있는 필수 어휘들입니다. 이 책을 읽었던 경험은 비슷한 수준의 다른 원서들을 읽을 때 큰 도움이 될 것입니다.

원서는 한 번 다 읽은 후에도 다양한 방식으로 영어 실력을 끌어올리는 데 활용할 수 있습니다. 일단 다 읽은 원서를 어떻게 활용할 수 있을지, 학습자의 주요 유형별로 알아보도록 하겠습니다.

리딩(Reading) 실력을 확실히 다지길 원한다면, 반복해서 읽어보세요!

리딩 실력을 탄탄하게 다지길 원한다면, 같은 원서를 2~3번 반복해서 읽을 것을 권합니다. 같은 책을 여러 번 읽으면 지루할 것 같지만, 꼭 그렇지도 않습니다. 반복해서 읽을 때 처음과 주안점을 다르게 두면, 전혀 다른 느낌으로 재미있게 읽을 수 있습니다.

처음 원서를 읽을 때는 생소한 단어들과 스토리로 인해 읽고 이해하기가 매우 힘듭니다. 전체 맥락을 잡고 읽어도 약간 버거운 느낌이지요. 하지만 반복해서 읽기 시작하면 달라집니다. 내용은 일단 파악해 둔 상황이기 때문에 문장 구조나 어휘의 활용에 더 집중하게 되고, 조금 더 깊이 있게 읽을 수 있게 됩니다. 좋은 표현과 문장을 수집하고 메모할 만한 여유도 생기게 되지요. 어휘도 많이 익숙해졌기 때문에 리딩 속도도 탄력이 붙습니다. 처음 읽을 때는 '내용'에서 재미를 느꼈다면, 반복해서 읽을 때는 '영어'에서 재미를 느끼게 되는 것입니다. 따라서 리딩 실력을 더욱 확고하게 다지고자 한다면, 같은 책을 2~3회 정도 반복해서 읽을 것을 권해드립니다.

리스닝(Listening) 실력을 늘리고 싶다면, 귀를 통해서 읽어보세요!

많은 영어 학습자들이 '리스닝이 안 돼서 문제'라고 한탄합니다. 그리고 리스닝 실력을 늘리는 방법으로, 무슨 뜻인지 몰라도 반복해 듣는 '무작정 듣기'를 선택합니다. 하지만 뜻도 모르면서 무작정 듣는 것은 엄청난 인내력이 필요합니다. 그래서 대부분 며칠 시도하다가 포기해버리고 말지요.

모르는 내용을 무작정 듣는 것보다는 어느 정도 알고 있는 내용을 반복해서 듣는 것이 더 효과적인 듣기 방법입니다. 그리고 이런 방식의 듣기에 활용할 수 있는 가장 좋은 교재가 오디오북입니다.

따라서 리스닝 실력을 향상시키길 원한다면, 이 책에서 제공하는 오디오북을 이용해서 듣는 연습을 해보세요. 오디오북의 활용법은 간단합니다. 그냥 MP3를 플레이어에 넣고 자투리 시간에 틈틈이 들으면 됩니다. 혹은 책상에 앉아 눈으로는 책을 보면서 귀로는 그 내용을 따라 읽는 것도 좋습니다. 보통 오디오북은 분당 150~180단어로 재생되는데, 재생 속도가 조절되는 MP3를 이용하면 더 빠른 속도로 재생이 가능하고, 이에 맞춰 빠른 속도로 듣는 연습을 할 수도 있습니다.

중요한 것은 내용을 따라가면서, 내용에 푹 빠져서 반복해 들어야 한다는 것입니다. 눈으로 책을 읽는 것이 아니라 '귀를 통해' 책을 읽는 것이지요. 이렇게 연습을 반복해서, 눈으로 읽지 않은 책도 '귀를 통해' 읽을 수 있을 정도가 되면, 리스닝으로 고생하는 일은 거의 사라질 것입니다.

이 책은 '귀로 읽기'와 '소리 내어 읽기'를 위해 오디오북을 기본으로 제공하고 있습니다.
오디오북은 MP3 파일로 제공되니 MP3 기기나 컴퓨터에 옮겨서 사용하시면 됩니다. 혹 오디오북에 이상이 있을 경우 helper@longtailbooks.co.kr로 메일을 주시면 안내를 받으실 수 있습니다.

스피킹(Speaking)이 고민이라면, 소리 내어 읽기를 해보세요!

스피킹 역시 많은 학습자들이 고민하는 부분입니다. 스피킹이 고민이라면, 원서를 큰 소리로 읽는 낭독 훈련(Voice Reading)을 해보세요!
'소리 내서 읽는 것이 말하기에 정말로 도움이 될까?'라고 의아한 생각이 들 수도 있습니다. 하지만, 인간의 두뇌 입장에서 봤을 때, 성대 구조를 활용해서 '발화'한다는 점에서는 소리 내서 읽기와 말하기는 큰 차이가 없다고 합니다. 소리 내서 읽는 것은 '타인의 생각'을 전달하고, 직접 말하는 것은 '자신의 생각'을 전달한다는 차이가 있을 뿐, 머릿속에서 문장을 처리하고 조음기관(혀와 성대 등)을 움직여 의미를 만든다는 점에서 같은 과정인 것이지요. 따라서 소리 내서 읽는 연습을 꾸준히 하는 것은 스피킹 연습에 큰 도움이 됩니다.

소리 내어 읽기를 하는 방법도 간단합니다. 일단 오디오북을 들으면서 성우의 목소리를 최대한 따라 하며 같이 읽어보세요. 발음 뿐 아니라, 억양, 어조, 느낌까지 완벽히 따라 한다고 생각하면서 소리 내어 읽습니다. 따라 읽는 것이 조금 익숙해지면, 옆의 누군가에게 이 책을 읽어준다는 생각으로 소리내서 계속 읽어나갑니다. 한 번 눈과 귀로 읽었던 책이라 보다 수월하게 진행할 수 있고, 자연스럽게 어휘와 표현을 복습하는 효과도 거두게 됩니다. 또 이렇게 소리 내어 읽는 것을 녹음해서 들어보면 스스로에게 좋은 피드백이 됩니다.

라이팅(Writing)까지 욕심이 난다면, 요약하는 연습을 해보세요!

최근엔 라이팅에도 욕심을 내는 학습자들이 많이 있습니다. 원서를 라이팅 연습에 직접적으로 활용하기에는 한계가 있지만, 역시 적절히 활용하면 유용한 자료가 될 수 있습니다.
특히 책을 읽고 그 내용을 요약하는 연습은 큰 도움이 됩니다. 요약 훈련의 방식도 간단합니다. 원서를 읽고 그날 읽은 분량만큼 혹은 책을 다 읽고 난 후에 전체 내용을 기반으로, 책 내용을 요약하고 나의 느낌을 영어로 적어보는 것입니다. 이때 그 책에 나왔던 단어와 표현을 최대한 활용해서 요약하는 것이 중요합니다.

영어 표현력은 결국 얼마나 다양한 어휘로 많은 표현을 해보았느냐가 좌우하게 됩니다. 이런 면에서 내가 읽은 책을, 그 책에 나온 문장과 어휘로 다시 표현해 보는 것이 가장 효율적인 방식입니다. 책에 나온 어휘와 표현을 단순히 읽고 무슨 말인지 아는 정도가 아니라, 실제로 직접 활용해서 쓸 수 있을 만큼 확실하게 익히게 되는 것이지요. 여기에 첨삭까지 받을 수 있는 방법이 있다면 금상첨화입니다.

또한 이런 '표현하기' 연습은 스피킹 훈련에도 그대로 적용할 수 있습니다. 책을 읽고 그 내용을 3분 안에 다른 사람에게 영어로 말하는 연습을 하는 것이지요. 순발력과 표현력을 기르는 좋은 훈련이 됩니다.

'스피드 리딩 카페'에서 함께 원서를 읽어보세요!

이렇게 원서 읽기를 활용한 영어 공부에 관심이 있으시다면, 국내 최대 영어원서 읽기 동호회 스피드 리딩 카페(http://cafe.naver.com/readingtc)로 와보세요. 이미 수만 명의 회원들이 모여서 '북클럽'을 통해 함께 원서를 읽고 있습니다.

단순히 함께 원서를 읽는 것뿐만 아니라, 위에서 언급한 다양한 방식으로 원서를 활용하여 영어 실력을 향상시키고 있는, 말뿐이 아닌 '실질적인 효과'를 보고 있는 회원들이 엄청나게 많이 있습니다. 여러분도 스피드 리딩 카페를 방문해보신다면 많은 자극과 도움을 받으실 수 있을 것입니다.

원서 읽기 습관을 길러보자!

일상에서 영어를 한마디도 쓰지 않는 비영어권 국가에서 살고 있는 우리에게 영어에 가장 쉽고, 편하고, 저렴하게 노출되는 방법은, 바로 '영어원서 읽기'입니다. 언제 어디서든 원서를 붙잡고 읽기만 하면 곧바로 영어를 접하는 환경이 만들어지기 때문이지요. 하루에 20분씩만 꾸준히 읽는다면, 1년에 무려 120시간 동안 영어에 노출될 수 있습니다.

영어원서를 꾸준히 읽어보세요. '원서 읽기 습관'을 만들어보세요! 이렇게 영어를 접하는 시간이 늘어나면, 영어 실력도 당연히 향상될 수밖에 없습니다.

아래 표에는 영어 수준별 추천 원서들이 있습니다. 하지만 이것은 절대적인 기준이 아니며, 학습자의 영어 수준과 관심 분야에 따라 달라질 수 있습니다. 이 책은 Reading Level 3에 해당합니다. 이 책의 완독 경험을 기준으로 삼아 적절한 책을 골라 꾸준히 읽어보세요.

영어 수준별 추천 원서 목록

리딩 레벨	영어 수준	원서 목록
Level 1	초 · 중학생	The Zack Files 시리즈, Magic Tree House 시리즈, Junie B. Jones 시리즈, Horrid Henry 시리즈, 로알드 달 단편들(The Giraffe and the Pelly and Me, Esio Trot, The Enormous Crocodile, The Magic Finger, Fantastic Mr. Fox)
Level 2	고등학생	Andrew Clements 시리즈 (Frindle, School Story 등), Spiderwick Chronicle 시리즈, 쉬운 뉴베리 수상작들 (Sarah Plain and Tall, The Hundred Dresses 등), 짧고 간단한 자기계발서 (Who Moved My Cheese?, The Present 등)
Level 3	특목고 학생 대학생	로알드 달 장편 (Charlie and the Chocolate Factory, Matilda 등), Wayside School 시리즈, 중간 수준의 뉴베리 수상작들 (Number the Stars, Charlotte's Web 등), A Series of Unfortunate Events 시리즈
Level 4	대학생 상위권	Harry Potter 시리즈 중 1~3권, Percy Jackson 시리즈, The Chronicles of Narnia 시리즈, The Alchemist, 어려운 수준의 뉴베리 수상작들 (Holes, The Giver 등)
Level 5	대학원생 이상 전문직 종사자들	Harry Potter 시리즈 중 4~7권, Shopaholic 시리즈, His Dark Materials 시리즈, The Devil Wears Prada, The Curious Incident of the Dog in the Night-Time, Tuesdays With Morrie 등등 (참고 자료: Renaissance Learning, Readingtown USA, Slyvan Learning Center)

'영화로 읽는 영어원서'로 원서 읽기 습관을 만들어보세요!

『인크레더블』을 재미있게 읽은 독자라면 「영화로 읽는 영어원서」 시리즈를 꾸준히 읽어보시길 추천해드립니다! 「영화로 읽는 영어원서」 시리즈는 유명 영화를 기반으로 한 소설판 영어원서로 보다 쉽고 부담 없이 원서 읽기를 시작할 수 있도록 도와주고, 오디오북을 기본적으로 포함해 원서의 활용 범위를 넓힌 책입니다.

『하이스쿨 뮤지컬』, 『코코』, 『라푼젤』, 『겨울왕국』, 『메리다와 마법의 숲』, 『몬스터 주식회사』, 『몬스터 대학교』, 『인사이드 아웃』, 『주토피아』 등 출간하는 책들마다 독자들의 큰 사랑을 받으며 어학 분야의 베스트셀러를 기록했고, 학원과 학교들에서도 꾸준히 교재로 채택되는 등 영어 학습자들에게도 좋은 반응을 얻고 있습니다. (EBS에서 운영하는 어학사이트 EBS랑 www.ebslang.co.kr 교재 채택, 서초·강남 등지 명문 중고교 방과 후 보충교재 채택, 전국 영어 학원 정·부교재 채택, 김해 분성 초등학교 영어원서 읽기 대회 교재 채택 등등)

Chapters 1-3

1. B The redheaded kid was wearing a mask and a homemade Super suit. Then Mr. Incredible recognized him. "Buddy?" he asked. Buddy, the president of the Mr. Incredible Fan Club, answered with a frown. "My name is INCREDIBOY!"

2. D As Buddy dashed for the shattered window, Bomb Voyage secretly clipped a small bomb to Buddy's cape. Mr. Incredible spotted the bomb. He raced after Buddy and grabbed the cape, yelling, "Buddy, don't!" But it was too late. Buddy jumped, activating his rocket boots in a shower of sparks and lifting Mr. Incredible into the air with him. Mr. Incredible fought to get hold of the bomb as he and Buddy streaked across the sky.

3. C Mr. Incredible took a deep breath and pushed open the chapel doors. Smartly dressed in a black tuxedo again, he took a step down the aisle of the large cathedral. Frozone, his best man, followed him. They walked to the altar, where Mr. Incredible's beautiful bride was waiting. The ceremony began. "Robert Parr, will you have this woman to be your lawfully wedded wife?" His wife-to-be, Elastigirl, also known as Helen, whispered, "Cutting it kind of close, don't you think?" Mr. Incredible smiled. "You need to be more . . . flexible," he replied with a wink. The ceremony concluded: "As long as you both shall live?" "I do," answered Mr. Incredible, taking Elastigirl in his arms.

4. A "This flash from the news desk: In a stunning turn of events, a Super is being sued for saving someone who, apparently, did not want to be saved. The plaintiff, who was foiled in his attempted suicide by Mr. Incredible, has filed a suit against the famed hero in Superior Court." On the crowded steps of the courthouse, a lawyer spoke to the media. "My client didn't ask to be saved. He didn't want to be saved," he said dryly.

5. D There was some protest in favor of the Supers, but finally, under tremendous pressure and a mountain of lawsuits, the government quietly initiated the Super Relocation Program (otherwise known as the SRP). Supers promised never to use their Super powers again, in exchange for anonymity. The Supers found themselves with new names and identities. From now on, they would live average lives, quietly blending in with the rest of society.

Chapters 4-6

1. A Bob thought for a minute, checked to make sure that the coast was clear outside his cubicle, and then quickly whispered to Mrs. Hogenson every possible loophole she could use to get Insuricare to pay her claim.

2. D Dash had been born with the Super power of lightning-fast speed. But of course, since Supers weren't supposed to be Super, he was never allowed to use it, and the Parr family had to keep it a secret. "What's this about? Has Dash done something wrong?" Helen asked the school principal when she got to the office, where Dash was waiting. "He put thumbtacks on my stool!" Dash's fourth-grade teacher, Bernie Kropp, told Helen. "And this time I've got him!" Mr. Kropp continued triumphantly. "I hid a camera!" He dropped a disc into a player. Helen and Dash held their breath and stared at the TV screen. There was Mr. Kropp, about to sit in his chair. He sat . . . and screamed. No sign of Dash at all.

3. C Violet was nowhere to be seen—but then, that was one of her talents. Violet had the power to turn invisible. This came in handy when she felt shy around boys, especially Tony Rydinger.

4. B In the kitchen, Bob was fixated on the newspaper. Under the headline PALADINO MISSING, Bob read, "Simon J. Paladino, long an outspoken advocate of Supers' rights, is missing." Bob couldn't help wondering what had happened. Simon Paladino was the secret identity of Gazerbeam, a former Super and one of Bob's friends.

5. A "What does anyone in our family know about being normal?" Vi interrupted. "The only normal one is Jack-Jack." Jack-Jack, the only member of the Parr family who didn't seem to have any Super powers, gleefully spit a mouthful of baby food onto his chin and giggled.

Chapters 7-9

1. C Lucius drove to a run-down part of the city and parked in an alleyway. He and Bob weren't really going bowling. Instead, they sat in the car and reminisced about the old days while a portable police scanner hissed dispatch calls.

2. B Bob suddenly ran full speed down the flaming hallway. Lucius was right behind

him. As they ran through the flames, Bob focused on the brick wall ahead. He picked up speed, gave a huge yell, and lowered his free shoulder into it. The heroes and their rescued fire victims smashed through the brick wall just as the burning building collapsed behind them.

3. D Helen closed her eyes. "You know how I feel about that, Bob! We can't blow our cover again!" Bob looked down at his singed coat. "The building was coming down anyway," he said, trying to explain. "You knocked down a building?" "It was on fire!" Bob argued. "Structurally unsound! I performed a public service. You act like that's a bad thing." "It is a bad thing, Bob. Uprooting our family again so you can relive the glory days is a very bad thing!"

4. C "Your customers make me unhappy, Bob." "You've had complaints?" Bob asked. "Complaints I can handle," Huph answered. "What I can't handle is your customers' inexplicable knowledge of Insuricare's inner workings. They're experts. Experts, Bob! Exploiting every loophole, dodging every obstacle! They're penetrating the bureaucracy!"

5. B "That man out there!" Bob said, his eyes on the victim. "He needs help. He's getting mugged." "Well, let's hope we don't cover him!" Huph said coldly as Bob suddenly stood and bolted for the door. "I'll be right back," Bob said. "Stop right now or you're fired!" Huph threatened.

Chapters 10-12

1. D "If you accept, your payment will be triple your current annual salary." Bob's jaw dropped, and he blankly scribbled "BIG $$$$" on a pad.

2. B "Uh, I . . . uh," Bob stammered. "Something's happened." "What?" Helen asked. Bob gulped hard. "Uh, the company's sending me to a conference out of town," he said finally. "I'm just gonna be gone for a few days."

3. A "The Omnidroid 9000 is a top-secret prototype battle robot," she told Bob. "Its artificial intelligence enables it to solve any problem. And unfortunately—" "Let me guess," Bob said. "It got smart enough to wonder why it had to take orders." Mirage nodded. "We lost control and now it's loose in the jungle."

4. C Bob returned home and felt like a new man. Over the next few weeks, he began

working out, getting in shape again. He bought the brand-new sports car he'd always dreamed about for himself and a new car for Helen.

5. C Bob held up his suit. "E, I just need a patch job."

Chapters 13-15

1. B Helen was home doing laundry. She was about to hang Bob's sports coat when she saw it: the glint of something shiny on his jacket—a long blond hair.

2. C She was tidying up Bob's den, dusting the glass case, when she noticed the case was open. She took a closer look and saw a long, nearly microscopic stitch in his old Super suit. Helen was shocked. It had been newly repaired. "Edna," she said to herself. Helen knew that type of craftsmanship couldn't have been done by anyone else. Helen decided that if Bob was doing Super work on the side, she wanted to know. There was only one thing to do. She picked up the phone and dialed a number she had never thought she would dial again. "Hello," Helen said. "I'd like to speak to Edna, please."

3. D "All I wanted was to help you. I only wanted to help! And what did you say to me?" Mr. Incredible remembered his words: "Fly home, Buddy. I work alone." "I was wrong to treat you that way. I'm sorry," the Super said. "See? Now you respect me. I'm a threat. That's the way it works. Turns out there are a lot of people, whole countries, who want respect. And they will pay through the nose to get it. How do you think I got rich? I invented weapons."

4. A Exhausted, he was looking for a possible way out when he saw the skeleton of Gazerbeam. He recognized the glasses that hung on the old Super's skull. He remembered reading that Gazerbeam was missing, and shook his head sadly. But Mr. Incredible had to hand it to his old hero friend—in Gazerbeam's dying moments, he had used his laser eyes to burn the word KRONOS into the cave wall. Mr. Incredible knew it meant something important, but what?

5. D Mr. Incredible heard the click, click, click of an electronic probe. It was entering the grotto. He quickly crawled under Gazerbeam's skeleton. The probe scanned the entire cave and then fixed on Gazerbeam's skeleton. Mr. Incredible held his breath and closed his eyes. The probe chirped and left. Above the waterfall, the probe returned to Syndrome.

"Life readings negative," it reported. "Mr. Incredible terminated."

Chapters 16-18

1. C "Shhh, darling, shhh!" E said as a small featureless baby mannequin in a tiny red suit emerged in a glass chamber, moving slowly from one side to the other. "I cut it a little roomy for the free movement." E smiled. The inside of the chamber erupted in flames. Helen jumped back. "And," E added, "it can also withstand a temperature of over one thousand degrees!" The flames were replaced by a barrage of machine-gun fire. "Completely bulletproof and machine washable, darling. That's a new feature!"

2. A "So," E said, shaking her head. "You don't know where he is. Would you like to find out?" she asked, holding up the homing device. Helen hit the button on the homing device.

3. B Syndrome's plan to unleash his new and improved Omnidroid on the world flashed onto the screen, followed by the status of all the Supers that Syndrome had lured to the island. They'd all been done in by the evil mastermind. He had used them all as test subjects to perfect his Omnidroid. Mr. Incredible shook his head. DYNAGUY: TERMINATED. GAZERBEAM: TERMINATED. The list went on and on. Then Mr. Incredible saw FROZONE: LOCATION KNOWN. He suddenly thought of Helen. He searched for her name. ELASTIGIRL: LOCATION UNKNOWN.

4. D Vi looked down at her suit and wondered. Then, making her hand invisible, she touched a finger to it. The suit disappeared in her hand. "Whoa," said Vi.

5. C "Who did you contact?" "Contact? What are you talking about?" asked Mr. Incredible. With a nod from Syndrome, a jolt of electricity went into Mr. Incredible's chest. He winced in pain. "I'm referring to last night at 2307 hours, while you were snooping around, you sent out a homing signal," Syndrome said impatiently, and jolted Mr. Incredible again. "I didn't—" said Mr. Incredible painfully. "And now a government plane is requesting permission to land here! Who did you contact?" Syndrome demanded in a rage.

Chapters 19-21

1. A Helen's expression suddenly changed. "Wait a minute, you left Jack-Jack alone?" she asked them. "Yes, Mom! I'm completely stupid," Violet said sarcastically. "Of course we got a sitter! Do you think I'm totally irresponsible? Thanks a lot!" "Well, who'd you get?" asked Helen anxiously as she dialed home. "You don't have to worry about one single thing, Mrs. Parr. I've got this babysitting thing wired," Jack-Jack's new thirteen-year-old babysitter said.

2. C Dash and Vi watched, amazed, as their mother stretched her body into the shape of a boat. They both climbed on board. Helen had Dash put his legs over the side and kick them at Super speed. The Parr family boat was moving toward the island of Nomanisan.

3. D "Put these on," she said, handing them their black masks. "Your identity is your most valuable possession. Protect it. If anything goes wrong, use your powers."

4. B "Mom . . . what happened on the plane . . . ," Vi said with tears in her eyes. She knew her force field could have helped if she had just been confident enough to try. "I—couldn't—I'm—I didn't—I'm so sorry."

5. B A guard was sliding a key card through a reader, and whoosh, the door in front of him opened. She needed that key card. It would let her access different parts of Syndrome's lair to look for her husband.

Chapters 22-24

1. D "Voice key incorrect," the bird said. "Voice key?" Vi repeated, and frowned. The bird's head mechanically swiveled toward Dash and Vi. Its eyes lit up red as its beak dropped open and it let out a shrill electronic alarm.

2. B She walked to the control panel and switched off the immobi-ray. "There isn't much time," she told Mr. Incredible, who dropped to his knees. It was Mirage. "No, there isn't," Mr. Incredible said, grabbing Mirage's throat. "There's no time at all." "Please . . . ," Mirage gasped. In a fury, Mr. Incredible lashed out. "Why are you here? How can you possibly bring me lower? What more can you take away from me?" "F-f-amily . . . survived the crash . . . ," Mirage gasped. "They're here—on the island."

3. A He saw a hanging vine ahead and reached for it as he zoomed by. Dash swung

around in a wide arc, surprising the last velocipod and causing it to veer off into the undergrowth. Immediately, another velocipod was hot on his trail. Dash grabbed another vine and was propelled forward. But the vine snapped and he rose into the air, suddenly realizing that he was no longer over land. He was falling fast off the edge of a cliff! Dash screamed. With a thud, he landed on the hood of a velocipod. He couldn't believe his luck. He was okay! A guard turned and took a swing at him. But Dash used his Super speed to duck every punch. He was beginning to get comfortable with his Super powers. He even managed to get in a few high-speed punches himself.

4. B A guard scanned the area with his rifle, looking for any sign of Violet. Invisible, Violet quickly clubbed the guard, knocking away his rifle and giving herself just enough time to run into the jungle. "Show yourself!" he commanded. He picked up his gun and fired, unleashing a barrage of bullets at a series of footprints that streaked toward the river.

5. C Stunned for a moment, Dash looked up to see the rifle pointed at his chest. The guard smiled and the trigger clicked. Violet leaped between them, throwing a force field around her and Dash, protecting them. Dash was amazed. Violet floated in midair, suspended in her own force field. "How are you doing that?" Dash asked as the bullets from the guard ricocheted off the force field. "I don't know!" Vi answered. "Whatever you do—don't stop!" Dash said enthusiastically. Dash began to run within the force field like a gerbil in a wheel, causing them to roll into the jungle, rumbling past the guards and down a hillside.

Chapters 25-27

1. C "Whoa, whoa, whoa!" Syndrome said, stepping out of the jungle. "Time out!" he shouted, firing his immobi-ray and suspending the Incredibles motionless in midair.

2. A "The robot will emerge dramatically, do some damage, throngs of screaming people, and just when all hope is lost, Syndrome will save the day. I'll be a bigger hero than you ever were!"

3. D "How about a rocket?" Dash suggested, pointing to a rocket in the launching bay. "I can't fly a rocket," Helen said. "You don't have to," Vi told her. "Use the coordinates from the last launch."

4. C Suddenly, Lucius saw a huge six-legged Omnidroid outside his window. He began opening his dresser drawers. "Honey?" he called to his wife in the other room. "What?" Honey answered. "Where's my Super suit?"

5. B Syndrome faked a punch while he secretly used the remote on his wrist to send a signal to the arm of the Omnidroid, which fell out of its socket, crashing into the street. The crowd went wild. Syndrome reveled in their cheers of appreciation. The Omnidroid, however, was still a learning robot. CONTROL STOLEN BY EXTERNAL SIGNAL, the robot began to process. It crunched the numbers and slowly turned toward Syndrome. SIGNAL SOURCE: REMOTE CONTROL, it concluded.

Chapters 28-30

1. A Helen released her hold on the landing craft as the van was disengaged. It now streaked through the sky and was headed for the freeway. The van hit the pavement in a shower of sparks, doing two hundred miles an hour. Bob struggled to maintain control as he hit the brakes. Tires smoking, he steered the van into freeway traffic.

2. A "I have to do this alone," Bob said sternly. "What is this to you? Playtime?" Helen asked. "No," Bob said. "So you can be Mr. Incredible again?" "No!" Bob snapped. "Then what?" Helen asked, confused. "What is it?" "I'm . . . I'm not . . . not strong enough!" Bob said finally. "Strong enough?" Helen asked. "And this will make you stronger? That's what this is? Some sort of workout?" "I can't lose you again!" Bob shouted at Helen. "I can't," he whispered. "Not again . . . I'm not strong enough."

3. B Elastigirl flung a manhole cover at the robot, destroying its laser beam, as Frozone swooped in to rescue Dash. The Omnidroid thundered down the street after them. The learning robot knew it needed to get the remote back. Then it was Frozone's turn to help out. He cut across the river, freezing a path and taking Dash along.

4. D The robot kept coming after them, but the remote did open the claw that had Mr. Incredible pinned down the street. He realized that the only thing that could penetrate and destroy the robot was itself. Suddenly, a rocket at the end of the claw was activated. That gave Mr. Incredible an idea. He struggled to control the claw and looked down the street toward his family and Frozone. The Omnidroid was bearing down on them. Mr.

Incredible pointed the claw and yelled to his family, "Duck!" The rocket fired, and the claw flew right through the center of the Omnidroid.

5. C Meanwhile, Helen was on the cell phone, checking the messages. The first was from Kari, the babysitter. "Hello, Mrs. Parr. Everything's fine, but there's something unusual about Jack-Jack. Call me, okay?"

Chapters 31 & 32

1. D "Shhh. The baby's sleeping," Syndrome said, holding Jack-Jack in his arms. "You took away my future," he said calmly. "I'm simply returning the favor."

2. C Syndrome froze as Jack-Jack suddenly transformed from fire to a hideous screaming mini-monster. Horrified, Syndrome tried to drop the baby, but Jack-Jack managed to cling to his rocket boots. Syndrome spun out of control as Jack-Jack began ripping the boots apart.

3. A "This isn't the end of it!" Syndrome shouted, having regained control. He stood in the docking door of his jet, his cape blowing in the wind. Then Bob reached for his beloved new sports car and flung it into the air. "I will get your son!" Syndrome shouted as the car hit the jet, knocking him off balance. "I'll—" Then he felt the tug at his neck. He turned in time to see the end of his cape sucked into the jet's turbines. It was his last monologue.

4. B Helen landed, and the Incredibles huddled together as the debris landed around them, erupting in a massive explosion. The Parr home was completely destroyed. But inside the wreckage, inches from being crushed, the Incredibles were alive. Vi had created her most powerful force field ever.

5. D Their Super identities were still secret, but their new confidence wasn't. "You're . . . Violet, right?" Tony Rydinger said to Vi at the school track meet. "That's me," Vi answered, holding her head up. "You look . . . different," Tony said. "I feel different. Is different okay?" "Different is great," Tony said, liking the person he saw. "Do you think maybe you and I . . . you know?" Tony stammered, feeling a little shy. "I like movies." Vi smiled, putting him at ease. "I'll buy the popcorn, okay?" "A movie," Tony answered. "There you go, yeah . . . yeah! So, Friday?" "Friday," Violet said with a big smile. Running

in the track meet that day was Dash Parr. His family was in the stands to cheer him on. "Go! Go, Dash, go! Run. Run! Run!" Bob, Helen, and Vi yelled after the starting pistol fired.

인크레더블(THE INCREDIBLES)

초판 발행 2018년 7월 16일

지은이 Irene Trimble
기획 이수영
책임편집 정소이 김보경
콘텐츠제작및감수 롱테일북스 편집부
번역 이인애
마케팅 김보미 임정진 전선경 정경훈

펴낸이 이수영
펴낸곳 (주)롱테일북스
출판등록 제2015-000191호
주소 04043 서울특별시 마포구 양화로 12길 16-9(서교동) 북앤빌딩 3층
전자메일 helper@longtailbooks.co.kr
(학원·학교에서 본도서를 교재로 사용하길 원하시는 경우 전자메일로 문의주시면
자세한 안내를 받으실 수 있습니다.)

ISBN 979-11-86701-83-6 14740

롱테일북스는 (주)북하우스 퍼블리셔스의 계열사입니다.

이 도서의 국립중앙도서관 출판시도서목록(CIP)은 서지정보유통지원시스템 홈페이지(http://seoji.nl.go.kr)와
국가자료공동목록시스템(http://www.nl.go.kr/kolisnet)에서 이용하실 수 있습니다. (CIP제어번호: CIP2018018724)